TEN YEARS IN EQUATORIA

AND THE

RETURN WITH EMIN PASHA

LANDSCAPE IN CENTRAL AFRICA.

TEN YEARS IN EQUATORIA

AND THE

RETURN WITH EMIN PASHA

BY

MAJOR GAETANO CASATI

TRANSLATED FROM THE ORIGINAL ITALIAN MANUSCRIPT
BY
The Hon. Mrs. J. RANDOLPH CLAY
ASSISTED BY
Mr. I. WALTER SAVAGE LANDOR

"We can only achieve what is most noble and great by modesty"
St. Hieronymus

IN TWO VOLUMES—VOL. II.

NEGRO UNIVERSITIES PRESS
NEW YORK

Originally published in 1891
by Frederick Warne & Co., London

Reprinted 1969 by
Negro Universities Press
A DIVISION OF GREENWOOD PUBLISHING CORP.
NEW YORK

SBN 8371-1514-0

PRINTED IN UNITED STATES OF AMERICA

CONTENTS OF VOLUME II.

CHAPTER I.

THE FALL OF KHARTOUM.

The carpenter of Dongola—May 1884—A life of penance—The standard of rebellion unfurled—Causes of disaffection in the Egyptian Soudan—The slave trade—Raouf Pasha and his measures—A Babylonian banquet—Abd-el-Kader Pasha—Defeat of the troops—Wise measures of the Governor—General Hicks' expedition—*Ti sebil Allah*—Trophies of human skulls—Osman Digna, chief of the dervishes—Plans concocted in Cairo—General Gordon—His mission—His intentions—Prestige of his name—Battle of El-Teb—Fall of Sinkat—Surrender of Tokar—General Graham—Abandonment of the campaign in the Eastern Provinces—Tactics; difficulties arising from the nature of the soil, from the climate and temperament of the enemy—Gordon cannot leave Khartoum—Relief expedition under the command of General Wolseley—Bombardment of Berber—Death of Colonel Stewart—Faulty division of the forces—The Mahdi's exertions—Wilson before Khartoum—The catastrophe—The soldier without fear and without reproach—The Geddal of the Mohammedans.

Pp. 1—14

CHAPTER II.

LIFE IN UNYORO.

Hostilities cease—The *matamure*—The king shows himself—Waganda and Wanyoro—Muanga and Kabba Rega—King Chua (Kabba Rega)—He remembers his friend Emin—Juaya—His royal palace—The morning greeting of king and people—The king's favourite occupation—"Thou art a shepherd"—Simulated piety and manifest avarice—His sons brought up by shepherds—No profane eye is to rest on the king's cows—The milkers—Reception at an audience—Object of my mission—The good Kategora—Covetous intentions of the king—I speak with the king—Occupation of Tunguru and Msua—Arrival of Biri—The king yields—Hopes reposed in Biri—Kategora poisoned—"He dies, he dies!"—Abd Rehman made proud—Vexations—Kisa and Gumangi—Emin believes in Kabba Rega's loyalty—The soldiers of Equatoria—Emin loses a good opportunity—The Shooli rebels defeated and subdued—Pantomime of the Lango—We are thirsty for blood—The dead fowl—The throne in danger—The queen-mother, a priestess and magician—The ceremony of the *mpango*—Kisa of Muenghe—Rejoicings and dancing—Burning of Juaya—A heap of ashes.

Pp. 15—35

CHAPTER III.

REGION BETWEEN THE ALBERT AND VICTORIA LAKES.

Uganda and Unyoro—Watershed between the Victoria Nile and Lake Albert—The region of forests—Mount Sedgiomocoro—The Kafu, the Ngussi, the Msiri—The peninsula of Magungo—Climate—Productions of the vegetable kingdom—The fauna—Destruction of hyenas—The chimpanzee—Professor Giglioli and the *Troglodytes Schweinfurthii*—Professor Reichart of Berlin—The *termes mordax*—The different tribes of which the people of Unyoro consist—The *Kinyoro* or language spoken in Unyoro—The francolin and the tortoise—The leopard and the dog—King Chua tells the story of the Golden Book of his family—The Wahuma—Customs of this tribe—From Juaya to Katua on the Ruitan Lake—The Virica of the Vacongio—The Ruwenzori of Stanley—Mountains of the Moon—Political government and administration of the Soudan—The order of the *Condo*—Sacrifices at every new moon—The magic spirit that disturbs the mind of the Queen-mother—Suuna and the hundred murdered—Bead culture—Three cudgel blows—Another locality selected—Cutting off the hands and blinding—A decree against pipes—The ceremony of the milk—Kamissua, son of Rionga, entrapped—The king eats—The Wanyoro—The *Tiumba*—The *Mbugu*—The ceramic art—Butter—The merchants of Zanzibar—Customs of the Wanyoro—The great dispenser of rain and his delegates—Funeral honours—King Kamrasi's sepulchre—The veneration of the people and the capricious superstition of the despot . . . . . Pp. 36—59

CHAPTER IV

DIFFICULTIES IN UNYORO.

A throne streaming with blood—Absolute power of the king—The *banassura*—Their increasing influence, their recruitment, and their conduct—The king desirous of pleasing—" Movement is life "—The way of deceit and treason—A fatal dualism—Pain destroys illusion—The boldness of yore encouraged by the paternal ghost—Alone in Juaya—Ahmed Akkad's good services—Willing and paid informer—The Dinka boy brave and affectionate—Shooting the thieves—An unpleasant nocturnal visitor—The expulsion of the merchants—I am accused of plotting against the king—A guard on the River Kafu—Biri's servant arrested—Chua will not have me—Plan to attack Wadelai—Emin informed of it by me—At Muimba, June 1, 1887—Obese women—The steamers *Khedive* and *Nyanza* on the Victoria Nile—Burning of the village of Rokora—Destruction of barges—Anger of the king—Letters seized—Biri on the road to Unyoro—Unavoidable danger—Fortunate meeting with my people—The young ruler ignorant of the way to govern—The Waganda resume hostilities—A Winchester rifle, psychical experiment—Joyful welcome—I obtain permission to remain in Unyoro—Fights—A deputation from Waganda—Oakibi and Kauta—The troops of Waganda—They march past my house—The *banassura* fighting—Emin at Kibiro—Alliance or invasion—My expulsion is requested—I am to exchange blood with his son . . . . Pp. 60—81

CHAPTER V.

KABBA REGA'S HOSTILITY.

Occupation of the region on the left bank of the Victoria Nile—Katongoli, the Lango man—A child as a holocaust—Guakamatera, prime minister of King Chua—" The king has ordered me to watch you "—The king reiterates his promises—Neither a single piece of ivory nor a cartridge—The guards' refusal—Attempt by night—Great imprudence—The king wishes me to become his guest—The merchant Hamis—Exchange of victims—The Victoria Nile placed in a position of defence—Sacred boats—Young students—Emin leaves on a visit to the northern stations—I ask for frequent despatch of messengers and steamers—Prisoners in Juaya—The raids at Menakulia—A caravan of Karagua people—Communications with Kafu and Kibiro are forbidden—Delusive hope—The 10th of December 1887—Noble conduct of an enemy—Advice given to Biri—The 31st of December 1887—I think of a friend—The king's wickedness against him—Stanley has arrived—Guakamatera's strange proposal—A goat and a fowl—The great drum gives no sound—A set trap. Pp. 82—96

CHAPTER VI.

A NARROW ESCAPE.

Sad farewell supper—Biri's illusions—" To-morrow I shall be with you "—Shall we turn back ?—The great priest of the Unyoro sorcerers—Opening of the royal gate—The signal is given—An unrestrained crowd—Tied to the trees—" Woe to you ! "—Orders to my boy—Grief and alarm of Biri—A more fortunate soldier—I save my shoes—Our sufferings must not be relieved—Bought by means of a coat—Payment of services—Guakamatera at my residence—Confiscation of all property—Return of the conqueror—" *Gobia, Gobia !* "—The place of execution—Meeting of my domestics—A piece of paper and a pencil—Flight—Followed and threatened—Kagoro protects us—At Kibiro—Lying message of Guakamatera—The breakage of a pipe—I give away my waistcoat—At the salt-pits—From Tokongia—Ntiabo, the wife of the king—Kapidi, the cripple—Neither food nor passage—Driven to the woods—Dinka girl—A plate of beans—Fadl starts in a boat—" *Majungo, Majungo !* "—A colony of Lur—" We'll not kill you "—A happy meeting—" Man dies only by permission of God "—Discouragement subdues us—" The steamer ! the steamer ! "—On the shore of the lake—Refreshing sleep—The *Khedive* in sight—Fresh anxieties—We are saved.
Pp. 97—124

CHAPTER VII.

THE ALBERT NYANZA.

Opinions of the geographers of the first half of this century on Central Africa—Speke and Burton—Discovery of the Tanganika Lake—A great sea—The Victoria Lake discovered by Speke—Rosher's explorations—The Nile flows

CONTENTS.

from Lake Victoria—Speke and Baker—Discovery of Lake Albert—Livingstone's hypothesis contradicted by facts—Gordon in Equatoria—Equatoria ought to find a commercial opening at Zanzibar—It opens a way by the Nile to the lakes—Romolo Gessi explores the Albert Lake—The steamers *Khedive* and *Nyanza* — Colonel Mason's exploration — General Stone's opinion—Stanley and the Beatrice Gulf—From Berber to Khartoum—The Nile between Khartoum and Lado—Difficulty of the traffic by water in the Nile Valley—The sources of the Nile—The Albert Lake—Conformation of its shores—The navigation of the lake—Storms—Crocodiles—Fishing—The lake boats—Kibiro salt-works—Salt trade—Tribute to the king—Cultivation—Products of the forests—Fauna—Inhabitants.

Pp. 125—139

CHAPTER VIII.

FIRST NEWS OF STANLEY'S APPROACH.

Woe to the vanquished—A dignified proposal—Unexpected answer—Faithfulness and disinterestedness badly rewarded—Proposals for the soldiers—Death of Hurshid—Cunning policy of the King of Unyoro—Its consequences—Ballula on the Vurvira mountain—Enchantment of Sunga and congratulations of Umma—The allied Lango — Contradictory news — Sunga's son—Arrival of Stanley—Emin's departure for Msua—Raids into the countries bordering on the Nile—Search for Stanley—Reticence of the natives—Interior condition of the Province—Major Rehan Aga—His declarations—His death—New misfortune—Major Hamid Aga—Demands of the soldiers—Ali remains—Emin does not accept advice from me—Fatal order—Pernicious lull—Demands and proposals of the first battalion—Emin at Kirri—His flight—The firman granting the title of Pasha—Defeat of Befo, chief of the Belinian—Stanley at Ndussuma—The wife of Mpigwa—The brave Mogo—The 27th of April 1888—Stanley's letter—Advice about the best thing to do . . . . Pp. 140—153

CHAPTER IX.

ARRIVAL OF THE EXPEDITION.

Emin appeals to the philanthropy and humanity of the English people—Stanley is summoned—The road to be followed by the Relief Expedition—There is no other than that of the Congo—Provisions fail—The Expedition separates—A disastrous road—Route proposed by Felkin recommended by Schweinfurth and Junker—Peters on the eastern road—Route by Kibali and the Bomokandi—The 29th of April 1888—Henry Stanley—Hope and joy—Emin is not decided about his departure—I remain with Emin—Stanley refuses to perform an act of courtesy by visiting the station—Emin does not explain the dissensions in the Province—His good faith is not justified—Jephson remains with Emin—Stanley's letter and sword—Stanley's proposals to Emin about the future—Scientific labours bear fruit—An angle of Lake Victoria—The arrival of Stanley increases our weakness—Stanley's error in dividing his Expedition—The post of com-

CONTENTS.

mander—Departure of Stanley—King Chua does not forget us—Horrible butchery at Kibiro—The arrogance of King Chua does not alter—He knows of our precarious condition—Minds are agitated—A complaint is made to Stanley—Consequent anger and indignation—Measures of excessive rigour—I cannot succeed in restraining Emin's hand—Jephson incredulous as to my experience and knowledge—The fruit of four years' work and observation—Faithful to the Pasha—Advice that I gave Emin.
Pp. 154—170

CHAPTER X.

EMIN'S ARREST.

An old slave of the Baggara—Beginning of the rebellion—A despot and a drunkard—Captain Fatelmula—The Pasha at Dufilé—Opposition of the soldiers of Kirri—Insult to the Governor—The station of Muggi and Abdallah Menze — Threatening attitude of the soldiers at Laboré — Return to Dufilé—Prisoners of the rebels—Ahmed Dinkani—Resignation of Emin—I hold the knife by the handle—I receive the sad news—I resolve to go to Emin—Conduct of the rebels at Tunguru—The news of Stanley's return and its subsequent contradiction—At Wadelai—Agreement amongst the Egyptians—My arrival at Dufilé—Permission to remain with Emin—Interview with Emin and Vita Hassan—A sitting of the revolutionary assembly—Surprise prepared by the factions—Dismissal of Emin Pasha—I advise Emin to sign his name—The new Governor—Violence against Major Hawashi—Fear of Stanley's return—My sympathy for Emin—Proposed transportation of the prisoners—I oppose the insane proposal—"I'll have him put in chains"—Search of the Governor's house and that of the doctor—Little Ferida—The commander of Msua retires to the mountains—The Mahdists in Rejaf waters—Horrible massacre—The three dervishes and Omar Saleh's letter—Emin's advice—They want war—Imprisonment maintained—Selim Matera and Solyman persuaded by me—Defeat of the troops—Emin and Hassan are enabled to settle at Wadelai—Departure from Dufilé . . . Pp. 171—192

CHAPTER XI.

CROCODILE HUNTING.

Bows and kissing of the hand—The crocodile hunter—The Bari of Bedden —The Dinka's whistling—The clerk Taib—A difficult position must not be attacked openly—Proposed abandonment of Wadelai—Yussuf Fahmi's mother-in-law—At Fagongo—Arrival of the steamer *Khedive*—Mahdists' discomfiture at Dufilé—Injunctions to the Pasha to return to Wadelai—Emin's refusal—Major Selim Matera's letter—Mahdist dollars—Evacuation of Dufilé—Captain Solyman—His death—Emin's fears—I do not agree with him—Lieutenant Saleh—Indignant revolutionists—The two factions—Execution of chief Sunga—His corpse on the shore—Kolikio and Katto—King Chua madly enraged—A slaughtered child—A black bullock and a girl twelve years old—The Lur of the mountain—Boki is dead—

CONTENTS.

Funeral ceremonies—Proclamation of the successor—Raids of the Unyoro—Emin an ornithologist—Jephson a hunter—Emin will not leave Tunguru—Stanley's return—His letter to Jephson—Emin left to himself—Jephson and Emin write to the chief of the troops at Wadelai—Jephson's departure—I advise Emin to take time—What an imprudence would cost us.
Pp. 193—217

CHAPTER XII.

STANLEY'S MANIFESTO.

News of the arrival of Stanley—Departure from Wadelai—Nomination of a commission to be sent to the head of the Expedition—Refusal of Emin Pasha—New perils—The means of avoiding them—Proposal accepted by Emin—The opinion of the officers of the Province asked—Departure for Msua—New intrigues—Emin concedes a pardon and amnesty—Selim Bey—The voyage to Were—Osman Latif—His equivocal conduct—He throws himself into the river—" You should have left this carrion to be drowned!"—Always the same—Counsels given to Emin—Emin shares my opinion—Emin goes to Stanley's camp—William Bonny—Danger of being assailed by the troops of the King of Unyoro—Bonny sent "not to fight, but to bring over the luggage"—Return of Emin to Were—Colonel Fatelmula and his menaces—Impression of the officers after their visit to Stanley—Letter from Stanley to the officers at Wadelai—Advice given to Emin—Difficulties of the situation—Flight of soldiers and servants—Departure of Vita Hassan—The road from Were to Buguera—Arrival at the encampment of the Relief Expedition . . Pp. 218—230

CHAPTER XIII.

DEPARTURE OF THE EXPEDITION.

Waterparting between the Aruwimi and the Albert Lake—The plateau of Buguera—Flora and fauna—The chimpanzee—Catching with nets—Drunk in the trap—A chimpanzee drummer—The Walegga, Wahuma, and Vavra—The Mount Virika—The camp of Buguera—Service of the camp—Transports from Were—Refusal of the Zanzibaris—Stanley *Bulamatari*—His character—Robbers rewarded—The departure is fixed—Even Captain Fatelmula wishes to go to Egypt—Conversation with Stanley—The officers complain—The Koran peeps out—Samadia—How to cure headache—A letter of recommendation to a Wahuma—The torture of the *tabatt*—*Bismillah il Rahman*—Final evacuation of the camp of Were—Stanley's fears—Emin's hesitation—The 5th of April—"I leave you to God"—The assembly—"As sure as my name is Stanley"—Rigorous watch—Those who leave—Omar the Shillook—Well-distributed bastinado—Abandonment and burning of the camp of Buguera—The river Tarara—Mpinga and Mazamboni—Flight of sixty-nine soldiers and servants—Council of inquiry—Mild sentence—Necessity of procuring porters—Stanley seriously

CONTENTS.   xi

ill—Fever and rheumatism—A furious hurricane—Chests of ammunition buried—Flight of servants—Arrest of Rehan—Summary judgment—The body thrown among grass . . . . Pp. 231—257

CHAPTER XIV.

THE VIRIKA MOUNTAINS.

Marching order of the caravan—Toil—Diseases—Hard treatment—Slighted complaints—The little Amina—Departure from Niangabo—At Joddo—Selim Bey's letter—The reply—At Buhogo—The attack of King Chua's *banassura*—The brave Oakil killed on the battle-field—Unlucky youth!—His tomb—The land before us—Western route—The study of the White Mountains—The Semliki river—Crossing of the stream—The Wamba country—The Bassua—At the foot of the Virika—Sanitary conditions of the caravan—Clerk Wassif—A horrible thing to relate—Fighting the Manyema—Lieutenant Stairs's exploration—Karalla, a servant, killed by the Vakongio with their lances—New victims—Stanley arms the servants to guard the caravan—Discontent augments—Exit from the forest—The Usongora—The sun shines on the Virika peaks—Lake Ruitan—The salt lake—King Chua's power—Salt trade—At Amkongo—Attack by the soldiers of the King of Unyoro—Return to Unyampaka—Moral and material conditions of the caravan—Abundance of food—Routes from Unyampaka—Selection of the route through Nkole . . . . . Pp. 258—271

CHAPTER XV.

FROM LAKE RUITAN TO LAKE VICTORIA.

The Nkole State—Conformation of the region—Wahuma and Wichinesi—King Ntali—A shepherd, not a king—Fear of strangers—" I will not flee, but wait for you "—Negotiations started in Unyoro—Hospitality granted to Uganda Christians—Mtesa driven away—Slaughters—Either circumcision or death—Karema—Persecutions against Christians—Muanza christened at the French Mission—A difficult path—The Mpogo swamp—The king's concessions to the caravan—Disorderly conduct of soldiers and Zanzibaris at Ruganda—Fight to rescue a woman—The king's son visits the camp—Murder of a Manyema and of a woman—The river Kagera—A girl carried away by a leopard—The mineral waters of Ntagata—Karagua's country—King Ndàgora a vassal of the King of Uganda—Carried in a hammock—Death by cold on the way to Batenga—The Urigi Lake—Fatelmula, a soldier, abandoned to the Mtara people's revenge—His horrible death—Requisitions end—Provisions are bought—Fatal effects of manioc—An Akka's flight—The Victoria Lake—At the British Mission—Mackay.
Pp. 272—287

CHAPTER XVI.

ARRIVAL AT BAGAMOYO.

David Livingstone and slavery—Humanity is one and the same everywhere—Explorers and missionaries—Robbers of men in Egypt and Zanzibar—The war in Africa—Europe intervenes—Persecution of the missionaries—Suppression of the slave treaty—The words of Cameron—The means must be adequate to the end—Want of news—Stanley decides on departing—Arrangements for the journey—The districts of Urima and Boniera—Attack by Negroes in the district of Kelia—Four days of hostilities—General flight of the natives—Atrocity committed by a Soudanese porter—*Adansonia digitata*—The chief Mitinginya—The Wanyamuesi—Evil school of the Arabs—The *tembe*—The Masai—Theft of three asses—A Masai saved from deserved punishment—Fauna and flora—The chief Icongo—The Fathers Giraud and Schynse—The forest of sorrows—The river of palms—The cisterns of Makomero—We leave the forest—A remembrance of the caravan for the Wanyamuesi—We set foot in Ugogo—Mualata—The Wagogo—The *tembe* of Ugogo—Sands and desolation—The chief Nianguira—A foolish pretext—Robbery of guns—The caravan at Unyamuesi—Letters from Wissmann to Emin—The village of Mussanga—The forest of Jonyo or of the salt water—A well-merited punishment—At Mpwapwa—Usagara—A lovely region—At Mrogoro—The French missionaries—Captain Gravenreuth—At Kingani—The explorer of the Cassai—At Bagamoyo—Accident to Emin—The return . . . . Pp. 288—313

APPENDIX.

METEOROLOGICAL OBSERVATIONS IN UNYORO . . . Pp. 315—334

INDEX TO VOLUME II. . . . . Pp. 335—350

LIST OF ILLUSTRATIONS—VOLUME II.

SEPARATE FULL PAGE ILLUSTRATIONS.

PLATE		TO FACE PAGE
I.	Landscape in Central Africa	(*Frontispiece*)
II.	Daily Greetings to King Chua by his Kinsmen	18
III.	View of a Village in Unyoro	28
IV.	A Village of Shooli, at the Foot of Mount Shooa	44
V.	Execution by Three Blows with Clubs	52
VI.	Milk Ceremony	54
VII.	Burial of King Kamrasi	59
VIII.	King Chua's Fattened Females	71
IX.	Emin Shells the Canoes of King Chua's Warriors	72
X.	Musicians of Rionga, one of the Chiefs of Unyoro	82
XI.	Transport of King Chua's Canoes	87
XII.	Casati with his Servants	93
XIII.	Mass of Gneiss Rock on Mount Logwek	125
XIV.	Rejaf, with Mount Logwek	128
XV.	Wooded Scenery of the Nile near Kirri	132
XVI.	The Murchison Falls near Shooa-Moru	136
XVII.	The First Meeting of Emin with Stanley	158
XVIII.	The Egyptian Station at Kirri	173
XIX.	A Bari Village	196
XX.	Casati, with his Negro Child, Vita Hassan, and Dr. Junker	229
XXI.	An Ape Paradise	232
XXII.	Negroes warming themselves by the Fire	255
XXIII.	Execution of a Deserter	257
XXIV.	A Negress of the Caravan carried away by a Leopard	281
XXV.	Casati Ill on the Return	282
XXVI.	A Slave Caravan	290
XXVII.	Warriors of the Urima District	294
XXVIII.	African Women of Various Tribes	298
XXIX.	The Banquet at Bagamoyo	313

LIST OF ILLUSTRATIONS.

TEXT ILLUSTRATIONS.

	PAGE
General Gordon	7
General Gordon's Head	13
Attending Chua's Sick Cattle	19
"We are thirsting for Blood"	30
A Human Sacrifice	34
Shooli Warriors	37
A Shooli Family	39
A Shooli Chief	42
A Shooli Chief	43
Shooli Vessels and Ornaments	46
An Unyoro Princess	54
Musical Instruments of the Shooli	58
Flight of King Chua	75
My Negotiations with the Chiefs of Uganda	78
Casati bound to a Tree	103
King Chua's Relatives in Court Attire	106
I am dragged along by the Guards	110
View of the Banks south of Fola	131
Landscape near the Albert Lake	135
A Shooli Girl	143
Major Hawashi Effendi	151
Emin and the Mutineers	175
Bari Women	195
Facsimile of Selim Matera's Letter	202
Ditto ditto	203
Coins of the Mahdi	205
Osman Latif	222
Little Amina	261
Fording the Mpogo Swamp	276
A Woman stolen	278
Ntali's Present to Stanley	279

LIST OF ILLUSTRATIONS.

	PAGE
Distribution of Goods	285
Negro of Urima	293
Attack on the Caravan	295
Village of Ugogo	305
Delivery of a Letter to Emin	307
Lieutenant Rochus Schmidt	309
Meeting with Major Wissmann	311
Bagamoyo, where Emin's Accident occurred	312

MAP FOR VOLUME II.

Map of the Return Journey from the Albert Nyanza
to the Indian Ocean.

TEN YEARS IN EQUATORIA.

CHAPTER I.

THE FALL OF KHARTOUM.

The carpenter of Dongola—May 1884—A life of penance—The standard of rebellion unfurled—Causes of disaffection in the Egyptian Soudan—The slave trade—Raouf Pasha and his measures—A Babylonian banquet—Abd-el-Kader Pasha—Defeat of the troops—Wise measures of the Governor—General Hicks' expedition—*Ti sebil Allah*—Trophies of human skulls—Osman Digna, chief of the dervishes—Plans concocted in Cairo—General Gordon—His mission—His intentions—Prestige of his name—Battle of El-Teb—Fall of Sinkat—Surrender of Tokar—General Graham—Abandonment of the campaign in the Eastern Provinces—Tactics; difficulties arising from the nature of the soil, from the climate and temperament of the enemy—Gordon cannot leave Khartoum—Relief expedition under the command of General Wolseley—Bombardment of Berber—Death of Colonel Stewart—Faulty division of the forces—The Mahdi's exertions—Wilson before Khartoum—The catastrophe—The soldier without fear and without reproach—The Geddal of the Mohammedans.

"MERCIFUL GOD has put the sword of victory into my hands; and to prove to the world that I am the Mahdi, He has marked my left cheek with a mole. In the confusion of battle, I shall be led by the luminous standard of Azraël, the angel of death, the exterminator of my enemies."

With these words the carpenter of Dongola, the hermit of the island of Abba, Mohammed Ahmed, announced to the world his divine mission to propagate Islamism and to found the reign of happiness and justice.

In May 1881 the attention of the Egyptian Government was turned to Mohammed Ahmed. Until then they had been pacified by the illusion that it was a passing bubble of fanaticism and religious commotion, which is often seen in the East, and, as such, easy to master and extinguish; but a warlike challenge of this description had to be met very differently.

On the anniversary of the Feast of Ramadan, the lean and squalid apostle who had spent a life of penance in the midst of privations and fastings, confirmed his mission, by baffling, sword in hand, all the efforts made to capture him, thus corroborating his claim to supposed sanctity.

Abu Saoud was defeated, and Rashid Bey, who attempted to check the triumphant march of the Mahdi, fell at the head of his troops, who were horribly slaughtered. The Mahdi unfurled the standard of rebellion at Jebel Kadar, in the Baggara region.

The causes of disaffection in the Soudan were numerous: the venality that prevailed in the appointment of functionaries, the unjust and oppressive manner in which the taxes were levied, and the preference accorded to the Egyptian element, fostered a silent but slow agitation, ready to become an open revolt against the brutality of the conquest and the hated oppression of the Egyptian Government.

The suppression of the slave trade had dried up the source of gain and spread misery through the country without producing any beneficial result. It was still further increased by heavy taxes. The feeling of hatred grew stronger every day, and the following precept from the Koran was echoed in the heart of all believers: "Kill those who wish to kill you. Kill them wherever you meet them; drive them away from the place whence they would drive you, for the temptation of idolatry is worse than death."

Folly, nay, madness, hastened the bursting of the tempest. The Governor, Raouf Pasha, by a stroke of his pen had destroyed General Gordon's heroic and intelligent work. The dismissal of Soudanese employés and their substitution by Egyptians; reduction of the number of officers in the regular army; excessive economy in all public offices; further imposition of taxes, and the sending of a considerable sum of money to Cairo, were the beginnings of his rule at Khartoum.

He was supposed to have propped up the crumbling edifice, and his ears were delighted by the songs of praise sung by the native poets in the midst of revels and concerts which were held in his honour; and when at last the cry of defiance and death roused his dull mind, the hand of fate had already written the Biblical words on the wall of the banquet-hall.

Raouf was succeeded by Abd-el-Kader Pasha (August 11). The rebellion was at its height, and the situation was rendered worse by the pompous and fallacious assertions which had been sent to Cairo by Giegler Pasha and also by the inefficiency of the measures taken by him.

On June 7, Yussuf Pasha's corps was surprised in a thick wood near Mount Kadar, and completely annihilated. The Mahdi, strengthened by the prestige of his victories, sent an expedition to Sennaar, through the ford of Abu Zeir, took possession of the north-west bank of the Nile, and occupied Kordofan.

Abd-el-Kader began the campaign with some success; he reorganised his troops; retook El-Obeid; liberated Sennaar from the hordes infesting it; and defeated the Mahdists at Duemme and Dara. Mohammed Ahmed again fell upon El-Obeid with great fury, cruelly slaughtered the garrison and inhabitants, took it, and settled there, making it the base of his future operations. The treason and defection of the chiefs had facilitated the victory. The Mahdi had won the sympathy of the people and confirmed the divine nature of his mission by deeds.

Then the battle of Tel-el-Kebir occurred, which brought British protection into Egypt. Colonel Stewart was sent to Khartoum to ascertain the causes of the rebellion and to suggest remedies, and was assisted in the work by Colonel Messedaglia, late Governor of Darfur, under Gordon. The reorganisation of the army, plans for the campaign, the preparations necessary to carry them out, were discussed and settled with the full consent of the Governor-General; and the negotiations entered into with the natives led to a political success. The battles of Mahatuk and Meshra-el-Dahi, and the victory of Segadi soon promised the near repression of the insurrection in the Eastern Provinces. But Abd-el-Kader was abruptly recalled to Cairo and Ala-el-Din Pasha appointed in his stead. General Hicks was entrusted with the continuation of the campaign in the Soudan, and he defeated the insurgents twice; but, ignoring Abd-el-Kader's plan of campaign, and the wise counsels of Colonel Stewart, he directed his entire attention towards the reconquest of Kordofan. He rejected the plan of operation upon Omdurman towards Dara, supported by Messedaglia with sound military arguments, and resolved to operate upon El-Obeid and along the valley of Abu-Hableh, which lies between narrow passes continually dominated by higher grounds.

The expeditionary force, consisting of 11,000 men, 500 horses, and 5500 camels, departed from Khartoum, September 9, and in twelve days arrived at Duemme, after having suffered the loss of a great many men and animals through the difficulties of the road and climate.

The march was continued in two columns, one proceeding by the main route and the other, under Ala-el-Din Pasha towards Melbes. Near Alloba, a detachment of Mahdists was defeated.

On November 2, General Hicks was suddenly assailed whilst crossing a woody region (three hours' journey in length), but defeated the rebels, who were compelled to withdraw in consequence of the resistance of the solid square of men. The want of water, however, compelled the General to hasten his march, but, Nov. 4, both columns were surrounded, in the valley of Kashgil, by a force of about 100,000 armed men, who cursed and derided them from the neighbouring heights with the cry *Ti sebil Allah*, the fatal invocation which preceded extermination. Every effort was vain; heroism was powerless in presence of the iron wall which barred every route. On the afternoon of the 7th, the attack was general and furious, till at last it became a horrid butchery, and not a battle. All the soldiers and the Generals themselves (Hicks and Ala-el-Din) were put to the edge of the sword. Mohammed Ahmed gathered the heads of his fallen enemies into heaps, as trophies of war, and then retired to El Obeid, forgetting, in the ecstasies of religious ceremonies, to turn his victory to further advantage.

The news reached Khartoum, Nov. 19, and caused general alarm. Divided counsels led to the wildest resolutions. The Prophet's cause was really believed to be protected by God. The insurrection gained ground, and the quietest tribes declared themselves in favour of the Mahdi. Even in the Eastern Soudan fortune smiled on the rebels; the Hadendowa, who had rebelled at the instigation of Osman Digna in the preceding August, seriously injured Captain Moncrief's column in the neighbourhood of Tokar, and, Dec. 10, they drove away the Egyptian troops, under Hassan Bey, who had been sent to relieve Sinkat. Baker Pasha then took the command at Suakim.

In Egypt, the situation of the Soudan Provinces was considered hopeless. Inability to subdue so formidable a rebellion was obvious. The British Government advised, and the Khedive accepted the proposal to withdraw all Egyptian functionaries and soldiers from the Soudan, as well as all the individuals who were directly connected with their Government, and the Christians of various nationalities. Heroic advice indeed, without even the probability of success! The exodus of 60,000 persons upon a long journey, through a poor country in a state of rebellion, with insufficient means of transport and defence, would only have hastened the final catastrophe.

General Gordon was appointed to carry out this difficult undertaking. The man of genius, with a generous heart and firm faith, the apostle of redemption, the soldier of mystical aspiration, with the sword in one hand, and the Bible in the other. The liberation of slaves and the defeat of God's enemies were first in his thoughts, and he willingly devoted his life to the holy enterprise, smiling in the midst of danger, heedless of the morrow. To evacuate the Soudan seemed to him a manifest act of cowardice, and he showed by his first acts that he meant to establish a native Government.

At Berber, he proclaimed the independence of the Soudan, and handed over the administration of Kordofan to the Mahdi, remitting all unpaid taxes and suspending the law about the repression of slavery.

He reached Khartoum, February 18, 1884. With his knowledge of military engineering he completed the defensive works of the fortress, superintended the reorganisation of the troops, and took measures for the supply of provisions. He took Colonel Stewart as his collaborator.

The prestige of his name paralysed the action of the rebels. Mohammed Ahmed dared not fight openly before he had strengthened his position by secret activity. His complete inaction during February, March, and

GENERAL GORDON.

April, inspired Gordon with hope; he thought his triumph was predestined. Excessive confidence in his own providential missions increased the fervour of his resistance, and encouraged him to give up all idea of evacuating the Soudan.

But in the neighbourhood of Suakim the situation was going from bad to worse. All Baker's attempts to relieve the beleaguered garrisons of Tokar and Sinkat not only failed, but resulted disastrously. Here is an account of the battle of El-Teb, in the words of Colonel Messedaglia, who was present at it :—

"The expeditionary corps was composed of 3500 men, the remainder having been left behind at Suakim and Trinkitat, to garrison those places. They had four Krupps, two machine, and two siege guns. But these were difficult to carry on account of the salt pools, which, though open to attack, it was necessary to cross for about two miles from the sea, in order to gain the interior; it was therefore resolved to construct a small fort south-west of the pools, in order to protect the passage of the ordnance.

"On the morning of February 4, the troops had hardly drawn up in marching order, when it began to rain heavily, and the air became so dense that it obscured everything. Eight hundred horsemen formed the vanguard, including the scouts; then came the artillery, together with the main body, the camels protected by the flanking companies, and then the rearguard. After about four hours' march, the rebels began to show themselves laterally in groups of forty or fifty, we fired four cannon shots at them; the fog becoming thicker and thicker.

"In the neighbourhood of the wells of El-Teb, about 300 rebels suddenly appeared on our left flank, and, soon after, another band came upon our right, which compelled Baker to fall back, at the trot, upon the main body. The noise of the fusillade, to which our troops were unaccustomed, and the hurried retreat of the staff, together with the vanguard, caused a panic in the expeditionary corps, which (as the enemy were between the vanguard and the main body) was increased by our soldiers firing upon one another; the camels added to the confusion. We had fallen into a clever ambuscade. The rebels had dug rifle pits along the side of the road, each of which was occupied by four or five men, who had covered themselves with leaves and branches of trees, and in consequence of the fog, the vanguard had marched past without observing them."

It was impossible to form squares; a hand-to-hand fight took place round the wells; numbers prevailed over valour, and Baker with difficulty succeeded in reaching Suakim with a few followers.

On February 11, Sinkat fell into the hands of Osman Digna. The brave garrison tried to break the ring formed round them by the enemy, but failed. and all fell. The garrison of Tokar, impressed by the terrible event, soon after surrendered to the victorious rebels. The relief corps under General Graham formed to collect the Egyptian troops in the territory of Suakim, and for operating eventually in the interior of the country, numbering 5000 soldiers with the transport service, disembarked there, February 21. The General marched to Tokar without delay, taking the route previously followed by Baker; and at El-Teb inflicted a memorable defeat upon Osman Digna, killing 2300 of his men. But Osman Digna, being reinforced by the fanatical dervishes who were accompanied by a large number of natives, attempted a bold and sudden attack upon the strong fort at Suakim, but was checked at Tamai, with heavy loss. The British, although victors, did not feel strong enough to proceed to Sinkat, and the campaign was thus closed. The opening of the road to the Nile, *viâ* Suakim and Berber, being considered impossible the British Corps returned to Suez.

The war and its development in several combats as well as in other insurrectionary events, clearly showed how improper it was to resort to the strategy of regular armies when a fanatical attack is to be contended with; and that, on the contrary, considering the superiority of the weapons of a regular army, the discipline of its soldiers and the confidence which accrues from their military training, quick tactics are advisable.

Slow movements encourage rebellious bodies, whose numbers increase from day to day, and their defeat, for this very reason, becomes more difficult; therefore, it is indispensable to attack first and promptly, and, of course, with all the energy necessary. In cases of this description, the charge of such an enemy is more like one of cavalry than an attack of infantry, and the change from defence to attack is often the cause of irreparable disaster. The tactical formations resorted to in fights with an irregular army must be such as to develop an extensive line of fire without interfering with the compactness required to resist a charge.

One cannot precisely give any rule for attacking an enemy with the main force ; one must be guided by the enemy's mode of fighting, his moral strength, and his arms. The square presents indisputable tactical defects ; to utilise it thoroughly, small reserves should be provided, ready to rush to the succour of any salient points menaced. Therefore, in presence of frequent and unexpected attacks from agile and dexterous assailants, it is always preferable to sacrifice mobility, rather than to run the risk of an immediate and irreparable disaster. The muscular vigour of such men facilitates the rapidity of their attack, therefore ground, easy of access, is less favourable for sustaining the shock of a charge, and for preparing counter attacks. The habitual tendency of cavalry to follow up a charge always generates an injurious confusion, which it is difficult to remedy, and which often results in a medley. The arms of cavalry soldiers should be composed of lance and sword ; the first being indispensable in the charges, the second in fighting hand to hand. But in these countries, in face of such enemies, in the heart of a general insurrection, the greatest peril is surprise on the march and sudden attacks. Hence, the most important maxim to follow is, diligent preparation against surprise, an active, bold, incessant and intelligent service of scouts, and concentration of forces, as their separation is always a cause of disaster.

The opportunity of a successful evacuation of the Soudan had been missed by General Gordon, and he was hemmed in on all sides. The British Government had submitted to the sad necessity of giving him up, but public opinion and the press demanded the preparation of an expedition to relieve him, and Mr. Gladstone yielded to the wish of the nation.

An expedition was then fitted out, the best route discussed, and, after a lengthy discussion, it was agreed to send a body of troops by way of the Nile, under the command of General Wolseley. The concentration of troops was effected in September. In November the General was at Dongola, and, December 16, headquarters were transferred to Korti. Meanwhile Gordon, being informed of the succour sent to him, despatched a flotilla, under the command of Colonel Stewart, in order to facilitate operations on the Nile. Stewart repulsed the rebels' attacks, shelled and destroyed Berber, and steamed off towards Dongola with only one vessel, sending the others back to Khartoum. But, having reached the Cataract of Merawe, the strong current and an awkward manœuvre hurled the vessel in a wrong direction, and it was wrecked upon the rocks. Colonel Stewart, the French Consul, and the crew were slaughtered by the Arabs of Monasir.

The year 1885 opened in the midst of great difficulties. The concentration of troops had not proceeded with the rapidity expected. The necessity of hastening the march suggested the idea of dividing the forces.

The nature of the sandy plains caused many obstacles, the hostility of the natives great fatigue and delay. General Sir Herbert Stewart took the road to Metemmeh, and General Earle the one to Berber.

But the Mahdi had not been inactive; he knew that the prestige of his name and the triumph of his cause were on a decisive trial. He reinforced Berber and entrusted it to the care of Nur Angara, a man of great courage and energy, already known for his ribaldry in Darfur. Metemmeh was fortified and garrisoned by numerous troops, Kassala beleaguered, and the Mahdi himself directed the siege of Khartoum. He knew that he could concentrate his efforts on the Nile, and that there was nothing to fear on the Eastern Nile, as he was protected by Osman Digna and his faithful Dervishes.

The British defeated the enemy at Abu-Klea, January 17, 1885, but were checked at Metemmeh, and were obliged to entrench themselves at Gubat.

Time pressed, and every delay might have proved fatal. Two steamers were sent up the Nile, under the command of Colonel Wilson, and on the 28th they were in sight of Khartoum, and were received with a brisk discharge of musketry and artillery. The town had fallen into the hands of the Mahdi, Mohammed Ahmed, and Wilson was compelled to steam back. His two steamers were wrecked upon the rocks, and he reached the British camp under great difficulties, the bearer of the sad news.

On January 26, Khartoum was startled by the sudden clashing of arms, heart-rending cries, people fleeing, and disorder on all sides. The square by the river side, where the Governor's palace stood, re-echoed with insulting fanatical howling. The rebels demanded Gordon, whom they called the enemy of God: threats were followed by deeds of violence, shots were fired, attempts made to open the gates; murders were committed, and, in short, it was a scene of hell. Treason was reaping its infamous reward, and the soldier with-

GENERAL GORDON'S HEAD.

out fear and without reproach was the victim of it, abominably sold by the very men whom his large heart had loaded with benefits. The palace gate was opened, and a man presented himself wearing the noble uniform of a soldier, with the sword by his side and a glittering array of decorations on his breast. That man was Gordon. With his arms folded, he stopped a few steps from the gate, calmly raising his head, with a serene and placid countenance. The majesty of the hero impressed even his bloodthirsty enemies, and silence prevailed, but it was the last token of respect received by the noble martyr from the rebels. A shot was suddenly fired, and Gordon, hit on the forehead, fell as if struck by lightning. His head was cut off, stuck on a pole, and placed at the entrance of Mohammed Ahmed's tent; his body was thrown.into the Nile. A dreadful massacre filled the unhappy town with horror for several days.

The Mahdi had triumphed; an undeniable proof of his sanctity; the herald of his victory, the Geddal, the Antichrist of the Mohammedans, had been conquered and was dead. The kingdom of justice and happiness was about to begin.

CHAPTER II.

LIFE IN UNYORO.

Hostilities cease—The *matamure*—The king shows himself—Waganda and Wanyoro—Muanga and Kabba Rega—King Chua (Kabba Rega)—He remembers his friend Emin—Juaya—His royal palace—The morning greeting of king and people—The king's favourite occupation—" Thou art a shepherd"—Simulated piety and manifest avarice—His sons brought up by shepherds—No profane eye is to rest on the king's cows—The milkers—Reception at an audience—Object of my mission—The good Kategora—Covetous intentions of the king—I speak with the king—Occupation of Tunguru and Msua—Arrival of Biri—The king yields—Hopes reposed in Biri—Kategora poisoned—" He dies, he dies!"—Abd Rehman made proud—Vexations—Kisa and Gumangi—Emin believes in Kabba Rega's loyalty—The soldiers of Equatoria—Emin loses a good opportunity—The Shooli rebels defeated and subdued—Pantomime of the Lango—" We are thirsting for blood "—The dead fowl—The throne in danger—The queen-mother, a priestess and magician—The ceremony of the *mpango*—Kisa of Muenghe—Rejoicings and dancing—Burning of Juaya—A heap of ashes.

THE sounds of war are hushed, the enemy has left the country ; the timid Wanyoro return from the caves and woods, to which they had fled at the first rumour of war, to their villages and fields, and with discouraged eyes contemplate at every step the horrors of devastation by fire and rapine, perpetrated by the furious enemies who had overthrown their country.

They anxiously seek for their hidden *matamure* (granaries), but the magic power of their adversaries (as they believe) has discovered and emptied them.

The spectre of inevitable famine overshadows the country, and slaughter adds to it the contagious smallpox ; for the miserable dead, according to their custom, lie unburied amongst the grass that borders the roads, shamefully covered with dirty rags. But the king has shown himself; he has emerged from the hiding-place that has protected him during the war. He promises to take vengeance for his injured country and to triumph over her enemies. Meantime he invites his people to return to the works of peace. Labour is resumed with fervour. Huts rise, villages are erected, men plough and sow the land; the herds return to their former pastures, the natives take up the thread of interrupted trade.

Waganda and Wanyoro! Two peoples who have a common origin, language, and customs. Muanga and Kabba Rega, their kings are of the same lineage, both powerful and equally ambitious and cruel.

Muanga, son and successor of Mtesa, a young man with a hard heart and warped mind, made it his study to destroy the little good that his father had done. The first thing he did was to reject the counsels of the old ministers, and to place foolish and badly disposed men in the chief offices.

After having caused Bishop Hannington to be assassinated, he began a persecution of the neophytes of the English Church and condemned them to death by hundreds. He ill-treated the missionaries themselves, and soon after made them practically prisoners. He then madly entered into a war with the King of Unyoro, thus increasing the misery and desolation of the country. A despotic monarch, cruel, and of vile habits, the enemy of all good, and hostile to foreigners, he did not hesitate to commit any enormity.

Chua, king of Unyoro (commonly known by the name of Kabba Rega), a bitter enemy of the Egyptian Government, for years and years kept the northern entrance of his kingdom closed, and, affairs in the Soudan having gone from bad to worse, he suddenly remembered Dr. Emin Effendi, who once visited him, and who was Governor of Equatoria. He did not remember this "friend," as he now called him, when he was receiving and favouring deserters from the Egyptian Provinces; but . . . . ivory was in abundance in the neighbouring station of Wadelai, and muskets and ammunition were in the hands of those soldiers, to whom every way of escape was closed.

Chua is a negro, cowardly, suspicious, a procrastinator, and of an irresolute spirit; narrow-minded, false in speech, and ever yielding to evil influences—a real compound of malice and cowardice.

Superstition and fear of the evil eye are strong in him, as in all the blacks; but if he perceives that any course of action may be useful to him, he alters his mind, gives up his belief, and takes any road that is presented to him.

The spirit of the dead Kamrasi had guided him in the choice of the site of his new residence, and, faithful to the religion of his ancestors, he had settled at Juaya, predestined to be the capital of his kingdom.

The royal mansion is entered by seven doors, each of which is reserved for a special caste of persons; among these are the door for the inhabitants of the district; for the *Magnoro*; for the Wahuma shepherds; the door for visitors from other countries resident in the realm; and lastly the door for the *mpango*, specially used by the *Mabitu* or the members of the royal family. It is in this section of the palace —the largest and most sumptuous—that human sacrifices are prepared.

Every day at sunrise it is customary for the king, attired in a traditional habit, head and feet bare, covered with a large *mbugu* (kind of toga) fastened with a knot on his left shoulder, to receive compliments and felicitations from his relations, amidst the blare of trumpets and the beating of drums. And the people cheer and bow to him before going to their daily work; calling him a Sovereign, absolute and potent, beneficent father, dispenser of every good, the jealous guardian of the rights of the State.

King Chua's favourite occupation, which absorbed the greater part of his day and consoled him when his heart was afflicted by the duties and cares (not always pleasant) of the kingdom, was the administration of the numerous dairy farms in his possession.

In the hall of the Wahuma he listened to reports upon the sanitary condition of his numerous cows, and the need of various reforms; he dispensed orders and prescriptions for sick animals, arranged for gifts and sales, and was prodigal of praises. He passed summary and severe sentences, which were often capricious.

"Thou art a shepherd, I am a warrior," said his brother, Kabamiro, to him (at the time when his father being dead, the country was agitated as to his successor), "leave the care and affairs of the kingdom to me, and I will give you all the flocks and herds."

But Chua wished for both herds and throne, and trafficked with Solyman Dand, the slave dealer, against his brother's life; Kabamiro fell, and the detestable monarch, attitudinising with a simulated pity, refused to pay the price of the horrid compact.

Chua (the son of a Wahuma woman) has a special love for cattle breeding; he possesses 150,000 large cattle, the result of continual raids into the regions of Lake Ruitan, and to the preservation of them he gives diligent care. His sons received their first training from the shepherds, wearing the traditional Wahuma costume, the skin of a calf finely dressed hanging from their backs like a small mantle.

DAILY GREETINGS TO KING CHUA BY HIS KINSMEN.

KING CHUA'S CATTLE.

No profane eye must gaze upon the beloved cattle, and when their presence in the road is announced by loud cries, those who are there must either fly or turn their backs on the sacred train.

The milk is collected by special people, who are forbidden to look at it, and it is carefully covered when sent or brought to the king's dwelling. A milker suspected of bewitching the royal milk was beaten to

ATTENDING CHUA'S SICK CATTLE.

death, without any form of trial. The distribution of it is made according to rules established by the king, who assigns the quantities for his sons and wives. His mother has her own dairies, over which she presides with an enthusiasm equal to her son's.

At the gate, looking upon a large open space, where the people usually assemble, he gives public audience, encourages his warriors, pronounces sentences, and distributes alms, though sparingly.

The 2nd of June, 1886, I was publicly received by the king. He wore a dress of elegant woollen cloth, finely worked and ornamented; his head was covered with a red tarboosh, according to the Arab custom. He sat upon a large seat, placing his august feet upon a very beautiful leopard skin. He was of colossal form, of gigantic stature, with a full and expressive face, and a smile more sarcastic than amiable. Ready of speech, correct in gesture, Chua awoke a sentiment of sympathy in whoever saw him for the first time. His eldest son sat at his left hand upon a wooden stool placed lower down. The great men of the kingdom formed a circle like a crown, inside the hut, seated on the ground in the Arab style of showing reverence, and covered with fresh papyrus.* Behind the monarch was a silk drapery of Indian manufacture, imported from Zanzibar, and from the rear of this the heads of curious boys occasionally protruded. Six young men of the royal family surrounded the throne, musket in hand. I was seated to the right of the king, at a few paces from him. The audience was short, but cordial.

Wishing to profit by the good disposition of Chua, I formulated, at the next audience, the demands of the Governor, who had sent me; they were a free and open road for the transmission of correspondence; the speedy conclusion of peace with Uganda, to obtain which object I induced the Governor to enforce the payment of the tribute; power of obtaining goods from Uganda and from the merchants of Unyoro; a free passage for officials and armed soldiers to Egypt; alliance with Ntali, in order that we might be able to use the road through the territory of Nkole, in case of the failure of the negotiations with Muanga; and the

* When the papyrus becomes dry or faded, it is changed.

despatch of a representative to Wadelai. But the inveterate hatred that prevailed amongst the Wanyoro since Baker made his armed appearance there, kept the king's mind in a state of doubt and uncertainty.

The good old minister, Kategora, tried to explain our pacific intentions to him, but the military party, led by a man named Abd Rehman, a Zanzibari, was in a state of agitation, and concocted shameful plots against us.

* * * * * *

The king consented to the transit of correspondence, but, at the same time, kept back letters coming from Uganda. He granted permission for the passage of the troops, providing that they were sent at intervals and in small numbers. He stated that negotiations with the King of Nkole were progressing favourably, but at the same time expelled Nguro, the latter's representative, and sent an envoy to Wadelai with friendly messages and promises to his "friend the doctor," as he called the Governor.

The fears I expressed when dissuading Emin from taking the road to the South and forming a friendship with Kabba Rega, were confirmed only too soon; it became necessary to frustrate his wicked projects, and to overcome our deceitful enemy by prudence and watchfulness.

I entered into arrangements with some Zanzibari merchants who were in the country, and by their means I was able to send and receive correspondence from the English Missions in Uganda. In this manner it came to my knowledge that Mohammed Biri had left Uganda with goods, but had been prevented from entering Unyoro by order of Kabba Rega, and that the king had made proposals to Muanga to unite with him in arresting and disarming the troops that would be sent through his country in small detachments. "The Governor," said I to Kabba Rega, at an interview on Oct. 10, "has instructed me to tell you that he does not now intend sending any soldiers away, and, instead, he begs you to agree to the other requests that he made you through me."

"Why will he not send the soldiers? Perhaps the road to Khartoum is re-opened," said the king.

"I do not know. He wrote thus to me, and I repeat his message to you."

"All right," he concluded, with a forced smile.

"Therefore," I resumed, "he asks you to allow two military stations to be built on the lake; one at Tunguru, in the territory of the chief Sunga, and the other at Msua, subject to Kisa."

"What do you want to do on the lake?" he asked.

"To concentrate the soldiers from the Northern stations, who are in daily peril of being attacked by the insurgents of Khartoum."

"But in this manner you would render yourselves masters of my territory," said Chua.

"Quite the contrary; our stay will be short. We shall leave upon the first favourable opportunity, and you will not only become the master of the countries of the Shooli and Lur, but also of the storehouses, well filled with ivory, iron, and brass; the two steamers will shortly be your property, and you will be in a position equal to that of the Waganda, and Cabaca will be inclined to Makama.* And now tell me what point has your treaty of friendship with Ntali reached?"

"A favourable one; the road by Nkole will soon be opened."

* Cabaca is the title by which the king of Uganda is known; **Makama** is that given to the King of Unyoro.

"But Nguro is gone, sent away (I am told) by you," I said.

"That is false. I have every possible interest in the success of this affair. The Arabs will be able to bring me rifles and powder; very difficult things to obtain at present on the confines of Uganda, in consequence of the evil disposition of Muanga."

The wicked king spoke falsely, but with rare tact guessed at matters in his own interest.

"Well, do not trouble yourself about us. For our interests, the Uganda road suffices; and that you have generously conceded to us. But why do not the messengers arrive? It appears to me impossible that Mackay should not be interested in our favour, after the promises and assurances given by him to us."

"It is that rascal of a Muanga who has put obstacles in the way of the departure of the messengers. But have the Arabs never delivered letters or brought you any news?"

"No. Without your permission I would not venture to avail myself of their services. We need not resort to Arabs after having received your word as a king—that is a sufficient guarantee for us."

"Yes; and rely on me. I am the friend of Emin Bey," he said.

"Then you will grant my requests?"

"From this instant I will do whatever my friend requires. You may occupy Tunguru and Msua. I will send orders to the chiefs to provide grain for the soldiers who are to be established there."

"I have another favour to ask you," I said.

"Speak; I am ready to do all that you wish."

"Biri left Uganda two months ago for this place. He is detained on the confines of your kingdom by your people. Give orders that he may be allowed to come here," I said.

"And how could you know that Biri is at Kudurma?"

"I know it."

"Who told you so?"

"No one," I replied.

"That is not possible."

"It is very possible. Listen to me. When Junker left us, he promised the Governor that he would send us our necessary goods by Biri. Therefore, by this time it is not only probable, but certain, that he must be very near us."

"But Biri is sent by Muanga to bring trouble into my kingdom; he shall never put his foot in it."

"You are wrong; he must come. We are here in consequence of the formal promise that you have made us; we expect that you will completely fulfil it."

"It is the merchants that will not admit Biri, and I cannot oppose them. I have too much interest in preserving their friendship," said Chua.

"It is that villainous Abd Rehman who will ruin your country by his fatal influence."

"I am king; I command, and have no need of anyone to advise me as to what I shall do," he declared.

"The truth, I know, wounds you, but you shall not on that account prevent me from speaking it. Emin Bey wishes that Biri should be allowed to enter the country. If you cannot comply he will be obliged to take other means."

"And what?" he asked.

"He will write to Said Barghash, to the Egyptian Government, and what will you say then?"

"But by what route can he send his letters if I close my roads?"

"By a thousand ways. If he applied to you first, it would be out of regard to his friend, and not because he was obliged to do so," I replied.

"You are more wicked than Baker. It is impossible that Emin would think of such things, unless you suggested them to him. It is you who are ruminating on all these new ways of injuring me," he exclaimed.

"Be not angry, O king. Emin may have personally a great friendship for you, but he is the representative of the Egyptian Government, and consequently, has duties before which his personal will must yield."

"And you wish that I, also, should yield?"

"Yes, in your own interest. It is a sincere friend who speaks to you. If I were otherwise, I should overwhelm you with civilities to gain your care and attention."

"Biri shall be here to-morrow," he assured me.

"And will you let him go to Wadelai the same day?"

"I cannot promise. We will see."

"Follow my advice. Friendship for friendship. Emin is at Kibiro* expecting him."

"After to-morrow he shall go to Kibiro, accompanied by my faithful Monyara."

"So be it; I thank you."

Biri came, and on the evening of that day (Oct. 12) he went to Kibiro, where Emin awaited him with a steamer. A few days before, the Governor had written, telling me that to return amongst his people without Biri, would be, not only a grief to him, but a grave injury. That night he wrote to me: "It is nine o'clock; but before retiring I will fulfil the duty of thanking you for the signal service you have rendered me by sending Biri."

* On the eastern banks of the Albert Nyanza.

Emin, in the excitement of success, always ready to commit imprudences, thanked the king and his ministers, thinking it a stroke of fine policy to send courteous words also to the wicked Abd Rehman, the perfidious counsellor of Chua, whom, in those days, I (thanks to the help of the honest Kategora) had succeeded in placing in a critical and inferior position. Would I had never done so!

The letter was the great news of the day. "The Governor implored his support and withdrew his confidence from me, his representative." The game paid, and the threads of the intrigue, which were momentarily broken and dispersed, were reunited for a more serious matter.

* * * * * *

On Nov. 14, my loyal friend, the old Minister, Kategora, died suddenly. The king sent a special messenger to announce the sad news to me, and assured me of his unalterable benevolence. But the public voice declared that Kategora had been poisoned. The king, the very morning of the assassination, had said that henceforward he intended to govern by the lower classes. He would no longer recognise the authority of the nobles. And while the Minister was dying in agony, a step only from the door of the palace, he made a party of boys sing the sad canticle (at that moment ironical and cruel):

"He dies! He dies!"

On Dec. 5, Biri departed for Uganda with a good quantity of ivory to exchange for goods, leaving a hope of better times to come in every mind.

But affairs proceeded differently in Unyoro; the king and soldiers, ancient enemies of the Egyptian Government, in the firm resolution of putting an end (at a favourable opportunity) to their unwelcome neighbour, with extreme levity (excited by greed for the immense quantities of ivory and arms), stooped to pretended compliances and friendly words, but now, terrified by the unexpected resistance to their evil designs, they tried to withdraw these ill-advised measures, and the most infamous plots were put in action; the grand master and leader in them being Abd Rehman, who in the eyes of the king appeared the only wise counsellor that could insinuate himself into the mind of the Governor and direct intrigues without generating suspicion. Babedongo, leader of the soldiers, having been recalled, prohibited the merchants from selling me goods, or holding any communication with me. A certain Abubeker, who brought goods for the Government from Uganda, was ill-treated, robbed, and driven back to the confines of the country; under severe penalties, the natives were prohibited from selling me grain or eatables, and the ivory given to the king, as a recompense for allowing the transit of Biri's caravan, was insultingly rejected.

"The horns of my cows," Chua sent to say, "are much longer than the elephant's tusks you have presented me. I do not know what to do with them; keep them for yourself."

"I regret," I replied, through the chief Bagonza, who was charged with this ridiculous refusal, "that the king should take so futile a pretext to disturb our relations. I advise him not to follow the suggestions of wicked men. As for the pieces of ivory, I will keep them at his disposal."

Hostile measures were not confined to these insults. In a great council of the chief men and soldiers, presided over by the king, they went still further.

The chiefs of Tunguru and of Msua were summoned to Juaya. Kisa and Gumangi were miserably killed, being found guilty of having made an act of submission to Emin Bey; the king's advisers instigated the negroes to refuse grain to the soldiers; they made a secret and extensive propaganda of rebellion amongst the Shooli and Lur; they at length ventilated the project of attacking the station of Wadelai, if the revolution triumphed; and they were masters of the territory of the Shefalu, at that time subject to chief Anfina.

Besides these plots, which I had clearly explained to the Governor, there was one that Emin, by a special messenger, should be invited by King Kabba Rega to visit Unyoro and his Court, under pretences of friendship and alliance.

It was not easy to dissuade the Governor from making this proposed visit, and it was only after he had been convinced by others of the treason designed against him that he lent faith to my disinterested exhortations.

Emin did not come, and I did not move. Our dignity and interests required us to keep a footing in Unyoro; to retire would be folly—it would be to confess ourselves conquered, and to allow the animosity of the blacks, hitherto curbed, to break forth to our injury under the leadership of King Chua.

* * * * * *

The presence of Mohammed Biri at Wadelai, and, still more, the quantity of goods that he brought to the Government, produced a salutary effect on the majority of Emin's soldiers. The negroes have a philosophy all their own; apathetic and passive by nature, yet of childish enthusiasm, with a mind void of sensibility and closed against every generous impulse, they are credulous even to superstition in all that strikes the imagination; but suspicious even to insolence in all that concerns material life.

It gradually dawned on them that the Government

VIEW OF A VILLAGE IN UNYORO.

watched over them, to deny it would be stupidity, and even the negroes dislike being called foolish; the Viceroy sent not only a letter, but Biri, a man of flesh and blood, not a mite, who, besides, brought cloth and glassware. He had come through Uganda and Unyoro —therefore the roads must be open—and he came with that soldier Surur, who had left with Doctor Junker, and who, after nine months, reappeared fat, robust, and merry as of yore.

Resistance was evidently overcome; in fact proposals for a general flight, of abandoning the Province and retiring by way of Khartoum, would not have found followers—would have been listened to with scorn. Some distinguished themselves, it is true, by obstinacy, especially amongst the officers, but rather from shame at acknowledging that they were mistaken than by conviction. The first step was taken; the thread that tied us to the future was fastened; and this fraction of the Egyptian forces could consider itself safe, if a firm and vigorous hand had been able to infuse confidence, to excite self-respect, and inflame all minds with a noble desire for active operations.

But Emin did not wish, or did not know how to seize the opportunity that presented itself of overcoming the differences that had provoked the quarrels in the provinces. He refused to arrest two factious officers of the first battalion, as I advised him, and he would not remove the chief commander of the second— a man who was generally known to be the originator of all the dissensions.

And this was bad for him and for all of us. His temporising in the continual hope of a better day shook his authority as a commander, more and more, and gradually brought him into general distrust. Indifference slowly filtered through the line of soldiers and officers, and obedience degenerated into a simple act of respect.

Chua did not hesitate to carry out the programme that he had drawn up; the signal was given and the Shooli arose; but, defeated at Fadibek, Fatiko, and elsewhere by the soldiers, who were always ardent and ready for a fight, they paid for their unfaithfulness with

"WE ARE THIRSTING FOR BLOOD."

many victims. Protshamma, the soul of the insurrectionary movement and of the insane attempt, fell also.

The end of the month of January was near.

"Not one soldier, or a single cartridge, shall you have to make war against Uganda," I said, one day to the king: he consequently hastened the departure of Mabuzi, the envoy of Muanga, with gifts and proposals of peace. And this consent to peace, which he gave so reluctantly—extorted from him, as it was, by the perilous situation in which the unlucky defeat of the Shooli had placed him—he resolved to seal with an ironical pantomime. Parties of the Lango people, their bodies tattooed in colours, performed sham fights, rushing towards the embassy of the Waganda, who were present at the tournament, as if in the act of striking them with their lances and long knives. Individuals, with hair dyed scarlet, rushed furiously towards the king, crying, " We are thirsting for blood, give us one of these villains." And the trumpets and choruses intoned the well-known song, " King Chua is powerful. He has reduced to slavery the Shefalu and the Waganda. He has obliged the soldiers to pay tribute; the only invincible ones are the Lango."

To which, with a marked and sonorous song, a youth of the deputation of the Waganda responded, " King Chua, murder us if it pleases thee; cast us into the burning pile as thou hast done with others—little we care. Cabaca lives to avenge us, his drum already beats for recruits; and—for the height of insult—when Mabuzi and his followers move to depart, let Chua cause us to be followed by this tipsy crowd of excited savages."

A fowl, with its throat cut, was found in the great dining-room of the royal palace on the morning of February 8. The Arabs were suspected of having secret intelligence with us, and two of them were expelled from the kingdom. The report gained belief that Biri had had charge of forming an alliance with Muanga in the name of the Governor of Equatoria, and that soldiers were already being organised to invade the country.

So many contrary rumours kept the mind of the king in constant anxiety, already overwhelmed as he was by the disaster that had befallen the Shooli, and inclined to superstition. The throne was threatened with certain peril; the spirit of his father, irritated, perhaps, by his son's past misfortunes, does not watch over the prosperity of the kingdom as he did in the past, but causes mourning and tears; it is necessary to appease him with sacrifices. The queen-mother is consulted. She is a great priestess and magician, and she decrees that they must have recourse to the monstrous ceremonies of the *mpango* or axe, in order to avoid the present evils and propitiate the favour of the defunct Kamrasi for the future.

The articles that they employ for this rite are—a drum, round which is wound a thick brass wire. It is also ornamented with talismans, consisting of pieces of wood, to which are attributed special magical virtues; a wooden stool covered with lion and leopard skins; an iron lance of about five feet in length, the handle surrounded with brass wire; and lastly, an axe (*mpango*) with the helve of wood covered with leopard skin, and with brass wire on the upper portion.

The tenth day of February passed. The sun hastened towards the west—a blow was struck on the grand drum, deep and solemn.

In a moment songs ceased, all sounds were hushed, the market was empty; every one went to his own habitation; the roads were deserted and for three long days silence and sadness reigned around. Only the slow dismal ring of blows struck at intervals on the great drum told that they were fulfilling the mysterious rites of the *mpango*, which caused the miserable inhabitants to shudder with fear.

It is the popular belief that the *nuggare* sounds without being beaten whenever the angry spirit of Kamrasi wishes to be appeased by human victims.

The period of the mysterious rites was passed; the sun approached the end of his journey; the great *nuggare* gave forth its deepest sounds; cries of terror mixed with reverence echoed everywhere, and spread from village to village, following one another like the waves of the sea; the miserable passers-by, the peaceful husbandmen, were seized, bound with cords, and their throats cut, as a holocaust to the Great Father.

In Juaya ten unhappy creatures paid tribute with their blood to this superstition. The rite is sometimes prolonged till the fifth day.

But the great sacrifice was not to be completed till the morning of the next day, when the king stood erect in the hut of the *mpango*, on the threshold of the large door of ingress, dressed in the traditional habit; a great mantle of stuff made from the bark of trees, surmounted by a leopard skin hanging at his back and round his neck; his head crowned with talismans, his wrists, neck, and ankles ornamented with large glass beads, and holding his lance in his right hand. The members of the *Condo* and all the nobles were arranged in a semicircle in the great court, sitting on their little benches; the guardian of the *mpango* stood at the right hand of the king, holding high the fatal axe; *nuggare* and a small chair belonging to the grand rite were placed in the front; a large cup was on the ground a little way off; terror and silence rested upon the assembly.

The king made a sign with his head; the great men rose, and, bowing in sign of reverence, approached him; he touched one of them with the point of his spear on the shoulder; the chief advanced and extended his neck; the horrid axe descended; the blood was caught in the cup; the king with his finger sprinkled some of it on his own forehead and cheeks, then on those of the great men; grasping the vase he poured the remaining blood on the drum and on the little seat. The sacrifice was complete; *nuggare,* seat, lance, axe, and cup were raised and carried to the residence of the queen-mother. At a sign from the king the sorrowing parents took away the body of the unhappy Kisa, late chief of the district of Muenghe. The drums and

A HUMAN SACRIFICE.

fifes sounded for a feast; they killed oxen, opened jars of beer, and the drunken people then danced and enjoyed themselves upon the ground just bathed with the blood of the victim.

* * * * * *

Men's minds being at ease, all thoughts and hearts returned to their ancient boldness. Confident of success, the madmen blindly relied on the security given by supernatural protection, and again took up the thread of their enterprises.

DESTRUCTION OF JUAYA.

When Chua thought that Emin's approach was near, he suddenly decided to abandon Juaya.

On the morning of March 6, the king immolated a boy of twelve years of age, with his own hand, in the interior of his dwelling, and also a white heifer at the entrance, as a holocaust to his dead father, to propitiate him and obtain his protection during his journey. Amidst the sound of fifes and drums, discharges of musketry, and the howls rather than cries, of an applauding crowd, he took a southerly route, carrying with him his paternal Lares, the infamous instruments of the *mpango*.

After wandering about some time he stopped at Muimba, planted his lance in the ground, and built himself a new palace, as the oracle had commanded him.

The removal from Juaya was completed about noon; the signal for its destruction was given, columns of smoke and fire rose from the abandoned royal residence, the conflagration spread from all parts, crackling and sending up immense spires of smoke, broken by flashes of flame that illumined the sky with a sinister light. The sad spectacle was prolonged for two days, when everything relapsed into obscurity and silence, and as the sole reminiscence of past greatness there remained a mass of ashes.

CHAPTER III.

REGION BETWEEN THE ALBERT AND VICTORIA LAKES.

Uganda and Unyoro—Watershed between the Victoria Nile and Lake Albert—The region of forests—Mount Sedgiomocoro—The Kafu, the Ngussi, the Msiri—The peninsula of Magungo—Climate—Productions of the vegetable kingdom—The fauna—Destruction of hyenas—The chimpanzee—Professor Giglioli and the *Troglodytes Schweinfurthii*—Professor Reichart of Berlin—The *termes mordax*—The different tribes of which the people of Unyoro consist—The *Kinyoro* or language spoken in Unyoro—The francolin and the tortoise—The leopard and the dog—King Chua tells the story of the Golden Book of his family—The Wahuma—Customs of this tribe—From Juaya to Katua on the Ruitan Lake—The Virica of the Vacongio—The Ruwenzori of Stanley—Mountains of the Moon—Political government and administration of the Soudan—The order of the *Condo*—Sacrifices at every new moon—The magic spirit that disturbs the mind of the Queen-mother—Suuna and the hundred murdered—Bead culture—Three cudgel blows—Another locality selected—Cutting off the hands and blinding—A decree against pipes—The ceremony of the milk—Kamissua, son of Rionga, entrapped—The king eats—The Wanyoro—The *Tiumba*—The *Mbugu*—The ceramic art—Butter—The merchants of Zanzibar—Customs of the Wanyoro—The great dispenser of rain and his delegates—Funeral honours—King Kamrasi's sepulchre—The veneration of the people and the capricious superstition of the despot.

THE spurs issuing from the chain of mountains, called by the ancients the Mountains of the Moon, descend and expand towards the north, forming more or less extensive valleys, traversed by copious streams of water, giving a prodigious fertility to this region, which comprises the vast territories of Uganda and Unyoro. Tropical forests—thick vegetation in the parts adjoining the lakes, with innumerable water-courses, that through narrow valleys open a road, amidst dense masses of papyrus, occupy the territory that borders the Victoria and Albert Lakes.

THE TERRITORY BETWEEN THE LAKES. 37

In the inner country are tall grasses, thickets of reeds, extensive plains on the summit of the hills, long valleys in a humid and productive soil, where the ancient trees of the forest zone are overshadowed by

SHOOLI WARRIORS.

Palma dôm, lofty sycamores, *Euphorbia venefica,* and varieties of mimosa. Wild thyme perfumes the hills, the plateaux and the sides of the mountains are covered by thickets of bamboo; and on the land, watered by rivulets, grow beautiful *Pistia stratiotes* and *Nymphea lotus*, with its rosy flowers.

The watershed between the Victoria Nile and Lake Albert runs in a northerly direction, and the highest point is in the district of Nusranduru, on Mount Sedgiomocoro. It was in this natural fortress, with its rocky sides, that Kabba Rega was entrenched, when (after his father's death) he disputed the Crown with his brother Kabamiro. The great watercourses that sweep the territory of Unyoro have their source in this neighbourhood; the Kafu, or River of Death, that flows into the Nile near ancient Mruli; the Ngussi, which, traversing the forest of Kiriangobi, falls into Lake Albert; and the Msiri, that descends in a south-westerly direction, by the territory of Muenghe, and then flows on to mingle its waters with the lakes. The land advances, in a series of hills shaped as terraces, towards the tablelands of Moranda, Nparo, Juaya, Kiriangobi, and Kitana, and from this line, that curves from a south-east to a north-west direction, it descends to the Victoria Nile, forming the peninsula of the Magungo, that is in the north-east extremity of Lake Albert.

The climate in this region is healthy and temperate. Rain falls abundantly, and even in the dry season the earth retains sufficient humidity, for the dews are heavy, and there are frequent light breezes. The rains are often preceded by violent storms of wind, almost always accompanied by thunder and lightning, and occasionally by a fall of hail. The continual dampness is favourable to the abundant growth and perfection of vegetable productions, causing their gradual development, and bringing them to maturity at the proper season. Maize, *Eleusina coracana*, *Batata edulis*, *Helmia bulbifera*, manioc, and various species of

VEGETATION AND ANIMALS. 39

vegetables, thrive there, and the banana, the staple food consumed by the people, yields abundance of excellent fruit. Tobacco (*taba*) yields a highly perfumed leaf when cultivated in elevated places, but one

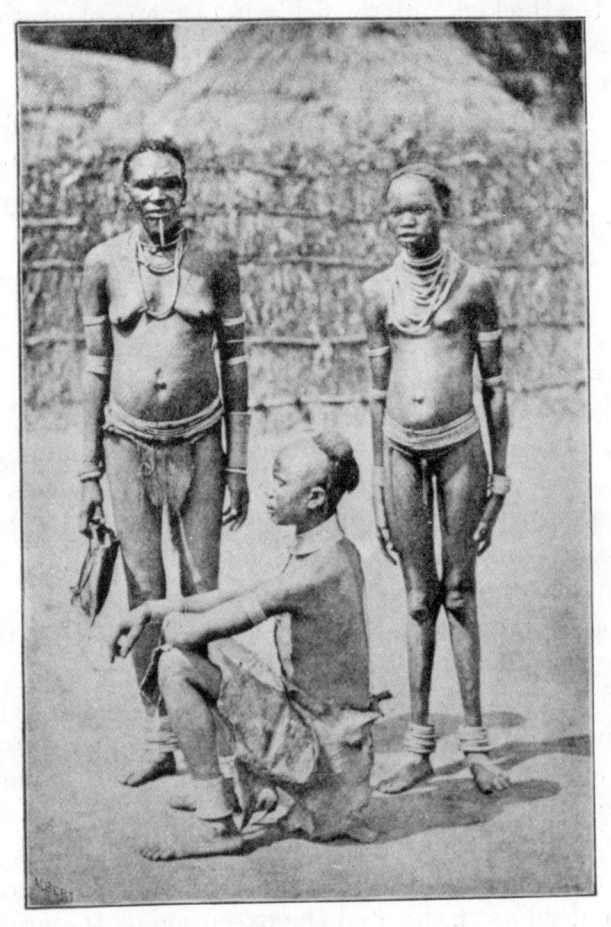

A SHOOLI FAMILY.

of a rather inferior quality when it is grown in low situations and valleys.

Elephants are to be found in great numbers in the woods of Kafu; lions prowl round the cattle enclosures in couples, leopards and hyenas, besides jackals, crowds of antelopes, gazelles, and wild boars, abound in the tablelands and valleys. Colonies of spotted monkeys make frequent pillaging incursions from the thickets into the fields and banana plantations, but a superstitious veneration keeps these quadrumana safe from the snares of men.

In one day, during a violent hurricane, I suffered the complete destruction of a field of maize by a troop of *Colobus quereza*. I had an opportunity of speaking to the king about this unpleasant visit, and with an air of sincere regret he said, " Do not kill any of those animals; it might bring misfortune upon you."

The grey parrots (*Psittacus erythacus*) fly in clouds, noisily screaming during most of the months of the year, and especially at the time of their double migration; multitudes of birds are to be seen, such as the weavers that build hanging nests; the lively swallows, that seem unwilling to make their return journey, as if tempted to linger by the softness of the climate, and the brisk wagtail, that on our very threshold chatters news from the far off fatherland.

After the king had abandoned Juaya, the neighbourhood of my habitation was changed into a meeting place for crowds of hyenas. The impunity accorded to monkeys I could not extend to these unclean animals, whose troublesome cries sounded like an augury of misfortune. Their destruction was decreed, and a dead ass facilitated the execution of the project. We injected strychnine under the skin of the dead animal, and then abandoned it to the wild beasts. For two consecutive nights the terrible cries of the dying gluttons deafened the air, then silence followed, and calm was spread around us. But the story

THE CHIMPANZEE.

was soon divulged, and the voices of the malignant natives at length reached Uganda, with the addition that the poison used in this instance had been given by me to King Chua, in large quantities; and the sale of salt at the markets on the borders experienced a palpable diminution for some time in consequence.

The woods of Farajak, on the tableland to the south of Kitana, and the forest of Kiriangobi, that descends from Juaya to the lake, at no great distance from Kibiro, and is crossed by the river Ngussi, are a favourite abode of the chimpanzee. Nevertheless, the terror with which this animal inspires the Wanyoro preserves it from being hunted as it is in the regions of the Mambettu and Sandeh, who pursue the chase of it in a surprisingly energetic manner. This monkey enjoys royal protection, the natives say, and it would be a crime to capture or kill it without an express order, because ages ago it formed part of the human race.

According to Schweinfurth, the chimpanzee of Central Africa differs from the *Troglodytes niger*, and must be considered as a distinct variety, that, in process of time, has been developed by natural selection in a given region. Professor Giglioli, of Florence, has classified it as a secondary species, naming it *Troglodytes Schweinfurthii*, in consequence of studies made on the skulls brought home by that illustrious scientist in 1872.

Professor Reichart, of Berlin, considers it identical with the *niger*. The chimpanzee found in Unyoro is the same as that in the basin of the Welle-Makua. From its resemblance to man it is called *niabantu*. The country is, in addition, infested with voracious termites, that supply a kind of food for the population. At the period of their transformation into winged insects, the natives capture them by means of fire, in the same manner that they do in the Mambettu region, with this single difference, that the chase is more carefully prepared, by raising straw conical sheds on the hills

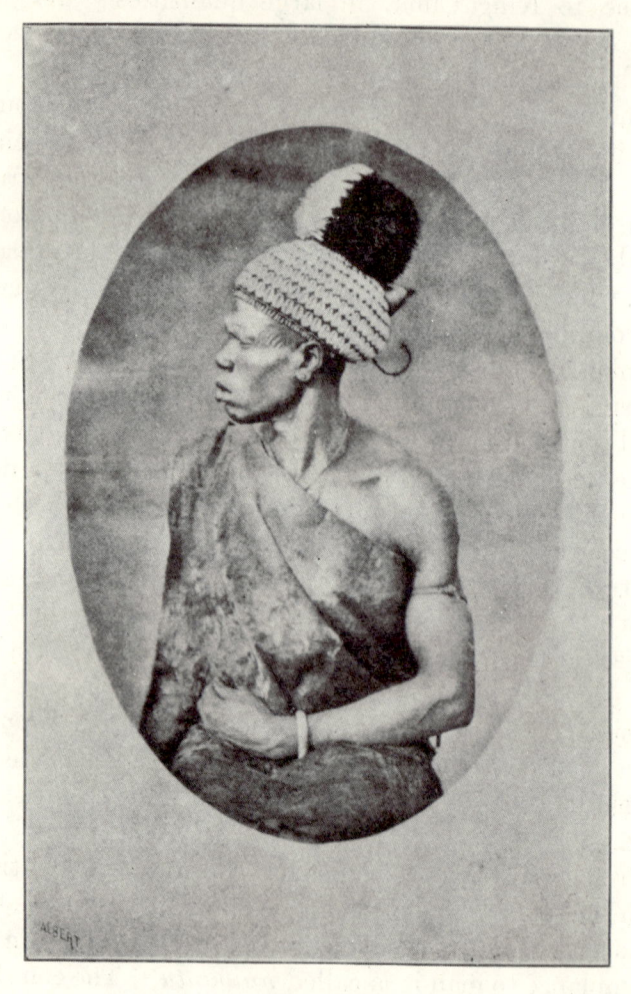

A SHOOLI CHIEF.

which swarm with them. The habit of feeding on dried termites has been the custom throughout Africa since the most ancient times. As the divine

THE POPULATION. 43

Dante rightly says in the *Inferno*, canto xxix.

> " And afterwards, as bards of yore have told,
> The ancient people were restored anew
> From seed of emmets."—*Cary's Translation.*

A SHOOLI CHIEF.

The population of the kingdom is a mixture of Madundi, Magaya, Wahuma, Shefalu, Magungo, and Wanyoro. There is also a strong colony of Shooli, emigrants from the territory of Fatiko, who left their homes on account of the oppressions and sufferings inflicted upon them by the soldiers of the Egyptian Government.

The Madundi and the Shefalu are especially spread along the banks of the Victoria Nile; the Magaya occupy the central tableland in the districts of Juaya and Baganghese; the Wahuma form the prevailing population of Muenghe; and the Wanyoro who are, it is believed, the aborigines, form the majority in the Nusranduru and River Kafu regions.

The language, which has had the triumph of overcoming or mixing itself with those of so many peoples of various origin and customs, is the *Kinyoro*, which, like the *Kiganda*, appertains to the family of African tongues called *Bantu*. The languages of the Wanyoro and Waganda differ very little, indeed, it might almost be said that those two peoples have an identical idiom.

The Rev. C. T. Wilson (missionary) writes thus on the subject:

"It is a composite idiom; all the inflexions of the verbs and other parts of speech are formed by a variety of affixes and prefixes which are united to the root of the word. In the case of the verb, there are separate prefixes which represent the subject, the object, and the relative pronouns, which are then joined to the root of the verb, so that what in most European languages would be a complete sentence, is in this tongue expressed by a single word, and consequently to a European ear it sounds like a very solemn language. The substantive is the most important part of the idiom, there being several species of nouns, each having its own special particle in the singular as well as the plural, which is joined to the root of the adjective, pronoun, or verb; thus, that which most strikes a European who hears this tongue for the first time is the apparent uncertainty of the forms of the adjectives, the change being at the beginning instead of the end of the word. The language when spoken is very soft, and resembles Italian in sound, for the vowels predominate, and

A VILLAGE OF SHOOLI AT THE FOOT OF MOUNT SHOOA.

there are no gutturals. Certainly, like all the savage languages, it has no literature and no form of writing, but we think that with an alphabet of twenty-four letters omitting 'q' and 'x,' all the words could be written."

I will here repeat two fables that I heard from the natives, which will suffice to show their lively intelligence:

The Francolin and the Tortoise.

"I am better off than thou," said the francolin to the tortoise; "I can both walk quickly and fly." "I congratulate you," replied the tortoise. "I draw myself along, and do my business in the best way I can."

Now, it happened that some men out hunting set fire to the grass of the plain. The increasing conflagration drew closer, and made the circle smaller and smaller. The peril of the two animals was imminent and certain. The tortoise drew himself into a deep wet hole, made by the foot of an elephant, and was saved. The francolin tried to fly, but the smoke and fire overpowered him and he fell down and died. He who boasts fails when tested.

The Leopard and the Dog.

The leopard confided her three little cubs to the custody of the dog, assuring him that he should have as a recompense for his services, plenty of meat; on condition, however, that he never gnawed the bones. The arrangement went on very well for some time, but one day the dog, yielding to temptation, gnawed a bone. A splinter flew from it, and, striking a cub on the head, killed it. He found it easy to deceive the mother on her return by bringing the two survivors up to her to be fed, one after the other—the first twice.

Soon the same fate befell the second cub. Then the

dog, seeing that his fault must be found out, fled and sought shelter with a man, who promised to protect and defend him, on condition that he did not leave the house. The dog promised, but a few days afterwards, seeing a heap of bones at a little distance, he broke his word and went out. The leopard, who had been in

SHOOLI VESSELS AND ORNAMENTS.

search of him for some time to avenge the death of her cubs, sprang upon him, killed and devoured him, and from that day the leopard has not ceased waging war on dogs, and eating their flesh.

"I am the eighteenth king of my family," said the despot of Unyoro one day to me.

The founder of the dynasty came from the countries beyond Lango, and established himself in Uganda. An expert huntsman, he taught the natives to kill the wild animals, and his fame spread so far that at last the queen was seized with a desire to see the brave stranger. He was a very handsome man, and the lady fell in love with him, and did not hesitate (for his sake) to poison her husband. On his marriage with her he ascended the throne, and had two sons, to whom, on his death-bed he gave, as separate heritages, the kingdoms of Uganda and Unyoro.

And thus Chua asserted, on the strength of tradition, his Galla origin. That emigrations of this people had passed through the lands of Unyoro is proved incontestably by the use (still common) of words of the Galla language, especially in the sale of articles of food.

The numerous family of the Wahuma undoubtedly had its origin in the great tribe of the Galla. It comprises a good number of people in Unyoro and Uganda, has acquired supreme power in the countries of Nkole and Karagua, and has succeeded in subduing the tribes of Vavra and Walegga in the countries west of Lake Albert. Having a strong predilection for rearing oxen, and no love for warlike enterprises, the Wahuma—though they have adopted the language of the people with whom they find themselves in contact—still in their habits and customs are faithful to the traditions of their ancestors. Disdaining agricultural work, they live on flesh and milk only, and their inclination for strong drinks, common to all the Africans, is largely satisfied by the exchange of their productions.

They rarely marry a woman belonging to other tribes, whom they despise, considering them of inferior race.

Their mode of dress—their hair constantly shaved, the use of sandals for their feet, and several superstitious practices before entering the house when they return after a protracted absence—make the Wahuma a distinct class, and separate them from the people amongst whom they live. The Wahuma women, from their physical beauty, their moral qualities, and domestic activity, are much sought after, especially by the chiefs.

The territory subject to King Chua beyond Unyoro extends to the lands on the eastern side of Lake Albert, to the district of Mruli and Toru, and stretches as far as Lake Ruitan, where a station was erected for soldiers, who had the privilege of selling salt, which abounds in the small lake of Kio. The district of Mboga on the left bank of the Semliki is also governed in Chua's name, and he receives tribute from the Lur of Melindwa, the chief of the western mountains that run along the coast of Lake Albert. It takes eighteen days to go from Juaya to Katua, the station established on the Usongora. The road runs down the western side of the chain, and passes at a little distance from Lake Albert, nearly parallel to it as far as Kieya, always in a southerly direction; there, by difficult roads on the heights, it stretches to Mruli, Toru, and the lake.

The king made frequent raids into these unhappy countries, once flourishing with abundant herds and tranquil homes. In one that the chief Ireta made there in the early months of 1887, 10,000 head of cattle were carried off. The Wahuma shepherds, voluntarily followed the victors, with their families, preferring to serve them in the capacity of cow-keepers, rather than to be separated from their flocks.

It was at this time that I first heard of the

white mountain with two horns, the Virika of the Vacongio, the Varicampanga of the Wanyoro, the Ruwenzori of Stanley. Of measureless height, of dreadful cold, there is peril of certain death awaiting him who attempts to climb those masses, inhabited by a powerful and malignant spirit, who keeps himself almost always enveloped in clouds; thus, at least, say those who return from Usongora, and they add that a fierce people, the Vacongio, with a white skin and a peculiar language, dwell on the rocks of the mountain, whom neither the men of Unyoro nor those of Uganda have succeeded in conquering. The King of Unyoro rules this extensive territory by means of governors appointed over every single district. The *magnoro*, as these administrators are called, are the chiefs of the various jurisdictions, which they govern in the name of the king, supply soldiers in time of war, and pay tribute in ivory, animals, iron, and food. To these are subject the so-called *matungoli*, who have a limited power over some divisions of the territory. The provinces must always be represented at the Sovereign's residence, either by the chiefs invested with their government or by their representatives, who have the title of *makongo*.

From amongst the *magnoro* the king selects his own secretary, the directors of the storehouses and armouries, the delegates who represent him in the tributary provinces, the chiefs of the missions appointed to the adjacent States, and the supreme commander of the troops during war.

The *magnoro* may be either hereditary, in the case of good services rendered by the dead father; or elective, as a reward for personal merits or from the special favour and benevolence of the king. The hereditary government is, however, given to the one amongst the sons of the late *magnoro* who offers the largest gifts to the avidity of the monarch.

The *magnoro* may be invested with an Order, called that of the *Condo*, which places him on a level with the king's relations. The members of this order are not subject to capital punishment ; they enjoy public respect, are the Crown counsellors, and reside with the *Mabitu*. King Chua, however, deviating from the usages consecrated by tradition, pronounced sentence of death, even upon these men, but he first practised the cruel cunning of degrading them from their order. The ornament that distinguishes the Order of the *Condo* consists in a leather ribbon studded with shells and various bead pearls, which descends from the top of the back of the head to both sides of the face, and is tied under the chin.

The number of members is fixed at seventeen, from which the victim for the grand sacrifice of the *mpango* (as an honourable distinction) is selected.

The power and greatness of the Sovereign and the happiness of the people of the kingdom, are believed to arise from the assistance of invisible powers, to whose sway is added that of the soul of the dead Kamrasi.

At every new moon human beings are sacrificed to propitiate their favour and ensure happiness. These immolations are not, however, distinguished by any particular display ; ordinary business is suspended for three days, and the rites of the new moon are performed inside the palace, by the sacrifice of some victim of propitiation and by killing out of doors, in the direction they wish to frighten away the evil eye, a variable number of individuals. They kill bulls on the king's tomb monthly, as a sacrifice, and human victims are often added to them.

On occasions of the illness of the king or of the

members of the royal family, human sacrifices play an important part.

On the 8th of May the magic spirit, whose emblems encircle the head of the queen-mother, angry, perhaps, on account of some want of reverence, disturbed her mind and made her ill. Two bulls, one white and the other red, were sacrificed, but in vain; the spirit was not appeased; and then human victims, in considerable numbers, were offered. This custom had been practised from a distant epoch.

Suuna, King of Uganda, father of Mtesa, being attacked with a slight malady, doctored himself, and ordered a hundred human victims of expiation to be killed daily to obtain his cure; for fifteen days (so long did the illness last) every sunrise saw the horrid butchery.

Fortune willed that death should put an end to these devout practices.

The Sovereign, whilst riding on his Prime Minister (for such was his custom) was entering his own residence upon return from a journey, when he fell, attacked with apoplexy.

It was during the reign of Suuna that the first Zanzibari merchant made his appearance in Uganda. He was incessantly annoyed by demands for beads, and told the king one day that he ought to cultivate them. The credulous monarch set to work, and not perceiving any result, took counsel of the merchant again, and he, having nearly concluded his business, and being on the point of leaving, continued the trick, and recommended the expedient of watering the field which had been sown; but the day having arrived on which the merchant hoped to proceed on his journey home, the king refused his permission; he repeated the request, and was told that he should go as soon as the beads germinated.

He was not at liberty to depart till the death of Suuna, and it was lucky for him that nothing worse happened to him.

King Chua's Court has not an aristocratic appearance, such as one meets with at the lord of Uganda's, but the iron hand of the despot falls inexorably, whether justly or unjustly, on the persons who have incurred the Sovereign's displeasure. Culprits, condemned upon bare suspicion, are barbarously slain by appointed executioners. They secure the doomed man with cords round his arms and legs, so as to oblige him to bend his back forwards; and then with a knotted club they inflict three heavy blows on the temples with surprising dexterity, which kill the victim instantly. The body is generally left on the place of execution as food for wild beasts and vultures; to only approach or stop to look at the dead bodies constitutes a crime that is punishable with death.

In the early days of my arrival at Juaya the grounds round my habitation were generally selected as the theatre of these monstrosities. In the silence of the night I heard distressing cries, the echo of three "blows of grace," and groans that were slowly stifled. One morning seven dead bodies lay, horribly disfigured, in the nearest fields. I went to complain of this to the king. He told me that I ought not to be troubled by it, as these people were not deserving of pity. I then made him understand the disgust that the fact produced on my mind; he smiled, but selected another locality for the horrible office. Thieves and seducers of women he corrected by amputating their hands, or burning the pupils of their eyes, not considering these crimes worthy of death.

On the evening of February 22, 1887, a column of smoke rose near the royal mansion; the hut of a

EXECUTION BY THREE BLOWS WITH CLUBS.

THE CEREMONY OF THE MILK.

clever worker in the ceramic art had caught fire through a lighted pipe having been left amongst the dry herbage with which the ground of their habitation is always strewn. The fire, however, was soon extinguished, but the following morning a decree was issued against pipes and smokers. The king's guards were occupied in breaking pipes and bastinadoing smokers for fully three days, without distinction of rank; the potter, in consideration of his skill, was not awarded a very severe punishment.

It is a mark of high distinction and of great trust to be admitted to the ceremony of the milk. The members of the royal family and the great chiefs do not enjoy such an honour. The having performed heroic deeds in war, the having shown an unalterable fidelity to the king, and, still more, the being in sympathy with him, are reasons which may admit men to this highest of all distinctions in the kingdom. Night having fallen, and the king's tables being set, those invited to the ceremony enter the grand hall of the royal mansion; the drums beat, the fifes whistle the royal march; the king takes a vase full of milk, drinks, and then passes it on to those present, who in turn drink also. When the ceremony is finished the doors are opened, and the friends of the great men are admitted to the daily entertainment of getting intoxicated on copious libations, the king setting the example.

The milk ceremony was fatal to Kamissua, the son of Rionga, Sovereign of Foweira, and tributary to the King of Unyoro. He had hardly arrived at Muimba, having been invited to this great honour, than he was arrested, conducted to Muenghe, and there murdered. Superstition in Unyoro even extends to the food. The king does not eat poultry; and woe to the chief that does not conform to a similar restriction. Moreover, he limits his dishes to veal boiled with bananas, *telabun* porridge, and banana beer, fermented with germinating corn, which is called *muenga*.

The beating of drums announces that the king is moving towards the room where the royal table is laid; the flight of the women and children from the royal court is general; the passages through which the king's dishes pass are deserted; his food is cooked by persons of tested faith, and is closely covered, in order that the evil eye should not cast a malignant spell upon it.

During the Sovereign's repast the Prime Minister watches at the door of ingress, turning his back upon the king while eating; and as an honourable recompense, he is allowed to feed on the royal leavings, seated upon the ground at his post of vigilance.

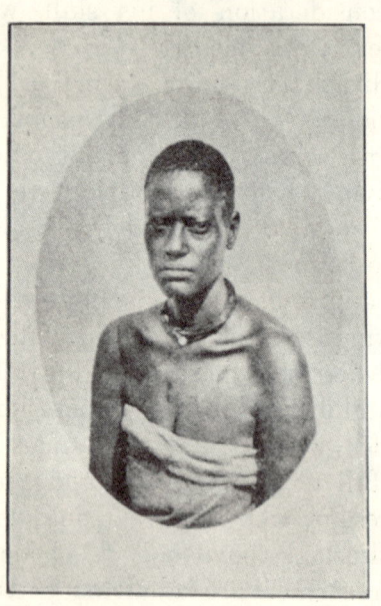

AN UNYORO PRINCESS.

The population of Unyoro lively by their natural intelligence, devoted and submissive to the king (more through fear than affection), are not lovers of bold, warlike enterprises, but only of a belligerent spirit in raids and pillaging. They exhibit their gifts in industries and commerce.

Numerous traders gather at the market-places with their produce; and flour, sesame, tobacco, hides, iron, and ivory can be purchased from them. A product largely consumed is beer made of banana juice; it is as

MILK CEREMONY.

necessary to the natives as food. In the Juaya market they used to sell about a thousand large jars of it daily.

The people are skilful tanners, and make dresses of skins that equal cloth in softness. The *tiumbe* are mantles formed by joining goat-skins, tanned, prepared, and sewn with such care as to present the seams well covered with hair; they also make these garments with ox-hide, which they render soft and light, to serve as clothes for the poorer classes. The working of such stuffs requires patient labour; and it is executed with the greatest skill by means of repeated rasping on the back of the skins, which are previously moistened and stretched by means of wooden pegs on the ground. The costume of dresses made of skin is taken from the Wahuma. The traditional dress, however, that is still used by the greater number of people, and always worn at the recurrence of festivals and public functions, is made of the bark of the *mbugu* or *ficus latia*. This is how the missionary Wilson, already mentioned, describes the mode employed to render this bark fit to use as cloth:

"They make an incision round the trunk in a part adapted for it, and another two or three feet lower down; they then make a longitudinal cut between the two incisions, and lift the bark in such a manner as to preserve the cylindrical form. Having a thickness of about half an inch, they raise the surface with care, and the front part, that is generally spongy and full of water, they place on a long plank of hard and very smooth wood, and there two or three men beat it with hammers with great force and rapidity. These hammers are of the hardest wood and have their ends fluted, so that the stuff comes out like morocco. The material stretches under this operation, and when it has gained the required firmness it is hung up to dry. After that they cut the edges carefully and mend the holes that by chance might have been made by beating the bark. If the piece thus obtained is not large enough to make a dress they join others to it. The trees from which they have taken the bark are immediately covered with banana leaves, which are left on it till a new bark has formed on the wound."

Various are the qualities of the *mbugu* cloth. The most beautiful and the softest, of a dark red colour, comes from Uganda and Msoga, on the right bank of the Victoria Nile; the strongest is made at Monyara, in the district of Mruli. Special artists attend to this manufacture, the production of which, though it is not very remunerative, nevertheless is a source of constant, if not great, profit. The ceramic art has also clever artisans, who make vases for milk, receptacles for water, cups, and most beautiful pipes, of various shapes and great brilliancy of surface. The clay they use is blackish or reddish, and the different colours vary in price, the latter being considered the more valuable. In the markets there is plenty of butter, which is mostly bought by speculators, who send it to Uganda. It is an item of business almost exclusively belonging to the Wahuma, who are possessors of cattle, or shepherds to the king or to the great of the realm.

Butter is made by shaking the milk in large empty gourds; it is preserved in a kind of wrapper formed by banana leaves covered with clay, mixed with ox excrement. The use of this tegument is general, it is a substitute for baskets. Tobacco, beans, sesame, corn, and salt are wrapped up in it to facilitate their transport. The coating of clay is only applied when they wish to guarantee the preservation of the different articles.

The merchants of Zanzibar have greatly contributed to develop the commercial tendencies of the natives, and the introduction of cowries (*Cyprea moneta*) has facilitated and extended business.

Brought into the country by the search for ivory, they did a good business in selling guns, powder, linen, and beads. They opened markets, which put them in contact with the population, and they knew how to acquire their confidence. Derogating somewhat from their own dignity, they made friends with the king, for whom they often committed secret misdeeds.

The various tribes scattered over the country, united by language and customs, and forming the people of Wanyoro, dwell in villages of no great extent, and like to build their abodes in banana woods. Their huts, of a conical form, built of bushes and grass, have high doors with a pent-house roof extending over them. The interior is well provided with utensils for domestic use, and is divided into various compartments. The women control the house, and attend to the work of the fields. The men, however, especially those of the poorest class, do not refuse to share in the heaviest labour. They are all devoted to drink, and a jar of beer is preferred to the most sumptuous food. Chiefs of high rank eat alone; but the greater part of the native men sit at the same board as their families. All make use of wooden spoons. As lovers of feasts and dances, they seize upon every occasion for satisfying this passion, and dance at births and marriages, and after having completed the rites of the new moon they dance for three days, and drink to excess.

The Wanyoro are very timid, and shudder at rain and dew. They never leave the house till the sun is high, and the roads in the hours of early morning are completely deserted, as they are also when it rains. They have a great respect for rain dispensers, whom they load with a profusion of gifts. The great dispenser, he who has absolute and uncontrollable power over the rain is the king, but he can confer and divide his power with other persons, so that the benefit may be distributed in various parts of the kingdom. One day a man arrived from the king, tired and breathless, and cried in the streets and roads that they might begin to sow, for Makama had ordered them to begin

MUSICAL INSTRUMENTS OF THE SHOOLI.

work in the fields at once. Rain had been wanted for a long time, it is true, but the sky remained bright, and the air calm. Nevertheless, next morning rain

BURIAL OF KING KAMRASI.

fell heavily, as if to confirm the supernatural power of the grand dispenser.

The burial of the dead is performed without a long mourning, and with little ceremony. They are interred near the house of which they are considered the guardians, and the family are comforted by the thought that the dead man watches over the prosperity of the relatives left behind.

Human sacrifices are not in accordance with the feelings of the Wanyoro, and if they perform them at all, it is only in imitation of a prerogative of the royal family.

When Kamrasi died, a large deep ditch or pit was dug in the king's abode, destined to receive the remains of the dead when the funeral rites were quite completed. Six of the dead monarch's wives were placed in it, and the body was fastened to their legs. A little boy kneeling at Kamrasi's feet held his pipe and tobacco jar. The horrible group was arranged (without a murmur from the unhappy victims), the pit was filled with earth, and on the tomb rivers of blood flowed from murdered human beings, to appease the dead monarch's soul, and render him propitious to the new despot. He still watches over the greatness and prosperity of the kingdom, and unhappy victims pay tribute for the veneration of the people to the dead Sovereign, and for the capricious superstition of the despotic heir.

CHAPTER IV.

DIFFICULTIES IN UNYORO.

A throne streaming with blood—Absolute power of the king—The *banassura*—Their increasing influence, their recruitment, and their conduct—The king desirous of pleasing—" Movement is life "—The way of deceit and treason—A fatal dualism—Pain destroys illusion—The boldness of yore encouraged by the paternal ghost—Alone in Juaya—Ahmed Akkad's good services—Willing and paid informer—The Dinka boy brave and affectionate—Shooting the thieves—An unpleasant nocturnal visitor—The expulsion of the merchants—I am accused of plotting against the king—A guard on the River Kafu—Biri's servant arrested—Chua will not have me—Plan to attack Wadelai—Emin informed of it by me—At Muimba, June 1, 1887—Obese wemen—The steamers *Khedive* and *Nyanza* on the Victoria Nile—Burning of the village of Rokora—Destruction of barges—Anger of the king—Letters seized—Biri on the road to Unyoro—Unavoidable danger—Fortunate meeting with my people—The young ruler ignorant of the way to govern—The Waganda resume hostilities—A Winchester rifle, psychical experiment—Joyful welcome—I obtain permission to remain in Unyoro—Fights—A deputation from Waganda—Oakibi and Kauta—The troops of Waganda—They march past my house—The *banassura* fighting—Emin at Kibiro—Alliance or invasion—My expulsion is requested—I am to exchange blood with his son.

THE acquisition of supreme power by violence and fraternal bloodshed, and the intimate friendship of King Chua with the slave dealers, which had become perfect (not only because he was their accomplice, but also from habit), were the motives which induced him to entrust his safety to foreign and mercenary guards. Moreover, the necessity of maintaining his prestige by terror over a population who had applauded the unfortunate Kabamiro, his innate cowardice and abject customs, were additional reasons for his confiding in strangers. Faith in the dynastic and national traditions, and, still more, the loyalty of old Kategora and others, had occasionally hindered imprudent changes of the ordinances of the kingdom. This displeased the despot, who, having at last given up all hesitation, was not ashamed to attempt the life of his father's friend, his patient and affectionate adviser.

From that day the power of the *banassura* in the Government was assured. The owners of the land were deprived of every customary right, and the king was happy in exclaiming, "I reign alone, since my ministers are the low and weak."

The institution of the *banassura* was originally intended to supply the king with a special guard, more as an exterior distinction than for the protection of the Court and his life.

In Kamrasi's time, the tranquillity and safety of the king were entrusted to the attention and devotion of the people to his sacred person. Parties of armed natives watched the royal residence in turn during the night, encamping round it with bright fires and singing national songs full of the king's praise. The duty of the *banassura* was then limited to a service of pageantry and keeping order at public assemblies; to receiving ambassadors, and forwarding royal despatches to the chiefs of the State provinces. Most of them were armed with lance and shield, only a few having muskets, more as an honour than as a practical weapon of defence. Their duties were limited to obeying the orders they received, and they were subject to the *magnoro* and *matungoli*, who were solely responsible to the king for the administration of the provinces entrusted to them. The *banassura* were mostly strangers in the country; they were looked upon with contempt by the natives, and had the character of being rather the king's slaves than soldiers of the country. The *banassura* were recruited from the deserters of the Egyptian troops, from runaway slaves, and riotous youths from the bordering States; in this corps of brigands there are Waganda, Bari, Shooli, Lur, Walegga, Lango, Madi, and Bongo men, by whom the Crown of Unyoro was supported, its subjects terrorised, and the main strength of its combatants obtained. The young king was an ardent admirer of the firearms carried by Baker's soldiers, the more so as the troops of General Gordon distributed along the Victoria Nile had shown their incontestable superiority; therefore he expended all the wealth of his treasury in acquiring powder and guns, and opened the barriers of his own State to the Zanzibar merchants, although adverse to them by jealousy and superstition.

Strengthened by the new weapons, and surrounded by hundreds of fusiliers, he felt convinced that he was the most powerful monarch in the world. His heroes saluted him with discharges of blank cartridge, and he meditated distant conquests, commanded numerous raids for slaves and cattle, challenged the once-feared Uganda warriors, and assumed the right of arbitrator amongst the tribes of the Lake district.

The military party became preponderant in Unyoro, and the *banassura* were considered indispensable for the preservation and grandeur of the kingdom; their numbers were increased to three thousand. They undertook to defend the throne and enforce the laws; thus, in the end every one's life and property were at their mercy, and their misdeeds were not only unpunished, but often even openly defended. They boldly prosecuted the guilty, and also the innocent in their eagerness to confiscate valuable property, and to perform summary executions; they were very audacious in their raids, and did not tolerate any authority except that of their worthy chiefs. They had neither feelings of honour nor love for the country in which they were strangers; in war they were rather unrestrained pillagers than brave soldiers. The king did not give them any direct recompense for their services, except supplying them with arms; but he allowed them to appropriate the goods of culprits, real or suspected. In this matter he exceeded every limit of decency; justice became a jest, impunity from punishment was sold, innocence and honesty were forced to pay a high price for safety. Moreover, the king, compliant and surrounded by the intrigues of the confederates, was as powerless to oppose them as to escape from them, and continued to maintain his ancestral glory by audacious and adventurous enterprises abroad, in order to satisfy their ever increasing avidity; and the circle of blood that surrounded him and separated him from his subjects more and more every day, increased enormously.

The guardianship of the king's dwelling by day and night and of public ceremonies, as well as the supervision of Government councils and administration of justice, were given up to military influence, and the chiefs, who were rather companions in his nightly orgies than subjects of the king, obtained the most insane and odious orders from his half-intoxicated Majesty, which had already been plotted in their private meetings. Chua acted as they required, rejoicing only in displaying the pomp of his own power and person to his people, who, faithful to the traditional awe of his ancestors, not only applauded but venerated the king. Movement is life, and even uncivilised nations are now and then influenced by internal commotions of greater or less importance, which gradually alter their usages and customs, and unconsciously open the way for new ideas, which, even if partly erroneous and inconsistent, change the character of the inhabitants and the customs of the country. There is a tendency everywhere to part unwillingly with old ways of governing and living, and if an attempt at their revival takes place, it is not only ephemeral, but crushes in its fall all the sophistry which was instrumental in bringing it forward, so that only that which is good and true triumphs permanently in the end.

Instruments of Providence, the chiefs are unconscious of the aim towards which they move, and woe to them if they could perceive it. In their superstitious ignorance they would recoil horrified; they rush on because their interest, vanity, or fear compel them.

When I went to Unyoro, the king, although he mistrusted us, was bent nevertheless upon a more or less friendly policy, which he considered as beneficial to the kingdom and himself. Taking advantage of these propitious circumstances, we obtained permission for the arrival of the merchant Biri from Uganda, for the passage of correspondence, and for sending a message of peace to King Muanga. If this state of affairs had continued, the barriers of the kingdom would have been opened; freedom of travelling and its beneficial results would have been accomplished facts. "But such friendship leads to ruin," exclaimed all the leaders of the soldiers, and the king was perhaps glad of an opportunity for returning to his old hatred and mistrust, sacrificing his minister, and adopting the policy of falsehood and treachery.

The military party resumed its influence in the management of Government affairs, with the full approbation of the king, who began to think he had committed a great political error when, forgetting the offensive conduct of the Egyptian Government, he had clasped the hand offered to him by the Governor of Equatoria. Then dualism, with its sad consequences, began to weigh heavily upon the country. The evicted owners of land secretly plotted against the soldiers who trampled on them, and were ready to rise if they only had an opportunity. But fear, and respect for the sacred person of the monarch, who was not only alive, but reigning, prevented them.

At the commencement of this sad period the most foolish projects were conceived and executed. But they all proved failures, bringing shame upon the king's advisers and champions. The war against Uganda was projected, but the landowners refused their acquiescence.

"You have your *banassura* and your guns," they said; "you have entrusted your defence, and that of your kingdom, to them for some time; now send them to war."

That was the answer given by the chiefs and people at the war council summoned by the great *nuggare*. But war had become inevitable on account of the young king Muanga, of Uganda. It was of short duration, but it sadly impressed King Chua's mind.

One day, when the intensity of his anguish tore aside the veil of illusions, he caused the following words to be conveyed to me:—

"My *banassura* like raids, because they profit by them. They are opposed to war, and contend that the territory should be defended by the landowners. I am a native of the east, and I would fain have returned to the country of my ancestors, if possible, without waiting for the result of the war."

When the king spoke in this manner he was under the influence of fear, discouragement, and doubt; but as soon as the danger was over he resumed his usual audacity.

"The spirit of his father," he said, "had guided his

warriors, blessed the campaign, and still held his hand over him."

And as if mad, he deviated farther still from the ancient mode of governing, ruling by oppression and treachery, rather than by reason; and to their united powers confiding the integrity and safety of the State.

My isolation was complete (March 6, 1887). I remained alone at Juaya with my domestics, two Government soldiers, and two of the king's *banassura*, whose instructions were to watch me rather than to render me any service.

The die was cast. The king was crossing the Rubicon, and had thrown off the mask. The party who had advocated execrable measures in the Council of January 25, had triumphed. Thenceforth, no more subterfuges, plotting, and ambiguous words were employed, but the rupture of every intercourse with Europeans, and the aggressions on the Government territories, were manifested openly.

King Chua's former policy, ambiguous, but timid and cautious, was given up and replaced by the frivolous, rapacious, and profligate proceedings of the *banassura*.

However, our affairs, in spite of so much animosity, were progressing favourably for the objects we had in view. At the beginning of the year hostile measures against us had been agreed upon by the principal people of the kingdom; but my first care was to assure the transmission and reception of our correspondence to and from Uganda. In this attempt I received the courageous and cordial co-operation of a certain Ahmed Akkad, an Arab from Oman, who had settled in Unyoro for commercial purposes. Thanks to him, we easily found messengers, who, for rewards in ivory, would take our letters to Mr. Mackay (agent of the British mission), and faithfully bring us those from Uganda. Suspected of intercourse with me, Ahmed Akkad was sentenced to banishment from the kingdom. But it was easy for me to obtain the revocation of the sentence through the mediation of the wicked Abd Rehman.

We did not purchase cloth and other goods in any considerable quantities, for the merchants' prices were too high, and also, because Biri's caravan was on the point of entering Unyoro; but for our most urgent needs it was an easy matter to elude the vigilance of the guards stationed even at night on the bank of the stream which separated us from the quarter occupied by the merchants. The most perplexing and important question remained; that is to say, we wanted to learn the foreign news, and still more to hear of the plots which were being concocted in the royal residence in rapid succession; but among the natives, and even the king's guards, there were volunteers and paid informers who undertook the dangerous task, so that every plot against us came to my knowledge as soon as it was projected, and before any attempt at carrying it out could be made. Although I was compelled to remain in my residence, watched by guards upon all sides, and every action spied upon, I managed to avail myself of a courageous Dinka boy, who, under the pretence of making some purchases in the market, cleverly found a way of speaking to our friends, and carrying out all our wishes. Being advised by him to grant interviews, I received nocturnal visits, after preparing the way for them, which was, I am sorry to say, by intoxicating my guards. I was not only informed of all that was useful to our interests, but also of the scandals and proceedings in the royal residence. As soon as the Government settled at

Muimba, the first nocturnal attacks upon my dwelling began. On April 28 I complained to the king about an attack which had been perpetrated the previous night, but he answered, smiling, "Shoot the thieves; night marauders of that description are not my subjects." And as a confirmation of the royal disapprobation, the following day had scarcely closed when the unpleasant visit was renewed and repeated for several months at various intervals. They were only interrupted at the time of the Waganda invasion.

Having been informed that these nefarious attacks had been inspired by the royal Court, either to frighten me and cause my departure, or, worse still, perhaps to remove me as a hostile spy, conspirator, or enemy, I showed an indifferent, and even smiling countenance to those who troubled me with their curiosity; but I increased my precautions during the night, which was difficult and painful work, as it spoilt the leisure of my servants and soldiers, but was chiefly carried out by myself with marvellous success, for I frustrated no less than eight attempts.

It was a rainy night; watch was to be kept by a young man who was easily overcome by sleep. I usually went out of my hut at different times (tormented by insomnia and the continual uncertainty of impending danger), in order to test not only the vigilance but also the fidelity of my sentry. Having seized my gun, I went out in the open and approached the lad, who was sitting down with his chin touching his breast, and having shaken him abruptly, recommended him to be more vigilant. Suddenly the noise of a heavy object moving close by, reached my ears. Turning round I saw the confused outline of several lions, and first fired in their direction and then at random. Complete silence ensued. Next morning we

THE KING'S ACCUSATIONS.

ascertained that a visit had been paid us by a whole family of lions. The poor lad, who had had such a narrow escape of his life, smiled, but with his lips quivering with fear.

* * * * * *

The king's peremptory order to depart from Juaya had not been obeyed by all the Arab merchants, and this fact irritated the suspicious despot, whom his perverse courtiers succeeded in inciting to fresh rigours and excessive interference.

On April 17, 1887, a detachment of *banassura* invaded the merchants' village, and drove away masters, servants, women, and children with clubs. They then fired the houses, collected the people like cattle, and with scorn and ill-treatment led them to Muimba, where they were compelled to obtain pardon from the royal clemency: these poor victims resigned themselves to the loss of their wealth, in order to save their lives.

On March 30, 1887, the king had accused me of conspiring against him. I did not attempt to defend myself, but answered his charge with a contemptuous smile. April 7, an armed expedition started for the conquest of the banks of the Victoria Nile, a region subject to the chief Anfina, and abandoned to the ambitious desires of the Unyoro king, by the impolitic concession of the Governor of Equatoria. On the 25th, a guard was stationed by the river Kafu to watch all arrivals from Uganda and seize our correspondence.

On May 2, Biri's servant was arrested, stripped, and flogged on the road as he was preceding his master, who was travelling towards Unyoro. Nor was this all, for on May 11, the king sent a letter to Emin full of charges against me, with the object of obtaining my recall. And whilst, with pharisaical compunction, he appealed to "his friend the Doctor," he ordered the chiefs Babedongo, Ireta, and Makavaro to muster a large force in order to seize the steamer at Kibiro, invade the Shooli country, and make a combined attack upon Wadelai. But man proposes and God disposes.

I had already informed Emin, some time previously, of the audacious plot, and he had consequently taken the necessary measures for defence, and entered into alliance with various chiefs on the banks of the Nile. Warned afterwards by me of the probable date when the King of Unyoro's troops would cross the river, Emin at once concentrated there a large number of regular soldiers and black troops, placing the steamers on the Albert Lake, a little above the mouth of the river.

On June 1, the king invited me to an interview at Muimba. The large village was enlivened by an unusual bustle; people were walking about excitedly questioning one another; caravans were removing the household furniture; women hurried away with supplies of corn, and babies across their right hip (held by their hand under the armpit), and herds of cows were on the road proceeding northwards.

I reached the square in front of the king's residence, and was told by a *banassura*, that the Sovereign could not receive me at that moment as he was busy making preparations for the journey of his wives and children towards Mruli, on account of the appearance of a Waganda army on the borders. The long procession of large and small caravans occupied three hours in issuing from the king's palace, armed men preceding and following each section of it. In the centre of the column was a palanquin, made of ox hide, fixed on two poles, upon which one of the royal wives sat wrapped in a bright coloured mantle of peculiar pattern, surrounded by the women of the household and by female slaves carrying

KING CHUA'S FATTENED FEMALES.

provisions and kitchen utensils; some leading little children by the hand, or dragging a dog or recalcitrant goat. It was a scene of deafening uproar; greetings and songs, confused beating of drums, shaking hands, and faces saddened by transitory weeping, that was suddenly succeeded by the habitual smile.

A crowd gathered at the king's door, and a cry of astonishment was uttered by everybody, as a woman, almost a shapeless mass of flesh, with immense limbs, and small eyes, sitting on a sort of sedan-chair, larger than the preceding one, and supported by stouter poles, was being carried across the royal threshold by four stalwart men. She was one of King Chua's obese women.

In the Courts at Uganda and Unyoro, the possession of obese wives is considered a thing worthy of the royal splendour. Such a luxury is considered as the emblem of wealth and as of extraordinary comeliness, for the possession of whom the monarch is particularly ambitious and greatly envied. This corpulency is attained by a special diet, regularly administered both as regards time and quantity. The accumulation of fat gradually proceeds so as to render the person unable to stand up; those who are afflicted by it are compelled to walk on their hands and knees, and even then they move with great difficulty.

After waiting some time, I was at last admitted to Makama's presence. He was sitting upon a large chair, with a sulky countenance, moving his feet restlessly, and convulsively grasping the edge of the mantle which covered him from his waist to his feet.

The courtiers, with bowed heads, hardly dared to look at each other. There was a long pause, and then at last the storm burst, and the king, forgetting the customary etiquette, addressed me vehemently in

Arabic, accusing me of conspiring with the Governor of Equatoria to ruin him and his kingdom.

What had happened? .... The steamers had suddenly appeared on the Victoria Nile, and the Expedition of the Wanyoro, which had already commenced to cross the river, had scarcely had time to retire. The natives' boats had been captured and destroyed, the chief Rokora had been driven from his own village, which was burnt, and some natives and *banassura* had been killed by the soldiers: these were the king's charges. The fact was not new to me; I was only astonished at the failure of the Government Expedition due to the commander's want of ability. The difficulty which surrounded us increased, and my personal position might become very perilous. I concealed my thoughts during the above string of charges, thanked the king for his attention in giving me such news, and begged him not to arrive at too hasty a conclusion respecting the facts, adding that the provocation to war might have been caused by Rokora's obstinacy in remaining in a country which was not his own, and mentioned that I myself had advised him several times not to risk difficult enterprises, and that the lesson which had been inflicted upon him might turn to his own benefit. Then he became still more gloomy and sulky, his eyes being reddened with fury.

" Have you not usurped my territories of Tunguru and Msua on the Lake ? " he asked.

" No, your majesty, we have occupied those two points with your consent."

" And you have appropriated them."

" No, they are still part of your kingdom ; some day we shall give them up, but we cannot do so just now. You gave us permission to pass through Unyoro, and

EMIN SHELLS THE CANOES OF KING CHUA'S WARRIORS.

you have not only prevented us from doing so, but have also intercepted our correspondence, therefore the Lake route is indispensable to us."

" What you assert is not true. I have never interfered with your letters."

" Why do you keep those seized at Kafu by Babedongo a few days ago, instead of delivering them to me ? "

" I have none of your letters."

" Why is Biri still on the border awaiting your order to enter the kingdom; an order a hundred times promised but not given ? "

" As to the Turk, I have already taken the necessary measures; he will come in a few days."

" And the letters ? "

" I have none."

" Yes, you have them."

" Well, yes; but I will never give them up."

" Your declaration is enough; I do not want the letters. One day, perhaps, somebody more powerful than I will settle the matter with you."

" Who ? "

" Said Barghash, for example."

" I am not afraid of him."

I moved in order to rise, but the king invited me to sit down. He said he was sorry to see me angry, and would speak to his minister about the letters. Our conversation then turned upon various subjects, and I left when the sun was already under the horizon. In order to reach Juaya, one had to travel for three hours in the midst of lonely country and marshy valleys, covered with cane plants. The king's persistence in advising me to delay my departure, his whispering to some of his guards—the moving to and fro of the latter —appeared to me a series of ominous signs after the grave offence given by the events that had happened on the Victoria Nile; therefore, after having walked a few steps, I begged the two *banassura* who were to accompany me to return and tell the king that I wished two vessels of good beer as a present. The two drunkards leaped for joy, and quickly went to him. I took advantage of their absence, to have my two guns loaded, which I had close at hand (carried by a faithful lad of mine and a Soudanese soldier), giving them summary instructions as to their behaviour along the road. Having arrived near a hill where the road, sloping, was hidden by high grass and thick reedy ferns, leading to a difficult and entangled marsh, I heard the well-known voices of my servants; they were alarmed at the unusual lateness of our return, and, being encouraged by one of the women, they all, soldiers, boys, and women, came out in search of us, and we were lucky indeed! For, later on, one of the two *banassura* who accompanied us that night, said to that very woman, "Accursed sorceress, if thou hadst not been alive, thy master would not be here to give us the trouble of busying ourselves for his sake."

Preparations for invading Unyoro had been in progress for some time. The presents sent by King Chua did not seem worthy of a great potentate's acceptance; such at least was the opinion of that little tyrant of Uganda, who, with his usual precipitation, assembled bands of armed warriors to invade, lay waste, and conquer Unyoro, and take prisoner its Sovereign, who had cracked numerous jokes about "the young man who was ignorant of the art of governing." As long as the danger was distant the braggadocios of Unyoro deafened everybody with their boasts and audacious schemes. When they heard, however, that the Baganghese district was invaded (June 9, 1887), their brag ceased as if by magic, and their only thought was of saving themselves, their women, children, and goods.

On June 20 the king abandoned Muimba, and retired to Nparo (not far from Juaya), on account of the aggressive march of the Waganda. He then sent me several messengers, with a peremptory order to prepare to retrace my steps towards the Government provinces immediately. From the messengers' abrupt manner

FLIGHT OF KING CHUA.

and sardonic countenances it was easy to see what were the king's intentions. I replied that I would not go unless the goods which Biri had brought from Uganda, and the ivory in my premises, were safely deposited at Kibiro; but at 5 P.M. another messenger arrived, bringing from the king an unopened letter, which the Governor had sent a few days previously, and repeating the order to depart from the kingdom, with threats in case I ventured to disobey. He would not have any further intercourse with us, " who," he said, "were good for nothing else than offering him idle words of encouragement and compliments when his kingdom was in danger."

It was a decisive moment, and hesitation would have been fatal. I took my Winchester rifle and one hundred cartridges, and sent them to the king as an opportune present, wishing him a speedy and complete victory. This was an effort to gain a point. If the king refused it, the game was lost—the cloth and the ivory on the road would have been forfeited; but if he accepted it, we at least gained time, and the continuation of the arrangement which connected us with the civilised world, however imperfect and precarious that might be. Next morning, before sunrise, I received a visit from the same messenger whom I had seen on the previous evening, and he invited me to go to Nparo at once, to meet the king. I did not delay one moment, and was received most cordially and joyfully by him. He thanked me for the gift of my rifle, and added that it clearly showed the interest I took in his success, and also that my intention to remain, while the Arabs had all fled at the first rumours of war, convinced him of the Governor's loyalty. He granted me permission to remain at Juaya, or to go to any other place in his kingdom. I also obtained a messenger to convey my letters to Wadelai, and the concession that Biri was to travel to Kibiro, together with the provisions collected, and thence to the residence of the Governor of Equatoria. We won once more, and our numerous enemies might well bite their fingers. But they had other matters to attend to, for the rapacious Waganda were on the point of attacking them.

On the 22nd of June the king sent me a message, asking whether I had any guns to sell him; but I answered that it was not becoming for me to act as a merchant, and sent him a good percussion gun as a present. On the 23rd he retired to Guamirma, whence he took refuge in the midst of the woods of Bidongo, near ancient Masindi. On June 27 the first battles took place in the neighbourhood of Muimba. There were numerous fusiliers. The blacks fled at the approach of hostilities, and the country became deserted by its inhabitants. On the 29th, Muimba was abandoned and burnt. On the 30th, and July 1, there were fights at Nparo and on the road to Masindi, and on the 3rd the entire invading army appeared at Juaya.

The column, which was a long one, descended the Moranda hills, and passed in front of my residence, on which the Egyptian Government flag was hoisted. The Wanyoro had suddenly ceased fighting in the neighbourhood of Nparo, and had succeeded in deceiving the enemy by means of a sham retreat. The Waganda then began to look for King Chua, who was generally believed to have reached the Ruwengabi-Coanga forest, in the Kiriangobi territory, but on their questioning me about it I confirmed their impression, which I knew was erroneous. If I had chosen to put an end to the tyrant's existence, a word or gesture would have been sufficient; but although my life had been continually plotted against, I would not act otherwise than as a loyal guest.

Next day a Waganda deputation brought the greetings of Oakibi, their general.* Kauto, their chief, offered to escort me to Uganda, but I thanked him and declined, though we entered into negotiations for the occupation of Kibiro, and for a future alliance, should Oakibi's arms eventually prove successful, and Unyoro be occupied for a long period. The missionaries of Usukuma assured me that on that occasion Kauto

* The Waganda call their commander-in-chief Kangao.

had received an order from Muanga to take my life, and that I owed my safety to the numerous Waganda Christians, who had been warned, and warmly entreated by the Uganda missionaries to do their best to defeat that horrible machination. On July 5 the Wanyoro attacked the Waganda. There were fights at Kibararo, Mount Sedgiomocoro, and on the banks of the

MY NEGOTIATIONS WITH THE CHIEFS OF UGANDA.

Ngussi, with varying fortune, but finally the Waganda marched towards the Baganghese district, and, July 19, the kingdom of Unyoro was clear of invaders. The Waganda army consisted of about 6000 men of all ages, from 15 to 60, with the greatest contrast of armament and dress. There were the king's guards in their white robes, with leopard skin and red cloth cartridge belts glittering, and heavy percussion guns, and the simple mountaineers armed with bludgeons, whose only dress was a rug made of bark fibres, hung round the loins. Between these extreme types, fancy an innumerable variety of old guns, shields, spears, worn-out and discoloured garments, and the traditional mantles of ox hide, or fig bark; glass ornaments and armlets, mostly consisting of ox or goat horn, with the famous conjuring powder. This was the army of the Waganda; this multitude was divided into corps, each commanded by a chief, easily recognisable by his better attire and finer ornaments, besides the *nuggare* carried behind him. Faithful to the idea of scattering themselves, in order to find food with greater facility, they covered immense tracts of land in their raids; but their depredatory instinct caused them to diverge too far, so that at the time of a fight most of them are distant from the spot where it occurs. For their object is more to plunder and spread misery than to struggle against the foe and acquire a reputation for valour, so that they search the dwellings and the *matamure*, seizing as booty everything they can carry away, and burning what remains, together with the huts. Goods such as tobacco or stuffs they consign to the flames, and they scatter corn or pulse amongst the high grass. They throw themselves upon the cultivated fields, and, having gathered sufficient food for the day, they pull down, upset, and destroy everything else; therefore starvation soon overtakes them, and compels them to shorten the duration of an invasion, thus reducing to nought whatever plan or bold enterprise they have formed.

They are fierce in battle, but only as long as reserves are in the rear ready to strengthen the weak and threatened positions; for should they be unsupported or hard pressed they quickly take to flight. The death of a chief also has a discouraging effect upon them. On the march, in camp, starting, and in the heat of a fight the deafening noise of the innumerable *nuggare* inspires them with courage. With such an army, it is obvious that the ambitious dreams of the lord of Uganda, and his desire to possess Unyoro, were very nearly hopeless.

Chua possessed more than one thousand guns, and they were in the hands of his guards, the *banassura*, who formed the army which fought against the Waganda, because the so-called landowners, who were only armed with a lance and shield, did not take part in it for various reasons. The arms of the *banassura* consisted of a large number of Remington rifles, a few Sniders, and a good many percussion muskets, either gathered from the deserters from the Egyptian Government or acquired from the Lango, who had several times defeated the soldiers. There were also some good breech and muzzle loaders bought from Zanzibar merchants.

The ancient and traditional tactics of the Wanyoro, are not to undertake serious engagements, and not to attack the enemy in a wooded country, but to prepare ambuscades in suitable places and then to harass him by sudden halts, in order to entice him to the places where the ambushes had been laid ; but it cannot be affirmed that the *banassura* practised such tactics successfully. Alarmed by the excessive number of enemies, and irritated by the refusal of the natives to join them, disheartened by their sufferings in the recent invasion upon the borders of the Victoria Nile, and still more impressed by the probability of being attacked in the rear by the soldiers of Equatoria, their compulsory retreat of May being still fresh in their minds—when the war-cry was raised they did not, for these reasons, muster in full force, nor did they behave in such a warlike manner as to deserve a good military reputation.

On July 7 Emin passed Kibiro, on his way to the Msua station on the western shore of the Albert Lake. This terrified the Wanyoro; and the king, who was at Buemba, on the banks of the river Kafu, with the object of placing an ambush for the retreating enemy, hurried precipitately to Kiani-Cassangora near Mruli for refuge, feeling certain that the country would be invaded by the Soudanese soldiers of Equatoria. From that place he announced to me that he was ready to enter into negotiations about the long projected alliance. I made known to him (in the Governor's name), through his messenger, our immutable decisions, which were, either alliance confirmed by exchange of blood, or a concession for us too ccupy Kibiro and the plateau of Kitana, because the freedom of our communications with Uganda was indispensable to us. In view of such an audacious proposal the grandees and military chiefs raised a tumultuous agitation, and decided to demand of the king my expulsion from the country, and the breaking off of all intercourse with the Government of Equatoria. But the Sovereign declined to carry out such resolutions, and on August 2 sent me presents, and a message, "My son will exchange blood with you. I want an ally, and accept your proposal. The last war into which I was led by the pernicious advice of Abd Rehman and the ambition of the grandees and the *banassura* was inconsiderate and foolish. I am the king, and my will is law. Ancient Juaya shall be rebuilt, and I will take up my abode close by you. Son of the great Kamrasi, my lip was never soiled by a falsehood."

CHAPTER V.

KABBA REGA'S HOSTILITY.

Occupation of the region on the left bank of the Victoria Nile—Katongoli, the Lango man—A child as a holocaust—Guakamatera, prime minister of King Chua—"The king has ordered me to watch you"—The king reiterates his promises—Neither a single piece of ivory nor a cartridge—The guards' refusal—Attempt by night—Great imprudence—The king wishes me to become his guest—The merchant Hamis—Exchange of victims—The Victoria Nile placed in a position of defence—Sacred boats—Young students—Emin leaves on a visit to the northern stations—I ask for frequent despatch of messengers and steamers—Prisoners in Juaya—The raids at Menakulia—A caravan of Karagua people—Communications with Kafu and Kibiro are forbidden — Delusive hope — The 10th of December 1887—Noble conduct of an enemy—Advice given to Biri—The 31st of December 1887—I think of a friend—The king's wickedness against him—Stanley has arrived—Guakamatera's strange proposal—A goat and a fowl—The great drum gives no sound—A set trap.

THE King of Unyoro decided upon the definite occupation of the countries on the Victoria Nile, formerly independent States, governed by Anfina, and Kamissua, the son and heir of chief Rionga.

"We were defeated near the great river, owing to the protection bestowed by our soldiers upon the Shefalu; but I was able to find out the secret conspiracy. The Great Kamrasi had invited us to undertake the enterprise; he had sent his son as an augury and guarantee of victory."

Thus spoke the king at a public meeting at Mruli; and Katongoli, a gigantic man of proved courage and savage ferocity, worthy of the Lango-Umiro tribe, had the leadership of the war.

In the region of the Equatorial lakes, it is believed

MUSICIANS OF RIONGA, ONE OF THE CHIEFS OF UNYORO.

that any warlike enterprise is destined by supernatural power to have a glorious end, if a human victim be offered as a holocaust on the frontier of the enemy, and is neither insulted nor taken away from the spot by them.

A child of unknown parents, stolen in a distant country, who, from his youth, is supposed to be pure and uncontaminated, is buried up to his shoulders on the road which the army must follow.

Along the route the scouts cautiously proceed, silent and watchful, always in fear of the danger of ambuscades. The column follows at a distance. They discover the little head of the innocent victim from afar; it leans on his shoulder—it is the head of a corpse—or perhaps, agonising, he still moves, uttering his last wailing.

The child being still there, according to their belief, was a sure sign of victory, and this was confirmed in their minds by the fact that the enemy had not even put in an appearance on the road, or expected an assault, whence they inferred that there was nothing to fear, and that ultimate victory was certain.

And trustful, bold, and raising their courage by songs to the dishonour of the enemy, they march past the wretched child of propitiation.

No one dares to succour him, nor even address a word of consolation, for fear of breaking the charm.

Katongoli fell as a thunderbolt upon his enemies —discomfited them, and proclaimed the power of his king all along the left bank of the Victoria Nile— September 1887.

In the court-yard of the palace at Kiani, all the grandees of the kingdom being present, the king appointed Guakamatera—one of the chiefs, who had distinguished himself in the war with the Waganda people—to be prime minister of the kingdom, and presented him with the axe, an emblem of justice, saying : " Make use of it with the greatest severity, against those who stubbornly refuse obedience and respect."

Guakamatera took up his abode at Juaya, near the river Kavarongli, and from thence sent me this message : " The king has appointed me chief of the country during his stay at Mruli, and has ordered me to take care of you ; you will let me know your wants. You are at liberty to purchase goods from any of the natives, as well as from Zanzibar merchants. I want to know you personally ; for the present I send you my regards."

An envoy from the king brought me his royal salutations, and repeated and confirmed his decision to enter upon a compact of alliance and to inaugurate a new order of things in the kingdom.

This was, perhaps, a sign of better times to come, of which I ought to have taken advantage; the opportunity, if missed, might disappear as easily as it had appeared. Obviously, as there was a struggle between two parties, our interest was to give our help, clearly, immediately, and unreservedly, in order to turn the balance in favour of that party which had become friendly to us.

I urged the Governor to send presents, to keep up frequent correspondence, and have trust in my work. The situation required an early answer ; as I did not receive any, I wrote, frankly : " If it is *urgent, indispensable*, and of the *greatest importance*, to make sure of the transit through Unyoro for the present, as well as for the future, a regular service of correspondence must be established. If the matter has only a *relative, secondary*, and *dispensable importance*, let us permit things to go as they will, as I consider it of no use to sacrifice myself any longer."

Emin was offended—as if I had meant to blame him, or usurp his power. His answer was : " I will not give a single piece of ivory, nor a cartridge, before blood brotherhood has been concluded."

Our enemies were on the watch. Babedongo and Matunzi, two military chiefs, were getting round Guakamatera to alienate him from us; the guards appointed for my service refused to accompany the soldier who was to carry letters to Wadelai.

On the 17th of October, four armed men attempted to kill me during the night, but they had to fly on account of the uninterrupted watch I used to keep, even during days of hope. A messenger I sent to the king never returned. Guakamatera was summoned to a secret council of the influential men, under the presidency of the Sovereign. . . . .

The month of October was an apparently calm one, but the silence that surrounded us on all sides was the forerunner of furious hostilities.

In the early part of November 1887, to make the situation more difficult and dangerous, notwithstanding the refusal I had sent him, Biri came to see me. He had been at Wadelai since July on his way to Uganda. That visit was a fatal imprudence, which caused him to be included in the schemes plotted against me.

Entering Unyoro without the king's permission or orders is considered a great crime, an offence to the sacred majesty of the king, and the punishment inflicted on the offender is generally death.

On the 11th of November, Guakamatera informed me of the king's anger at such proceedings, and, whilst promising his support for Biri's journey to Uganda, he expressed the king's wishes to have me as a guest for a few days. I have no doubt that it was a snare; nevertheless, had I had at my disposal the presents asked for so many times (not to increase my personal influence, but for the general welfare), I should have risked the chances of the visit.

At one time I had made the black king at Nparo smile with the splendour of a Winchester rifle!

That King Chua would not have hesitated to remove any obstacle in order to avenge his offended dignity, was not only probable but certain; it had been shown by a recent event.

Hamis, a merchant, went towards the territory of Mboga, on the right bank of the Semliki, for his own business, having been tacitly authorised to do so by the chief Babedongo, who had recently become his friend. The king, being informed of it, sent for one of his bravos, and ordered him to pursue the merchant, murder him, and take away the goods he had with him. The victim was overtaken without delay, and imprisoned in a hut, prudence inducing the assassin to perpetrate his crime during the night; but Hamis escaped and hastened to throw himself at the king's feet.

"You wish to kill me," he said; "well, then, avenge yourself;" but the king, not at all embarrassed by the failure of his scheme, called the fellow, saying:

"Why did you want to murder this defenceless man?"

"Because such was your command," answered he. "Who would dare to touch a foreigner without your order?"

The faithful emissary was put to death. The king's word, however, was not enough to enable the merchant to consider himself quite safe, and, without taking any further care of his business, he left immediately for Uganda.

TRANSPORT OF KING CHUA'S CANOES.

The king, being now master of the Victoria Nile, gave great attention to fortifying suitable points on it for its defence and for the concentration of troops. He mustered a great number of boats in the protected locality, in order to prepare all that was required for the passage of numerous soldiers to the opposite bank.

Out of caprice he ordered that two canoes of extraordinary size, built in the Kiriangobi forest, should be carried from the shore of the Albert Lake to Mruli on the Nile. The enterprise was not an easy one; steep hills, intricate woods, and rivers with high banks, interrupted the great distance between the two places in a thousand ways; but the king's will was law. It was said that a baby and a pot of milk were found at the bottom of the tree from which the large boat, called *ngata*, had been made. This strange and marvellous story attracted hundreds of earnest workers, who swore that they would launch on the Nile, not only the larger canoe, but also its fellow-boat of smaller dimensions.

Amidst rejoicings and copious draughts of beer (after many days' work interrupted by festivities), the two boats were triumphantly carried to the appointed spot. It is true that many lives were lost in the transit, but the king's whim was satisfied and numerous presents were showered on Guakamatera, the director of the pious enterprise.

Everything concurred to render it more obvious that Chua, having repented his promises, had again given way to the customary polities of intrigue and deceit. The pressure of his faithful servants and the uncertainty and carelessness on our part had encouraged him, but he hesitated to proceed to open violence. A thread, though a thin one, still bound him to us.

From the first day of my stay in Unyoro, six youths

belonging to the best families of the kingdom had on my advice been sent to Wadelai to receive literary instruction at that school. Two of the pupils had died of small-pox during the epidemic which ravaged the country in the last months of 1886; the other four were still attending the school, to their benefit, and the satisfaction of their teachers. The king had several times expressed a wish to see the young students for a short time, and I, without giving a formal refusal, had always encouraged Emin to keep those precious hostages, as a check on any wicked intention of the king. But on the 1st of November, Emin sent back the four lads from Kibiro, and at the same time informed me that, by request of the officers and employés of the first battalion, he purposed visiting the northern stations in the hope of restoring order among the troops, and bringing them to reason.

At the close of the letter he hinted at his expectation of persuading those people, by telling them that the firman for the title of Pasha had been conferred upon him, as the letters of the Egyptian Government had announced in a despatch from the British Consul General at Zanzibar, which I had forwarded to him.

I answered Emin that, notwithstanding the ever increasing danger threatening our safety, I was ready to do all in my power to help him in his painful situation. I advised him to grant a general pardon to some officers and officials, punished too severely, and to rid himself of the Major commanding in Dufilé, because he had been the author of the prolonged disorders. I exhorted him to keep in mind the wickedness of King Chua, which was not less than that of his advisers; a disposition which could only be checked by impressing fear on his cowardly mind; I requested him, therefore, to order that a messenger should, without fail, be sent

DANGER AND ANXIETY.

to Kibiro every week, and that every fortnight a steamer should anchor there, with the express order to await my consent for its departure; and I added that he had better send me, at once, choice elephants' tusks and a case of cartridges as presents for the king.

Emin wrote, promising to do all I had asked him, and left Kibiro.

On the 2nd of December I sent a messenger with the firman and Government letters to Kibiro. No courier had arrived from the Pasha; no steamer had made its appearance in the roadstead.

Even now, whilst I am writing, the remembrance of those days makes me shiver and affects my heart and mind with grief.

Violence was substituted for intrigue, and crime ended the horrible drama.

On the 28th day of November, Biri and a soldier were prevented by the *banassura* from going to Nusranduru, a village where the merchants were residing. To overcome this resistance was a question of dignity; and almost resulted in a quarrel, but they were allowed to pass.

The chiefs Babedongo and Guakamatera made raids on the boundaries of Uganda, in order to seize the Zanzibar couriers, waiting at Menakulia for the king's permission to enter Unyoro.

A man named Meikambi was searched, robbed, and beaten, on the Kafu river, whilst on his journey back from Uganda with letters for us. A caravan of Karagua people was dispersed, and some of the party were arrested under the suspicion of conveying correspondence.

Two men, named Rubanga and Katto, accused of supplying me with news concerning the king's affairs, were barbarously murdered. Ten rifles were presented by the king to Ballula, a notorious Shooli chief in rebellion against the Government, who at the same time received instructions for an impending rebellion.

A large number of soldiers were mustered around Juaya, on the road to the Kafu and Kibiro.

We never heard from the king; not a single friendly word was addressed to us; the bold, grinning black faces of the three guards watching us, every moment reminded us of our pitiable condition.

The sole relief from our distress was the hope of the longed-for arrival of a steamer from Kibiro, to defeat all designs made against us, and to delay our complete ruin.

Every evening we used to retire with this illusion, and every morning we woke to witness a new scene of the drama, which was quickly approaching its end.

Vain hopes! The steamers had remained guarding Dufilé, and had afterwards taken the Governor back to Wadelai, for, being threatened with imprisonment by his soldiers, he had had to escape by night from Kirri.

The departure of the steamer from Wadelai had been postponed on account of important repairs. The chimneys and hulks had been varnished like new, for show at the approaching voyage on the lake.

Matters went on like this till the 10th of December, on the evening of which day we were told of the fate awaiting us, by a servant of the merchants.

At Kiani, near Mruli, in the great audience hall, in presence of all the great men (who always assembled on emergencies), as well as of Abd Rehman, the evil genius, a *banassura* made most serious accusations against me before the king, declaring that I despised the Sovereign and intrigued against him; that I spread a propaganda of rebellion; had secret intercourse with

Muanga; was plotting to dethrone Chua; and that I had gathered armed men in my house.

Biri was accused of being my accomplice in the horrible plot.

"I know," said the king, "and I know also what I must do."

He sent for one of his bravos, and in a majestic tone, said:

"Thou wilt go to Babedongo and relate to him what thou hast just heard. Tell him that I order the white man's house to be surrounded, and he and the Turkish merchant to be sent away; and, if necessary, to kill them both. Tell him to fear not, as I will take the responsibility."

Three days afterwards, the messenger communicated the king's wishes and orders to Babedongo, but the former promptly answered:

"Return to Makama and tell him to entrust this affair to some one else. He will have to repent of such an action assuredly. He has called the white man into the country, and he (the white man) has not given any reason for complaint. He only wishes to be allowed to receive letters from Uganda and to send some there, of which the king has been aware since the day of his arrival."

The justice loyally done me by a man who had always been one of my worst enemies, was the only relief left to me in my burdensome work and daily sufferings.

I advised Biri to withdraw to Nusranduru among his friends, the Arabs. By their means and with presents, when away from me he could win Babedongo's favour, and avoid the danger now threatening him.

Overwhelmed by grief, and mastered by anxiety

for his ivory (still at Kibiro), Biri could not make up his mind to anything. He wept, but lived in hope.

On the 19th of December 1887, his servant, Manjaliva, on his return from having taken letters to the confines of Uganda, and now the bearer of correspondence, repeated and confirmed to him the news which the Arabs had sent; but even then he did not come to any decision.

The year closed with gloomy prospects (31st December 1887).

King Chua was on the point of throwing off the mask. He had failed in his continued attempts to get rid of me, as well as of the ties which he had voluntarily contracted with the Government of Equatoria. His underhand intrigues had proved fruitless, and he remained as covetous as ever of the ivory and guns of the province, as well as of the possession of the Shooli. Now that he realised his strength in the positions on the Victoria Nile, and was certain of the alliance with the Shooli, owing to the rebel Ballula's friendship, and trusting also to the help of the Lango people, he intended to challenge the province, and, having a perfect knowledge of the weakness of the Government forces, was convinced that he would be successful in his attempt.

The storm had already begun.

The king was still at Juaya, again meditating flight, conflagration, and the whole series of deceptions which had made me so anxious for many months, and had been the cause of grief and ruin.

I had gone to the royal audience, I do not remember for what reason.

"Makamba," said Chua to an old man who was entering the place, "you come to see your friend, for

CASATI WITH HIS SERVANTS.

if he were not here you would never have thought of coming."

"Friend, friend; once you too used to call yourself his friend," he answered.

"Yes, it is true; but since I have learned that he would cause the ruin of my kingdom, I am no longer his friend."

"What will you? I am not yet persuaded that you are right."

I remembered that man, and his words. It was necessary for me to find him. He had been kind, and might be useful to me.

It was New Year's Day (1888), and as a matter of habit and necessity I wished my people to celebrate it with plenty of beer.

My *banassura*, with a respectful manner for the occasion, were abundantly presented with drink, and soon fell under the influence of Bacchus. I then sent my faithful boy to make inquiries about good Makamba. In disgrace with his king, he had been banished beyond the Muenghe country, probably destined to the same end as the unfortunate Kategora.

On January 3 a messenger from the chief Mboga stopped at Juaya for the night. He was going to Mruli, and brought news that in Lendu, on the way to the Walegga country, some Europeans had appeared, followed by many armed men dressed in the Zanzibar fashion. No doubt it was Stanley with the relief expedition. Our joy caused us to forget our sad condition. We entertained new hopes. I thought that the king would perhaps postpone the execution of his nefarious projects, and I was pleased to see poor Biri smile, he who had been drowned in sorrow for such a length of time, in fear of his life, for the safety of his family, and for the fate of his ivory.

Already since November 24, Guakamatera, through one of his confidants, had proposed for me to enter into the bond of blood, but secretly, as he warned me, in order not to incur the king's wrath.

I accepted the proposal with the utmost pleasure, like a wrecked sailor who clings to any piece of wood the waves throw within his reach.

Such a length of time had elapsed that I had forgotten the strange offer when, on the morning of the 4th of January 1888, the same man came, as the bearer of his chief's wishes. After having had a pot of beer put on the ground, he communicated to me with majestic gravity his master's decision to hasten the much desired ceremony.

On the 6th of January he made his appearance again with a goat and a pair of fowls. He whispered to me:

" To-night."

" All right," I answered.

" The Vizier," added he, " wants you to go by yourself; he is greatly frightened. When you hear the great *nuggare* beat, go to his house by the path along the stream."

Astonished at so many conditions being imposed on me, I could hardly utter a word; but I soon grew calm again, and quietly but resolutely, looking straight in his face, I answered:

" Tell the Vizier that to-night, when the *nuggare* are beaten, I shall be at his house. Thank him, and present my compliments to him."

He bowed and left. I could clearly see that he was anxious to get away.

Until then I had never mentioned the strange proposition to Biri. But when the messenger had departed, I told him of it.

"What do you think of doing?" said he, opening his eyes widely.

"To go."

"How?" he asked.

"I will take the revolver with me."

My boy, who had overheard the conversation, said: "Shall I go with you?"

"If you like. Biri will give you his revolver, and we will go together. After all, the devil is not as black as he is painted. As we stand we might have a chance of leaving some souvenir behind us. Let us trust in our good star. If a steamer arrived at Kibiro to-day we should be safe. It might, because news in Unyoro has wings."

The goat and the two fowls were cooked during the day. The thought of the morrow did not worry us much as far as our meals were concerned.

Neither during the evening nor in the night did we hear the drum. The *banassura* Mohongoki arrived, whom I had sent on the 10th of December to inform the king that the false reports made to him about me had come to my knowledge; and that I protested against the cowardice and meanness of my maligners, and appealed to his loyalty and justice. After some hesitation, he told me that, having delivered my message, the king told him that he was considering what was the best thing to do.

The answer was too short and meaningless to be considered a sincere one.

On the morning of the 8th, a *magnoro* of Mruli announced himself as an envoy from the king, with this message:

"The resumption of hostilities with Uganda is impending, and I do not wish that Biri, my guest, should suffer any injuries. Guakamatera, being a fainthearted man, has lost my confidence, and is about to be punished.

"You will go to Juaya, and make arrangements with the Pasha's representative."

A meeting was arranged for the next day at the Vizier's residence.

CHAPTER VI.

A NARROW ESCAPE.

Sad farewell supper—Biri's illusions—" To-morrow I shall be with you "—Shall we turn back ?—The great priest of the Unyoro sorcerers—Opening of the royal gate—The signal is given—An unrestrained crowd—Tied to the trees —" Woe to you ! "—Orders to my boy—Grief and alarm of Biri—A more fortunate soldier—I save my shoes—Our sufferings must not be relieved—Bought by means of a coat—Payment of services—Guakamatera at my residence—Confiscation of all property—Return of the conqueror—"*Gobia, Gobia!*"—The place of execution—Meeting of my domestics—A piece of paper and a pencil—Flight—Followed and threatened—Kagoro protects us—At Kibiro—Lying message of Guakamatera—The breakage of a pipe—I give away my waistcoat—At the salt pits—From Tokongia—Ntiabo, the wife of the king—Kapidi, the cripple—Neither food nor passage—Driven to the woods—Dinka girl—A plate of beans—Fadl starts in a boat—" *Majungo, Majungo!* "—A colony of Lur—" We'll not kill you "—A happy meeting—" Man dies only by permission of God "—Discouragement subdues us—" The steamer ! the steamer ! "—On the shore of the lake—Refreshing sleep—The *Khedive* in sight—Fresh anxieties—We are saved.

" DEAR BIRI, very probably this is the last time we shall sup together at Juaya," said I, turning towards my guest, while we were sitting at our humble table.

" But why ? " asked he ; " do you think that I will not return from Uganda ? I have promised to do so, and I mean to keep my word."

" I do not mean that, but I am convinced that you will not go to Uganda."

" For what reason ? "

" For a very simple one ; to-morrow there will be no departure, but something much more serious."

" What ! Do you believe that the arrival of the *magnoro* from Mruli is a mere fiction ? "

" Certainly."

" And the permission to make arrangements for my return caravan ? "

" Also fiction."

" And why should these gentlemen deceive us ? "

" To cause us to fall more easily into the net."

" But since we are already in their hands, why so many subterfuges ? "

" It is not strictly true that we are in their hands; we are only their prisoners."

" I don't understand you."

" I will explain. Guakamatera has the order to do away with us; nocturnal attempts have failed, as also the trick of blood-brotherhood; for he was afraid. Now, since he has a peremptory order to deliver the king from our presence, he thinks that he may coax us with a proposal which, according to his idea, must meet with our full consent. If he obtained our removal from this house, he would be free to act according to his own will."

" Then what do you intend to do ? "

" Not to accept the invitation for to-morrow, but to stay at home till the arrival of the steamer, the appearance of which at Kibiro cannot be delayed for long."

" But if the proposal of my departure for Uganda were a sincere one, we should make a mistake, which would prove very detrimental to ourselves."

" Why ? "

" Because Guakamatera will be angry; he will threaten us and, worse still, act with violence."

" No; do not believe it. It is quite true that he will threaten us, but it will only be by words; he will not have the courage to lay his hands upon us, as long as we remain barricaded within our home."

AN ARGUMENT WITH BIRI.

"I believe the contrary."

"But, dear Biri, he is certain that we conceal a good number of armed men. None of his *banassura* are bold enough to approach if they see one of us gun in hand; and then, in presence of any unforeseen event, Guakamatera would make a report to the king, which would enable us to gain time."

"But if they besiege us, how could we long resist? It would be impossible."

"I know that the defence could not be protracted, but the Pasha's messenger will be here before long. We have in the house corn enough to last one month; water is close at hand, and we can supply ourselves with it during the night, for the *banassura* would be afraid of some resolute action on our part, and would watch us from a distance, especially after dark."

"But we should place ourselves in a difficult position. I should ruin my business in Uganda, and, besides, cut off the road for my return."

"Still, in my opinion, there is no better expedient in the terrible circumstances in which we are placed. With regard to Uganda, you may come with us and join Stanley's caravan. You can go to Uganda from a thousand points."

"Ah! I think your fears have no foundation. Formerly the king wished very much to get rid of us, but now circumstances have changed. Stanley's arrival frightens him, and he is desirous of amending his conduct, and entering into cordial intercourse with the Governor; therefore he will comply with his wish and let me go to Uganda."

"Biri, do you forget the offence you gave the king? You entered his country without permission. Can he forget that? To pardon you does not depend upon him; the national traditions and the royal dignity could not allow it."

"But I suppose he would, if he were compelled by political reasons; and he is in fear."

"You are mistaken. King Chua once feared us, now he hates us. He wants to close the borders of his kingdom again. His strength, like that of all Negro kings, is found in isolation; to attain his object he will not hesitate to commit a crime. Thirst of power guides him, not reasons of State."

"Then what will become of us?"

"You will know to-morrow."

"You mean a great misfortune is impending?"

"Quite so; unless, I repeat, we trust to chance and decline the invitation for to-morrow. If I were to decide for myself, I would not hesitate a moment."

"But that would be to give ourselves up to certain death."

"Not necessarily; but if we gave ourselves up to Guakamatera, we would surely be put to death."

"To what a point the policy of the Governor has brought us!"

"Events have influenced his conduct. The dissensions of the province have tied his hands, and prevented him from acting on a consistent political plan. For this reason he has always been disinclined not only to resolute actions, but even to give presents freely, as I advised him. The King of Unyoro and his Ministers are not to he bought by fine words, but by rich and substantial gifts."

"And we bear the consequences of the mistake."

"What can we do? I, as well as you, have come here as a volunteer; we must have courage. We must be prepared for something worse even than death. When the sacrifice has been consummated, our name, instead of being uttered with feelings of sympathy and gratitude, will be reviled as the name of persons who have been the cause of ruin; but listen to my advice, and let us resist."

"No; indeed, it would be our worst course. Let us be prudent; for if we are destined to be struck down by misfortune, no action of ours will be of any avail. My resolution is to go to-morrow and present myself to Guakamatera."

"We shall go to ruin."

"Perhaps, but I will go. If you will not accompany me, I will go alone."

"No, dear Biri, I will not forsake you; I will go with you."

At 6 A.M., January 9, 1888, accompanied by my faithful boy, a corporal of the Egyptian troops, and the three *banassura*, Wando, Rehan, and Singoma, I took the road to Guakamatera's residence. Having crossed the stream and ascended to the esplanade, whence the Vizier's abode could be perceived in the distance, we saw, with great astonishment, that the place was full of armed men. Our hearts throbbed violently for a moment, and we looked silently at each other. Biri uttered a faint "Let us go back," but it was useless; we were bound to go on, and hastening our steps we reached the gate. The cries ceased, some of the warriors gathered on our way; some saluted us, and we approached the audience hall.

Not far off, at the foot of some ancient trees, majestic for their imposing height, and the wealth and beauty of their foliage, sat the high priest, surrounded by crowds of his subordinate sorcerers. His head was covered with a rich turban of red cloth, adorned with beads and shells, and from each side of his forehead protruded two ox horns, from which hung small wooden talismans. In his left hand he held a large horn full of the magic powder, and in his right the conjuror's small wand. He was dressed in an ample mantle of ox skin clasped on his left shoulder, and was sitting on a small stool, with a severe countenance that became his dignity.

The gate of the royal house was opened. We heard the flourish of a trumpet, and the Vizier came forth with a suite of grandees and warriors. The people scattered about the open space, gathered round at a short distance, forming a compact circle; some of the men were armed with guns, some with lances and shields, and others with bows and arrows. They amounted to several thousands. Perfect, icy silence, foreboding a solemn event, prevailed; and they all looked at ·Guakamatera, who was conspicuous amongst the armed courtiers by his high stature and large head.

"There is treachery," I whispered to Biri. "May God help us; any other hope is useless. However, let us show courage."

About ten minutes after the Vizier's appearance he suddenly stretched up his right arm. That was the signal agreed upon, and the air resounded with horrible cries. The unbridled crowd pounced upon us. We were seized, and barbarously tied to the large trees, close by the great magician. I was stripped of my tarboosh, and my pockets were rifled. My neck, arms, wrists, knees, and ankles were bound to a tree with such atrocious force that I was unable to make the least movement. The rope round my neck was so tight that my respiration was hindered, and one of my arms was twisted and tied in a painful position.

Poor Biri, entirely stripped of his clothes, was tied

CASATI BOUND TO A TREE.

to a tree close by, with ropes round his wrists, neck, and feet, and my boy Oakil was treated in the same manner. The corporal, with his arms bound together, was also tied to a tree near Biri.

I uttered an imprecation, directing a glance at Guakamatera, who stood coldly by, upbraiding him for the cowardice of tying a boy, and begged him to have Biri's bonds loosened. The arms of the former were then freed, and the latter was somewhat relieved. But, on the contrary, the *banassura* Wando, having called the Vizier's attention to the barbarous manner in which I was bound, he, with a needless burst of anger, ordered that even my body round the middle should be fastened to the large tree with a rope. His remorseless satellites, intoxicated with joy, were ready to carry the order out; but I could not refrain from smiling, consoled by the fact that the cord which bound my neck, being a new one, yielded to my efforts, and permitted me to breathe more freely.

Then Guakamatera approached me nearer.

" I am going to your residence by order of the king," said he. " I know that you have there many armed men who have arrived stealthily and at intervals from Wadelai, on whom you rely for conquering our country. Woe to you if they make the least resistance ! You shall be immediately put to death."

" Considering the circumstances," said I, " to which you have reduced us by order of your king, I cannot answer for what will happen if you go to my residence ; therefore I advise you to take this boy with you, who will give my message to the soldiers there, by whom he will be readily believed and obeyed."

" Very well, give him your orders ; " which I did, saying :

" Let the Government soldiers give up their arms,

and you, my boy, obey without hesitation anything Guakamatera may command. I wish that there should be no resistance, no bloodshed."

The Vizier departed, accompanied by his troops, leaving about 300 armed men to guard us.

The pain caused by the cords; the rays of the sun, which on that day seemed to be more scorching than usual; the thirst which tormented us, and the continual derision of an inebriated mob thirsty for blood, were our Calvary for several very long hours.

Poor Biri sometimes recited the prayers of the Koran, but more often he sobbed, remembering his children and his lost ivory, and abandoned himself to despair, as if he beheld the spectre of death approaching.

I tried to infuse courage and hope into him, and begged him not to exhibit a degrading spectacle of cowardice; but, indeed, I was myself very afflicted at seeing us the laughing-stock of a ferocious and superstitious tyrant.

"If a steamer had been sent from Dufilé, as you requested, we should not be in such a plight. The Pasha had been warned of the danger." So spoke Biri, and he gave vent to expressions of anger and disgust.

Corporal Surur, less unhappy than we, was somewhat comforted by the words of his fellow-negroes. They urged him to make his submission to the king, who was ready, not only to pardon him, but also to show his consideration for his character as a soldier, and gave him cups full of water at his pleasure.

Still that crowd, apparently so elated and frantic, wavered at the bottom of their hearts from great fear. One of the boldest amongst our guards, having approached me, tried to loosen the strings of my shoes, probably to carry them away. Indignant at such an attempt, and unable to move at all, I shouted, staring angrily at the villain. The crowd then stood back till one of the chiefs, whose sense of duty triumphed over that of fear, after much hesitation and circumspection,

KING CHUA'S RELATIVES IN COURT ATTIRE.

overhauled the pockets of my trousers, and assured his companions that there was no bewitched article in them, except a piece of paper; whereupon I could not refrain a laugh, which was loudly taken up by the whole crowd, and even poor Biri himself enjoyed a gleam of cheerfulness.

At about three o'clock P.M. my boy returned, and in the name of Guakamatera gave the order for loosening our fetters. The guards protested loudly against such a concession, which they could not believe to be true, and demanded the presence of one of the Vizier's *banassura;* meanwhile our torments were increased, in order to satisfy the caprice of a fanatical crowd; and for about an hour the stream of insults and threats continued.

When the boy returned, accompanied by the guard Singoma, cries of dissatisfaction were uttered by all. Singoma gave the order to loosen the cords which bound my arms; the chief of the men who had remained to guard us protested, yet said that he would not only do so, but leave my arms free if the usual payment was handed to him. My coat was asked for, and I agreed to give it up, but they wanted it beforehand, which was impossible unless the ropes with which I was fastened were removed. At this there was a fresh explosion of violent outcries, but at last I was untied, deprived of my coat, and tied again, except my arms, and the same was done to Biri, whilst the corporal was set at liberty.

It is the custom of the Unyoro country, and the king tolerates it, that the jailors of those who are imprisoned may practise the hideous trade of afflicting their victims with torments, to compel them to satisfy their covetousness; so that if an unfortunate individual or a criminal has the power to satisfy their greed by a ready and substantial payment, his sufferings are allayed, for a short time at least, and even for a longer period if the victims continue to give presents; but should the unhappy prisoner be poor, and therefore unable to satisfy the greediness of his jailors, he is sure to undergo greater cruelties and molestations than those ordered by the monarch. It is thus that the officials of the king are compensated, and he is spared the burden of paying salaries. This system of extortion is extended to every branch of the public service; to the inspection of districts, messages to the chiefs, domiciliary visits, arrests, and transport of royal property; consequently dissatisfaction prevails everywhere in Unyoro, and were it not for the fear of the considerable number of guns possessed by the Government, public peace would be continually jeopardised.

The boy briefly informed me of what had happened at our residence after our departure until the arrival of Guakamatera. We had scarcely left the house when it was surrounded at a distance by about two thousand warriors, brought down from Mruli, Muenghe, and from the Kafu districts.

When the Vizier was close by the house, he stopped with his followers on the adjacent hill, whence he sent some soldiers, together with the boy, who was still in fetters. The arms of the two soldiers, and my own, as well as the cartridges, were brought before the commander; my effects and Biri's, those of our servants and of the soldiers, were arranged on the open space near our dwelling, and the domestics were ordered to leave it, and taken into custody at a place apart; detachments of armed men entered the premises, and closely searched every spot, striking with the butt-ends of their guns every point of the ground, in order to ascertain whether there were any subterranean hiding-places.

Guakamatera's anxiety subsided when he learned by the firing of shots and the beating of drums, that the search in our house had been fruitless.

He then descended the hill, crossed the river, and went to rest himself triumphantly in my house. The ill-treatment and cruelties perpetrated against our people were worthy of the frame of mind of that savage horde. All my property was carried to the Vizier's residence, and I saw brought in successively my arms, boxes, provisions, and the ivory which belonged to the Government.

Biri's effects were gathered at Nparo on the Mruli road.

As Guakamatera was about to return, I recommended firmness to my boy, and advised him to run away in order to carry the news to Wadelai of Stanley's presence in the southern region of the Albert Lake.

It was about five o'clock P.M. The Vizier, surrounded by the priests, holding a small bunch of herbs in their right hands, arrived on the spot.

The pipes and a trumpet sounded, the drums were beaten, the guns fired, and the crowd vigorously applauded the conqueror.

Guakamatera cast a glance at me, and observing that my arms were free, went into a passion, and ordered them to bind me again, which was done amidst the jubilant shouts of my tormentors; then, having put off his warlike equipment, and donned an elegant garment made of cloth, he came out from the dwelling, sat down on a large chair, and gathered the warriors and the people round him:

"This man," said he, pointing me out, "together with the other (alluding to Biri), brought the Waganda into our country; he was the cause of your children and wives being ravished, your goods stolen, and your crops destroyed. For these crimes the king has struck them with his justice, and entrusted his vengeance to my arm."

A stunning, howling noise, full of threats and curses, filled the air, and we were assailed with the words, "*Gobia, Gobia!*" (traitor!)

Guakamatera called the corporal, but I never knew what he said to him; then he called the boy, and told him that I was going to be escorted to Kibiro, adding that the next morning all my effects would be sent to me. He ordered them to unbind me, and also Biri; but as soon as the

I AM DRAGGED ALONG BY THE GUARDS.

order was executed four *banassura* took hold of me, bound my arms and neck again, and dragged me away. I tried to speak to Guakamatera in favour of poor Biri, but without success, for the executioners, by dint of blows and pulls, dragged me off, my boy and the corporal following.

At seven o'clock we passed across a colony of Shooli, and reached a place where criminals used to be executed; an encampment of warriors was close by.

Having entered the enclosure, we found the two

Egyptian soldiers and our domestics, who, by giving up their clothes, obtained from the *banassura* the removal of my ropes. I appeared to them as a man risen from the dead. At seeing me they were elated with joy, and forgot their past sufferings. My boy very kindly offered me a little paper and a pencil, which he had succeeded in concealing during the confusion of the pillage.

The place where we were was not of good augury; the *nuggare* that we saw were stained with the blood of executed victims, so that naturally the idea of escaping entered our minds. "This thorny wood is the only place not guarded by armed men," said my boy, on his return from reconnoitring. "Well," said I, "let us fall on our hands and knees and crawl through it." It was done as quickly as it had been said; we issued in evil plight from the wood and found ourselves on the road; but soon had to struggle through the ambushes placed by the landowners, from which we were unable to defend ourselves; we therefore abandoned the road, and proceeded for a long distance hidden amongst the tall grass, in which at last we stopped. Corporal Surur had left us, and fled. We heard far, far off the echoes of the curses of the warriors, who had lost every trace of us, but gradually the sounds of their voices died away, and complete silence prevailed.

After three hours' rest we resumed our journey, and, crossing the Farajak district, we reached Kitana, where, thanks to a few glass beads which some women detached from their necks, we were enabled to appease our hunger with sweet potatoes (*Batata edulis*).

At noon on January 10, 1888, we reached the top of the mountain whence Kibiro and the immense blue extent of the lake can be seen. We descended as far as the first terrace, when suddenly armed men appeared from behind the rocks and paths, taking up positions all round us. They numbered about a thousand altogether, partly *banassura*, armed with guns, and partly natives with lance and shield.

They ordered us to go back, and on my decided refusal they clamoured and threatened, but I did not answer. They had been sent by Guakatamera, Barabra, chief of Juaya, and Roconcona, chief of Kitana, and they accused me of having run away, declaring at the same time that they would take me back by force. The affair seemed to forebode a tragedy, and we thought that perhaps it was the last and fatal phase of our misfortunes; any hesitation would have been our ruin. I gathered my people, who were greatly frightened, declaring resolutely that even at the cost of my life I would not go back, and as I stepped forward to continue the descent, they followed me.

The warriors uttered loud cries, as leaving their positions, and jumping from rock to rock, they converged towards us, obviously bent on carrying out their threats of violence, when suddenly two individuals appeared, lance in hand, messengers sent by Kagoro, the great chief of Kibiro, who claimed my person, and extended his protection to me because I was in his territory.

The rushing crowd stopped, and we descended to the village, followed by our enemies, now reduced to silence, though disposed to dispute the prey.

Kagoro gave us shelter in a comfortable dwelling, and sent us two goats, besides three baskets of flour and some tobacco, with this friendly message: "Take some rest, and have no fear; I have no orders from the king about you."

That day and the subsequent night passed off without incident. The village teemed with armed men, excited by drink and quarrelling amongst themselves, but my house was under the custody of guards. Various chiefs who came to see me poured into my ears the strangest news. I was betrayed by my own soldiers; people, speaking in the Governor's name, said things quite different from those said by me; the proposal of exchanging blood was a whim of mine; I was plotting with Muanga against the king; Emin was in perfect agreement with Chua, and disapproved of my conduct; Abd Rehman, the Zanzibari merchant, the friend of Babedongo, and adviser of Chua, had directed and witnessed my capture from Guakatamera's house; my effects and the Government's ivory were to be confiscated, and sent to Mruli.

The Vizier, when he seized the goods within my house, said to the two Egyptian soldiers who were present:

"Tell the Governor of Wadelai that the severe steps which the king has ordered me to take are required for the safety of the State. The Governor's envoy hoisted the flag of his Government, and aimed at the overthrow of our Sovereign, by plotting with Muanga. Tell Emin that he has insulted and otherwise offended the king, and that he tried to make himself popular amongst the natives in order to cause rebellion; but the king will not break the friendship and alliance which connect him with the Pasha, and an envoy will be sent to Wadelai in order to strengthen it."

This foolish, false, and infamous message was not altogether without success; some persons believed the assertions contained in it, for a failure influences the minds of the foolish and of the wicked, and there had been a great deal of talk about that rag of a banner.

I had hoisted the Egyptian colours during the war with Uganda, with the full consent of the king, granted at Nparo, when I went to visit him. When the hostilities ceased the country was overrun by bodies of Magungo, who from the Baganghese district travelled home to that of Anfina, recently conquered. The want of public security, the complete abandonment in which I was left by the king, and the conspiracies incessantly fostered for bringing about my ruin, induced me to hoist that flag for my protection. My decision, submitted to the king, was fully indorsed by him, and confirmed later on by Guakamatera himself.

January 11, 1888.—To break another man's pipe is considered a very great offence amongst the Wanyoro. The case is submitted to the king with these formal words: " He has injured, or killed, my companion;" and the fine amounts to a goodly number of oxen. When the offended party does not agree with the judgment, or if neither applies for it, serious wounds, or even murder, are the final result. Often such an offence is resorted to as a provocation, when for some reason an individual wishes to draw another into a quarrel.

Early in the morning a lively dispute was going on between one of Guakamatera's guards and one of Kagoro's followers. The *banassura* had arrogantly and intentionally, without the least provocation, wrested a pipe from the mouth of an inhabitant of Kibiro and dashed it to the ground. The quarrel becoming worse, I went to the door, and the guard immediately invited me to act as judge between him and his opponent; but I, well knowing the habits of the country, guessed the trick, and excused myself on the ground of indisposition, begging to be left alone, whereupon they went away to settle their contentions elsewhere. At about eight o'clock a number of guards came up begging for cowries to buy beer; I threw my waistcoat to them, for I did not possess anything else; they were not satisfied, but went away. We were soon after ordered to depart, and did so, a crowd of armed men accompanying us to the shore of the lake, where two boats had already been prepared for us. I was ordered to embark in the smaller one and my people in the other, but I objected to comply with their treacherous request, declaring that force alone would compel me to do so, and I appealed to some Kagoro chiefs, whom I perceived in the crowd. We were then driven like a herd of cattle to the salt pits, and left there in custody of sentries posted at some distance round. The crowd retired and assembled in front of the house belonging to the chief of the village, to hold a consultation.

Although exposed to a scorching sun, permission to obtain a little water from the lake close at hand was denied us, and thus several hours passed away without any change in the situation. At about 3 P.M. a servant was sent in search of a little fire, in order that we might seek relief in smoking the tobacco presented to us on the previous evening by Kagoro, but he did not return. At four o'clock two ruffians from Guakamatera, presumably the chiefs of the band, approached and bravely stole a box containing the few clothes belonging to the two soldiers; half an hour later we saw our assailants meandering, one by one, up the mountain path and disappearing successively.

The bay of Kibiro was then restored to its habitual monotony, but no one came near us, because we were accursed and banished by the king.

At about five o'clock the chief sent me a native as a guide to the next village; at about eight o'clock we reached the residence of Tokongia, who gave us some fish and allowed us to spend the night in a large hut; but although peace and tranquillity seemed to prevail everywhere, we decided to watch in turn. The strange events of the last three days crowded on my mind, but the sorrow of having lost my notes grieved me more deeply than any other of my misfortunes.

At cock-crow, January 12, 1888, we started, accompanied by Tokongia, and at about 7 A.M. we entered the village of Ntiabo. Ntiabo was one of the king's wives, who, according to usage, had had bestowed on her, the possession of a district as an appanage, which she rules and visits occasionally, taking up her residence there at fixed dates. In her absence she is represented by a delegate, who rules in her name and sends her the produce of the district. The king grants lands as fiefs, not only to his wives, but also to some of his favourites, from whom he receives a fixed payment, besides the assistance of fighting men in time of war.

When we reached Ntiabo, the king's wife was absent at Mruli with her husband. We were received with indifference and suspicion, because the people knew of the judgment which had been pronounced against us, and they avoided us as if we had been lepers.

Tokongia procured us a guide, who early in the afternoon left us, on reaching the palace of a chief called Kapidi, a tall big man, lame in the right foot, a cunning and facetious chatterer. I asked him to conduct me to the Boki country, and though not absolutely declining to do so, he excused himself on the ground that he had no one on whom he could rely, and also because he was unable to make a long journey; however, he supplied us with some food, and the day passed away without any incidents. Soon after sunset, two of Guakamatera's messengers arrived, told our crimes, the king's sentence, and announced what was to be done in these words,

"Neither food nor passage." The future seemed more gloomy than ever, for the ferocious tyrant did not forget his victim.

On January 13, keeping along the shore of the lake escorted by Kapidi, with two of his faithful followers as guides, a little before noon we stopped in front of a small island, the residence of Melino, one of the most feared chieftains of the Magungo. He wished me to go to his residence, but that did not seem to me quite prudent. He made us wait for several hours, and at last granted us permission to continue our journey, accompanied by two guides.

At four o'clock we entered a small village, ruled over by a certain Amara, but as soon as we had advanced a few steps, all the natives in a crowd rushed at us in a threatening manner, to make us go back. The guides abandoned us, and the difficulties increased. The savage villagers, crying, "You shall neither be fed nor pass," proceeded from threats to deeds, struck us with their sticks, and drove us from the road towards the woods, till at last, after having followed us for a long way, they left us.

Having restored our minds to the calm so much needed after our abrupt expulsion from the village, we journeyed through the bush, and succeeded in again finding the road to the lake. At about sunset we were in presence of groups of miserable huts. I sent one of the soldiers and my boy to parley with the inhabitants, for the latter understood the language of the country pretty well; and having received no hostile reply, we camped out not far from the village. During the night we were regaled, to our great surprise, with a large plate of beans, for which we warmly thanked our generous Amphytrion.

In that village resided a young Dinka woman who

had run away from the ill-treatment of an Egyptian official of the Equatorial Government, and had been married by the chief's son. She was generally esteemed for her kindness, and her activity in performing domestic duties. She assured us of her husband's kind disposition towards us, adding his father was similarly inclined, and gave us the precious news that on the 11th the Pasha had reached Tunguru with the two steamers.

Our courage revived. Every one of my followers declared his willingness to be obedient, and hope made our rest sweeter.

Meanwhile the chief Melino, having mustered a large number of warriors (January 14, 1888), arrived at the village during the night, and at sunrise called together the neighbouring chiefs, to a meeting to decide on our fate. The most ferocious wanted to kill me at once; others suggested that we should be escorted as far as the village of Rokora, on the Victoria Nile. After lengthy discussions, interrupted by excited altercations—neither party being able to arrive at a definite conclusion satisfactory to all—they agreed to expel us from the district, and, taking rods in their hands, drove us away. But our persecutors were soon tired. The furious crowd vanished by degrees, and we remained alone.

We walked for about two hours, then, turning into a secluded and difficult marsh, we stopped to hold a consultation about the most proper thing to do, and agreed that it was urgent to try and get a boat, in order to cross the lake, reach Tunguru, and ask for assistance there. After searching for some time, we succeeded in finding an old boat in very bad condition, and even without oars. But brave Fadl, an Arab from Dongola, did not hesitate to undertake the arduous management of it, and after sunset we issued from our hiding-place, and waded through pools and sloughs, continually sinking into holes made by the feet of hippopotami, thrusting our way through the high grass, thorny hedges, and clusters of reeds, sometimes wheeling to the right or left at the sudden appearance of large amphibia, occasionally lying down, alarmed at the sight of buffaloes. At last, towards midnight, we reached a little hill near the lake. Plenty of water was our substitute for food.

On January 15, 1888, two of the unhappy Biri's servants joined us on the road, and accompanied us. I advised them to go during the night to the hospitable house of the Dinka woman, in order to obtain a little food; the place was not far distant and the Melino and Amara hordes had left the district, but they declined. At dawn we perceived four canoes a long distance off, obviously shaping their course with the intention of crossing the lake; it might have been a good opportunity for us and probably our deliverance, but Hurshid, the Circassian soldier, had swollen feet and could scarcely walk, and I could not be cruel enough to abandon him. Our condition was going from bad to worse; discouragement was obtaining a hold on the minds of my unfortunate companions, and they were all deeply affected, except young Oakil.

The sun rose, and we again threw ourselves amongst the *ambatsh* and reed thickets, searching for roots to suck, when suddenly the howling of savages warned us of the approach of new persecutors. Parties of armed men were beating the bush, precisely as when a search is made for game, and surrounded the place where we were hiding, crying " *Majungo, majungo!* " (the foreigner, the foreigner!)

I then emerged from my hiding-place and faced the

Magungo people, who were irritated at the disappearance of their boat, but their anger decreased when they saw I had not gone away. My companions, who had fled in all directions, then came back.

The cursing and threatening continued; the tone of it was somewhat improved, but the substance was the same. The wildest suggestions were discussed, such as to seize the women as an indemnity for the loss suffered; to bind us in a row and take us to the chief Melino; or to put an end to the matter by taking a well-merited revenge. By dint of discussing, promising, and pointing out the probability of danger, I succeeded in calming some of the most influential men, and the crowd finally resolved to escort us out of their territory.

I felt happy at having escaped from danger this time also, without hurt, and shaking hands with some of the chiefs, we proceeded towards the slope of a hill. We walked for about two hours, and then our guides left us in the neighbourhood of a village inhabited by the Lur and Lendu men.

They would not receive us, and yet would not set us at liberty. We asked for food, and some was shown us, but was quickly taken away with jeers. A boy was struck, and on my remonstrating, I received a blow from a stick. Then they assembled in council, and the chief abruptly proposed that I should be executed.

"Makama," said he, "has ordered this fellow to be killed at Rokora beyond the river, but it would be as well to do away with him at once. To carry his dead body there is an easy matter; we should neither be troubled all day on his account, nor incur the royal displeasure."

This proposal was translated to me by Hurshid's servant, who knew the language of the Lur.

I then stepped forward and said: "If you have the

courage to carry out your resolution, come forward, I am ready; but remember all of you that the king has ordered you to send me to Rokora, and that such disobedience may cause punishment to the whole village."

"No, no," cried they unanimously, "we won't kill you."

"Well, send away that man who suggested such an unjust resolution, and then we will talk together."

Cries of disapprobation pierced the ears of the *matungoli*, who thought it best to beat a retreat.

A young man who had a smattering of Arabic and had been an interpreter in the service of Mergian Aga Danassuri, late commander of the military station of Magungo, offered to act as an intermediary between me and the Lur, from whom he obtained permission for me to be restored to freedom on condition that he should compel me to take the road to Rokora. My companions grumbled, protested, and even thought that I had gone mad; but I encouraged them in the best way I could, and exhorted them to trust in me, assuring them that if a way of safety were possible I would find it. We walked slowly; my companions were tired, for long fasting had decreased the vigour both of their bodies and minds.

"Man dies only by the permission of God," said I to the Mussulman, Hurshid, who was troubled more than the others with a painful feeling of discouragement. He smiled sadly, shaking his head; his face wore an aspect of sorrow like the country which surrounded us. A few dry wild berries of a reddish colour, from a thorny shrub, were the cause of our little caravan being suddenly scattered; but the eagerness with which they were picked up soon stopped, for the caustic effect which they produced on the tongue increased our sufferings.

The soldiers who formed our escort urged us to hasten our march, and I begged them to have compassion. As the distance from Rokora decreased, so our hope decreased, for in a couple of hours we should reach the spot destined for our martyrdom.

We silently ascended the last hill which separated us from the Nile, when all of a sudden we saw its ridge covered with warriors. I begged our young interpreter to precede us, and to make them understand that we were not going to oppose them—that we intended going down the river, and hoped that they would not increase our misery. He promised to say what I told him, and started. His arrival on the opposite side was followed by lively disputes, thundering cries, movement to and fro of warriors, and the sudden appearance of men from behind the bushes. But soon after the crowd dispersed, and took to flight.

What had happened? Our young interpreter returned jubilant. "The steamer! the steamer!" he cried, as he descended the hill and approached us. He then informed us that the news had spread of the appearance of a steamer on the lake, adding that it was coming straight towards us. Our brave guides simply took to flight, and the interpreter, after having shown us the way to the lake, did the same.

The last rays of the setting sun warned us to hasten our steps. As we descended the slope we discerned an unusual commotion amongst the inhabitants, who were carrying away furniture and provisions, and driving off herds of cattle. They took no notice of us. Their ferocity of the morning had vanished. We spoke to some of them, but they did not answer, and hastened their departure, anxiously exclaiming, "The steamer! the steamer!"

Was the steamer really on the lake? Were we on

the point of being rescued? We looked eagerly, but the darkness of the night rendered fruitless all our efforts to see her. Restored to life after a deadly anxiety—strengthened by hope—forgetful of past sufferings—jesting at the fears of our persecutors, who had been so threatening in the morning, we walked on, till at last we reached the shore of the lake at about 11 P.M., and sat down on the sandy promontory appointed as the place of our meeting with Fadl. Our thirst was quenched by the clear waters of the sandy-bottomed lake, and a crackling fire made with materials brought from the neighbouring huts comforted us, and we fell asleep amidst the stillness and darkness of the night, with the certainty of a happy morrow.

The stars were still shining in the sky, but our impatience was such that already we were walking to and fro on the shore of the lake, looking anxiously for a black spot on the horizon. The sun was just emerging at our back in the fulness of its splendour. A few timid natives in canoes were flying towards the islands, almost hidden in the creeks. The cruelly lengthened expectation made us silent. Our sad thoughts re-asserted themselves, but the pangs of hunger overwhelmed sentiment. I ordered that some aquatic herbs, resorted to by the Negroes in time of scarcity, should be collected, and cooked in a large vessel taken from one of the houses in the village.

If the steamer did not appear by noon, our plan was to construct an ample raft of *ambatsh*, and to entrust our safety to the waves—an operation of easy execution, for the frightened and fleeing natives would not have troubled us.

At about nine o'clock a shrill cry interrupted the flow of thoughts that had harassed my mind. It was caused by the sight of a streak of smoke on the horizon. A little later the chimney of a steamer was discerned, and then on came the vessel herself, fully showing her outline, and shaping her course by the signal we had hoisted on the top of a pole—the white and red handkerchief of poor Hurshid. All eyes were fixed on her, when suddenly she began to move with uncertainty, and even seemed to stop; her dimensions decreasing gradually, till at last she disappeared. My unhappy companions uttered a cry of anguish and despair. I tried to make them understand that the steamer was taking soundings to find sufficiently deep water, but my words were of no avail. Their scanty repast was interrupted, and the poor creatures presented a lamentable appearance, sitting gloomily and silently on the ground with bowed heads, their arms encircling their knees, and their hands clasped together.

I withdrew from them, praying Heaven that the speedy reappearance of the steamer might shorten their sufferings. One hour later the *Khedive* was again in sight, steaming safely, and at a satisfactory speed. We saluted her by waving our flag, and our salutation was returned by the usual whistle, which we applauded clamorously.

She cast anchor at a short distance from the shore, and a boat conveyed us to her. Emin Pasha, with many of his officers and officials, had attempted our rescue in spite of its apparent hopelessness, and rather to fulfil a pious duty than with any expectation of success. Joy at our unhoped-for safety made every one mute, and fear only vanished by degrees, as if there was still a doubt as to what had happened.

> " And as a man, with difficult short breath,
> Forespent with toiling, 'scaped from sea to shore,
> Turns to the perilous wide waste, and stands
> At gaze; e'en so my spirit, that yet fail'd,
> Struggling with terror, turned to view the Straits
> That none hath passed and lived."—DANTE, *Inferno*, Canto i.

MASS OF GNEISS ROCK ON MOUNT LOGWEK.

CHAPTER VII.

THE ALBERT NYANZA.

Opinions of the geographers of the first half of this century on Central Africa
—Speke and Burton—Discovery of the Tanganika Lake—A great sea—The
Victoria Lake discovered by Speke—Rosher's explorations—The Nile flows
from Lake Victoria—Speke and Baker—Discovery of Lake Albert—Livingstone's hypothesis contradicted by facts—Gordon in Equatoria—Equatoria
ought to find a commercial opening at Zanzibar—It opens a way by
the Nile to the lakes—Romolo Gessi explores the Albert Lake—The
steamers *Khedive* and *Nyanza*—Colonel Mason's exploration—General
Stone's opinion—Stanley and the Beatrice Gulf—From Berber to Khartoum
—The Nile between Khartoum and Lado—Difficulty of the traffic by water
in the Nile Valley—The sources of the Nile—The Albert Lake—Conformation of its shores—The navigation of the lake—Storms—Crocodiles—
Fishing—The lake boats—Kibiro salt-works—Salt trade—Tribute to the
king—Cultivation—Products of the forests—Fauna—Inhabitants.

GEOGRAPHERS of the first half of this century were generally of opinion that the central region of Africa was formed by an immense internal sea, as large as half Europe. This great lake extended from the southern end of the Nyassa, having its northern limit and its greatest bulk of water in the Equatorial zone; but no European explorations had confirmed this supposed distribution of the river basins.

It was in 1858 that Speke and Burton, having started from Bagamoyo, on the east coast of the narrow channel which separates the African continent from Zanzibar—with the purpose of making discoveries about the great question of the sources of the Nile, which was still a mystery—discovered Lake Tan-ganika, but were unable to settle its northern borders. On returning to Tabora, the two explorers, whilst occupied in comparing and arranging former studies with the information they had received about the countries surrounding the region explored by them, were given some vague hints concerning the existence of a great sea, much larger than the Tanganika, at a distance of not more than fifteen days' march towards the north. Burton was prevented from joining the enterprise on account of the deplorable state of his health. Speke departed alone, and succeeded in discovering the Victoria Lake, of which, however, he could see but a small part.

From that time explorations, crowned by discoveries of lakes, followed each other rapidly, and the circumnavigation of them led to the division of the grand African Mediterranean into a series of great lacustral basins. In 1859 Livingstone reached the southern shore of Lake Nyassa, and almost at the same time Rosher explored the eastern banks of the Tanganika.

Speke had conjectured that the Victoria Lake might be the reservoir from which the Nile had its origin, and as soon as he arrived in England he projected an expedition, which started in the early months of 1860. Feeling himself thoroughly competent, he did not hesitate to accept the mandate of the Royal Geographical Society; and associated Captain Grant, his friend, in the enterprise.

He reached Uganda, by the route through the country of Karagua, and the Kagera river; and on the 28th of July 1862 he crowned his mission by witnessing the Nile flowing from the Victoria Lake at the Ripon Falls. He then went to the north-west, and the expedition reached the mountainous part of the Nile, near the spot where Miani, an Italian, arriving from the north, had engraved his name and the date of the event on the historical tamarind.

BAKER'S DISCOVERIES.

Sir Samuel Baker, a valiant hunter, fond of adventure, and wishing to study and make known the Soudanese countries (shut in by the desert and by the difficulty of communication), started an expedition to the region of the lakes, with the almost certainty of meeting Speke and Grant. He arrived at Gondokoro on the 2nd of February 1863, where a few days afterwards he greeted the two brave explorers. On being informed by Speke of the existence of a lake (in accordance with the statements of the natives), west of Unyoro, into which the great river flowing from the lake poured itself, he conceived the idea of completing the discovery of the sources of the Nile, both for the love of study and as a compensation for the troubles and expenses he had undergone. The explorations which he and the brave Lady Baker carried out, amidst all kinds of sufferings and dangers, led to the discovery of a new lake, which he called Lake Albert. Whilst Stanley and Cameron ascertained the boundaries of Tanganika and Victoria Lakes, Gessi in the year 1876 completed the exploration of the Albert Lake. The sources of the Nile were no longer a mystery, and Livingstone's hypothesis, that it had its origin at 12° S. lat., had thus been contradicted by facts.

On Baker's return, Ismail Pasha, Khedive of Egypt, sent Colonel Gordon to pursue the exploration of the Upper Nile, to establish a strong government in those regions, and to put an end to the slave trade. Gordon began his government with energy and intelligence. He occupied Bor, north of Gondokoro; established a station on the river Sobat; concluded peace with the Bari tribe; ascertained the course of the Nile from Khartoum to Rejaf, as well as the junction of the two lakes, Albert and Victoria; and laid the basis for opening up communications with them.

Having transferred the seat of government from Gondokoro to Lado, he established a series of military stations for the protection of the Nile route. Rejaf and Bedden at first, then Kirri, Muggi, Laborè, Dufilé, and Magungo, secured the way to the Albert Lake. The road to Unyoro and Uganda was opened later on by the Panyatoli, Foweira, Kirota, and Mruli stations. Gordon was of opinion that Equatoria would find its outlet on the road to Zanzibar. From Lado he wrote, "The only valuable part of this country is that formed by the tablelands of the kingdom of Uganda, whilst the country south of Lado and Khartoum is but a miserable marsh." The execution and completion of this plan, prepared by a diligent exploration of Lake Albert, was entrusted by Gordon to Gessi Pasha.

Before this voyage of circumnavigation took place, many geographers were still of opinion that the lake discovered by Sir S. Baker did not belong to the Nile hydrographic system, and that the Victoria Nile discharged its stream directly into the Nile of the mountains. The adventurous journey, and the observations made at Magungo, were not conclusive enough to settle every doubt. Gordon had first entrusted Chippendale and Watson with the exploration of the lake, but, as they did not succeed in carrying out this arrangement, he confided the enterprise to Gessi, who, with two iron boats and a small escort, brought to completion the tour of the lake amidst the greatest difficulties, unfavourable weather, and the continual hostilities of the natives. In the course of a few days Gessi accomplished his task, having ascertained the length of the lake to be 141 miles (224 kilometres), and its greatest width 50 miles (80 kilometres), thus showing the erroneousness of the dimensions given by Sir S. Baker. He confirmed the existence of impenetrable

MOUNT LOGWEK NEAR REJAF.

marshes at its southern end. At the same time Gordon undertook to explore the Victoria Lake, but through unforeseen circumstances he was prevented from carrying out his project. A short time previously the lake had been explored by Stanley, who for this purpose had obtained from King Mtesa an escort of 2000 men.

Gordon, in order to prepare for the complete exploration of the Albert Lake, had, since the year 1875, given orders that the steamers *Khedive* and *Nyanza*, left by Sir S. Baker, should be carried to Dufilé. The enterprise met with immense difficulties—hostilities from the natives, obstacles in the navigation, and insufficient means. The steamers were broken into sections, and the several pieces were dragged a long way over the road by men, and where the river was navigable they were placed on large boats, and thus transported. When the sections of the *Nyanza* had been brought beyond the Fola Fall they were put together, and the boat was launched in the Dufilé waters.

Towards the end of the year 1876, Colonel Mason, of the Egyptian staff, accomplished the second circumnavigation of the Albert Lake on board the steamer *Nyanza*. The results obtained differed partially from Gessi's, and geographers were undecided in accepting the conclusions of either one or the other traveller. The authority of General Stone made the scale incline in favour of the Italian explorer.

On the 9th January 1876, Stanley discovered the watersheds of the Lakes Victoria and Ruitan (Albert Edward Nyanza), which latter he called Beatrice Gulf. He went down on the table-land, which is at the altitude of about 1000 feet (300 metres) above the level of the lake, but was prevented from pursuing the enterprise any further by the refusal of the Waganda people to accompany him. This is the most distant of the basins where the Nile has its origin, and, as we know, communicates with the Albert Lake by the river Semliki. In the year 1889 the geographical question as to the sources of the great river, which for a long series of years had by its mystery attracted the attention and the studies of geographers, and enlivened the emulation of distinguished explorers, was solved. The distance between Berber and Khartoum is about 250 miles (400 kilometres). According to Sir S. Baker's calculations, the velocity of the current of the Nile varies between 10 and 13 miles an hour, and is interrupted by the Sixth Cataract.

Captain Watson, speaking of the navigation between Berber and Khartoum, says : " After remaining a few days at Berber, we went by steamer as far as Khartoum. There the river flows through a range of hills, which, by diminishing its width, increase the speed of its current. When the Nile is low it is impossible to pass those rapids, except in boats of very little draught, on account of the many sub-aqueous rocks. We went from Berber to Khartoum in six days, but the journey may easily be made in three or four."

By steamer the journey from Khartoum to Lado takes sixteen days. The country through which the river flows presents various aspects, according to the high or low level of the water. The extension of the Nile, generally called Lake No, or Mokren-el-Bohur, forms a large channel, the width of which varies with the changing conditions of the current. It is bordered by extensive grassy banks, floating on the water.

The Nuer tribe camp on this mobile land.

The shape of this lake is very irregular, owing to the force exerted by the mass of waters to open a wider mouth when the river is swollen ; the Bahr-el-Ghazal, rushing against the grassy surface, is powerless to break the thickly intertwined herbage, but at that point causes the channel to form an acute angle towards the east.

In the succeeding part, as far as Lado, the navigation of the river is not very difficult, but throughout a perfect knowledge of the route is required, in order not to deviate into one of the lateral branches that are frequently met with, especially in the ad-

VIEW OF THE BANKS SOUTH OF FOLA.

vanced season of the rains, and also to avoid the many sandbanks.

The country between Lado and Rejaf, and from that place to Bedden, is slightly undulating, and its cultivated fields extend to the banks of the river. In the dry season steamers cannot go beyond Gondokoro; but boats at this time of the year go as far as Bedden.

On account of the rapids, the change of boats takes place at Bedden, from whence navigation is easy up to Kirri, near which place the open ground, sloping slightly towards the river, narrows it, and renders its passage hard and difficult. The country comprised in this locality and the villages Muggi and Laboré slope gradually, and it is only at a short distance from this last place that we observe a steep declivity on both sides of the river. The many rapids of the Nile, though not difficult to pass, make navigation on it uncomfortable and dangerous. Between Laboré and Dufilé these rapids succeed each other frequently, and the Fola cataract at its confluence with the Assua, enclosed between the sides of a narrow neck, makes navigation impossible. For a space covered by two hours' walking the road runs over a limited tract of land on the side of the chain of mountains which slope towards the western bank, and after that becomes still more mountainous. Near the cataract a rock bars the way, and, leaving the bank of the river, the road winds down the wild-looking hills in the neighbourhood of Dufilé.

About 2½ miles south of Fola the river is free from obstacles and flows slowly; small islands of papyri are scattered over its course, which has frequent windings. The western bank is picturesque, owing to its fine and extensive cultivation, whilst the opposite shore is wild and desolate, and scattered over with bushes of papyrus.

The Nile, on account of its cataracts, from the great number of its rapids, and the scarceness of forests where fuel might be obtained, presents a series of difficulties to traffic by water.

In 1875 Colonel Gordon wrote: " Navigation from Lado to Khartoum is almost impossible; firewood is scarce, and becomes more so every year; there are numerous sandbanks."

The sources of the Nile are formed and flow from a vast basin partly surrounded by a semicircle of moun-

WOODED SCENERY OF THE NILE NEAR KIRRI.

tains. In the eastern segment the range of heights describes a curve diverging from the Abyssinian mass of mountains and from the surroundings of the Blue Nile, reaching its highest altitude in the Equatorial lake region. Tracts of alluvial land, and ranges of hills sloping down to the plains, extend between the greatest line of heights and the Nile.

These plains in the season of the rains are flooded by inundations. To the south of this region between Lado and Dufilé, the spurs of the range of mountains slope down to large meadows, cut by numerous streams of water, and scattered over with small isolated hills, forming the region bounded by the Victoria Nile.*

Westward the country extends in flat plains covered with trees to about 62 miles (100 kilometres) from Lado, surrounded by a line of heights which from the north-east run parallel to the river as far as Dufilé. There the range of mountains forms a small plain near the river, and, turning towards the south-west, passes at no great distance from Wadelai, skirts the Albert Lake, and with the heights of Wallegga forms the valley of Semliki, and borders the western and southern shores of the Ruitan, or Albert Edward.

The Albert Lake, enclosed on the east by the heights forming its waterparting with the Victoria Lake and on the west by the mountain ranges of the Lur and Wallegga countries, is a vast elongated basin, stretching from north-east to south-west. It is narrow at its origin, but gradually expands, forming ample bays; and then becomes narrower again at its northern end.

At the point of junction with the Victoria Nile, the water is stagnant in an inlet, and the accumulation of sand makes the entrance to the lake difficult for large

* This information is partially taken from "Notizie sulle provincie Egiziane del Sudan, Mar Rosso ed Equatore, del Corpo di Stato Maggiore." Roma, 1885.

boats at the time of the lowest water. The eastern shore is formed by protruding sandbanks and terraces, on which successive phases of the action of the waters are delineated by parallel lines. It appears that, even now, whilst on the western coast the waters are receding, their advance on the eastern shore increases. Kibiro is situated on the eastern coast of the Albert Lake on a level shore of small extension. Behind it, to the south, rises Mount Kitana, its steep sides cut into large and successive terraces, difficult to ascend. The coast is formed of undulations of varying height, with woods between the water and the hills, the average distance between the lakes and the heights being about a mile.

The uniformity and continuity of this configuration are broken here and there by great rocks, covered by *euphorbia*, wild date palms, and the beautiful flowers of the yellow stramonium (*Datura humilis*).

At three hours' journey from Kibiro the Kiriangobi forest appears on the ridge of the sloping mountains, and casts its dark shadow along the shore, its gigantic trees broken here and there by the silvery falls of the river Ngussi, and of several minor streams. The land then slopes gradually to the Muenghe territory. At Kieya the aspect of the lake is that of a marsh, covered with a growth of papyri and *ambatsh*, which becomes thicker towards the south.

The western side of the lake is almost everywhere bordered by a continuous range of mountains, rising like a wall, and sheltering the waves from the north-westerly winds. This line of heights proceeds tortuously, and forms plains of various size between the foot of its hills and the waters of the lake. The force of the water (not so strong perhaps on this bank as on the other) and the great number of rivulets, together with the action of the rainfalls which carry down the detritus, cause a perceptible progress in the extension of the western shore, and a consequent advance of the waters on the opposite bank. The thick Tunguru wood, with its high and leafy trees, screens from the winds of the north-east the village of the same name built on the borders of the lake, in the midst of rich and thriving fields of grain, bananas, and cotton.

Navigation along the western coast is made difficult

LANDSCAPE NEAR THE ALBERT LAKE.

by the many sandbanks protruding in the lake to a great distance, and of varying and uncertain size. When the point of Msua is passed the high mountains of Juguro rise almost perpendicularly from the water, and bar the passage near the shore. Further south the heights of Melindwa, which follow the bank of the lake and join the Kavalli hills, leave a narrow shore on which are erected several villages inhabited by fishermen. Numerous streams, like bands of silver, rush down from the rocks in cascades and waterfalls, in the midst of strips of still more vigorous and bright vegetation.

The lake cannot be freely navigated at Nsabe, Nyamsanzi, and Were, because it is there a mere marsh scattered over with papyri and *ambatsh*. From Cape Mina, on the western shore, the lake is deep and navigable at any season.

"The spirit of the lake may cause winds to blow furiously, and upset the boats with your soldiers," the king said to me one day; and he added, whispering, "The people of Kibiro are wicked, and will take vengeance on your men if they use any violence to them."

It is a general belief—to which King Chua himself seems to give credence for the convenience of his government—that an evil spirit inhabits the depths of the lake, and at his caprice unfetters the fury of the waves and raises storms. Veneration and devotion may avail, however, to calm and prevent his anger, and for this purpose sailors throw glass beads, fowls, &c., in the water.

The king's envoys throw in a certain kind of large cornelians called *genetot* by the Arabs, the use of which is forbidden to others.

Violent winds, generally from the north-east, but sometimes from the south, blow suddenly on the lake; the water becomes dark, waves fall one upon the other, and the storm rages, whistling and thundering, the bearer always of desolation and affliction. It often appears so quickly that boats at a short distance out have no time to reach the land.

The lake is inhabited by enormous crocodiles, which at the mouth of the Victoria Nile are to be seen by thousands. These reptiles, however, are not actively

THE MURCHISON FALLS NEAR SHOOA-MORU.

hunted, there being in the country a large supply of fish and hippopotamus flesh.

For fishing they use big iron hooks fastened at intervals to a long line, which is left in the water all night, and taken away very early next morning.

The lake is rich in varieties of fish, some of which are of immense size. The flesh is preserved by drying at a fire or by smoking it. The taste and smell acquired by the fish during this preparation may be improved by wrapping it up in earth for a few hours before cooking it.

Boats, some of considerable size, are formed from trunks of trees hollowed out; they are large enough to allow the natives to carry on commerce between the two coasts, especially the salt trade, an important branch of industry diffused over distant points of this extensive region. The greatest quantity of this article is obtained from the Kibiro salt-mines, and is the main source from which the inhabitants of that land obtain their livelihood.

At Kibiro, the natives gather some whitish earth from the ground, permeated by a stream of mineral water which flows from Mount Kitana, and spreads its wealth in the neighbourhood. This earth is placed eight inches thick in rectangular trenches, prepared for the purpose, and constantly filled with water. After a certain lapse of time, sufficient to saturate it with salt, this water is taken out and boiled for a long time in earthenware vessels.

The salt precipitated by evaporation is then dried, wrapped up and moulded into blocks, which are hung from the roof of the huts to keep them dry.

The chief of Kibiro annually pays the king a tribute of one thousand of these blocks, weighing about twenty-two pounds each. The monarch distributes this salt to the Wahuma shepherds, to be given with water to their cattle; for the service of his household, he uses Usongora salt. The chief of the salt-works carries on a very active trade in this product, which he exchanges for corn, sesame, oxen, tobacco, wood, cloths, &c. This business is not limited to the region of the lake, but extends to Uganda, where on the confines of the country there are many much frequented markets.

The king, besides the quantity fixed as a tribute, purchases more, giving oxen in exchange.

The land, flat or nearly so, bordering the shores of the lake, is brightened by fields of grain, *Colocasia esculente*, sweet potatoes (*Batata edulis*), and groves of bananas. A variety of nutmeg-tree grows in the woods of Msua; Indian canes, bamboos, and tamarinds here and there break the majestic obscurity of the forests.

Flights of cranes and wild ducks are seen in the reed thickets and the swampy spots of the shore, while on the sandy banks plovers, the foretellers of storms, pursue each other shrieking. Birds of various plumage, innumerable butterflies, flit about in the bushes, and fly merrily over the grassy level land. Elephants and buffaloes come out at sunset from the recesses of the forest in crowds to drink at the waters of the lake, but at night they spread ruin over the crops of corn and the banana groves, joined in their mischief by numerous hippopotami, colonies of chimpanzees, and several varieties of dog-headed apes which live in the Juguro bushes at Msua, and in the east of the Kiriangobi forest. Populous villages are dotted about the coast of the lake.

The Magungo Baba occupy the country from the Victoria Nile peninsula as far as the Muenghe territory, which is inhabited by the Wahuma. The Lur live on the western coast, and although they do not belong to the kingdom of Unyoro, they recognise the supremacy of that monarch.

The chiefs Boki, Tukende, and Acoi pay annual tribute to King Chua. Melindwa, the most powerful chief of the Lur on the mountains, is a faithful ally of that great tyrant.

The southern regions of the lake by Kavalli, Mpigwa, and Katonzi, formerly rich in cattle, were devastated several times by the raids of the Unyoro men, whose king they acknowledge from motives of fear and interest, although they have never been subdued by him.

CHAPTER VIII.

FIRST NEWS OF STANLEY'S APPROACH.

Woe to the vanquished—A dignified proposal—Unexpected answer—Faithfulness and disinterestedness badly rewarded—Proposals for the soldiers—Death of Hurshid—Cunning policy of the King of Unyoro—Its consequences—Ballula on the Vurvira mountain—Enchantment of Sunga and congratulations of Umma—The allied Lango—Contradictory news—Sunga's son—Arrival of Stanley—Emin's departure for Msua—Raids into the countries bordering on the Nile—Search for Stanley—Reticence of the natives—Interior condition of the province—Major Rehan Aga—His declarations—His death—New misfortune—Major Hamid Aga—Demands of the soldiers—Ali remains—Emin does not accept advice from me—Fatal order—Pernicious lull—Demands and proposals of the first battalion—Emin at Kirri—His flight—The firman granting the title of Pasha—Defeat of Befo, chief of the Belinian—Stanley at Ndussuma—The wife of Mpigwa—The brave Mogo—The 27th of April 1888—Stanley's letter—Advice about the best thing to do.

Woe to the vanquished, and I was one of them! The joyous reception soon came to an end. The message which the soldiers Fadl and Hurshid had heard from Guakamatera himself was believed, and strengthened the believers' hope in the future. I was accused of having rendered the position of the Government difficult by my extremely harsh behaviour; of having carried on, stubbornly and foolishly, the negotiations with the King of Unyoro and his grandees; of having ruined the future of the Province, wasted the ivory, lost the advantage of an arrangement for conveying the correspondence and for revictualling the storehouses, and of having alienated the heart of a friendly and benevolent king. Emin joined in the accusations, but added that the matter would have no serious consequences; that Chua had acted only from personal aversion; that intercourse with him was about to be resumed by the despatch of a more acceptable ambassador, and that the prince of Unyoro contemplated with pride the idea of an alliance with "his friend the doctor."

On my arrival I proposed sending one of the steamers to Kibiro with a letter for the king, requesting him to give up, within fifteen days, Biri, the soldiers, the guns, and the ivory of the Government, which he had seized, and also my personal effects, with the threat that, if he did not yield within the fixed time, the Governor would maintain his right by force and avenge the outrage.

This just proposal was unanimouly supported by the most distinguished amongst the officers, who were burning with the desire to give a well-merited lesson to the inhuman tyrant; but the reply of the Governor did not answer the general expectation. According to him, I ought to be quite satisfied with having got out of the scrape alive, and the most urgent matter was to resume a friendly intercourse with Unyoro on account of the transit of the correspondence through Uganda. This, according to him, was an easy undertaking, which rested entirely with him. Emin's behaviour at that time was ungrateful and presumptuous; I therefore maintained a dignified silence, feeling convinced in my conscience that I had fulfilled my mission with circumspection and prudence, without intrigues or cowardice. I did not wish for either thanks or recompense, but was profoundly wounded to find these accusations supported by a friend in whose service I had risked my life, and referred to with a cunning smile, as if I had been a child. It is true that in my distress I derived much consolation from the friendly words and letters written to me by the officers and employés.

I sent a request to the Governor that he would reward the two soldiers who had been my companions in the flight from Unyoro, and obtained, not without difficulty, the consent that Fadl should be promoted to the rank of an officer and Hurshid to that of a non-commissioned officer. But the latter died shortly after in consequence of an illness he had contracted during those days of terror and grief. From that day, when King Chua began to crave the arms, ivory, and territory of Equatoria, he turned all his attention to acquiring the friendship of the tribes bordering on the Nile and the lake, and fully obtained his object, either through respect or fear.

The natives avoided the military stations; refused to pay tribute of corn, or to serve as carriers, waging thereby an indirect war; and whenever they felt themselves strong enough they openly became the attacking party. This situation was rendered more serious from the arrogance and want of discipline among the soldiers, whose continual violence and extortions sowed the seeds of hatred and revenge.

Whilst the country lay open to the agents of the King of Unyoro, the Governor could neither get a faithful messenger nor obtain reliable information.

The chiefs Sunga, Boki, Reja, and Okuza were more or less manifestly allied to our bitterest enemy.

Ballula, who had entrenched himself on the Vurvira mountain, attacked the soldiers of Dufilé with muskets, assisted by a strong body of Shooli, besides other men sent by Chua. Okuza laid an ambush for the soldiers who were searching for corn on the Tunguru mountains. Two attempts to send letters to Unyoro failed, and what the king was planning, or what was going on, remained an impenetrable mystery.

When asked for news, the natives answered humbly,

DECEIT OF THE NATIVES. 143

and with apparent eagerness, but gave the most contradictory intelligence.

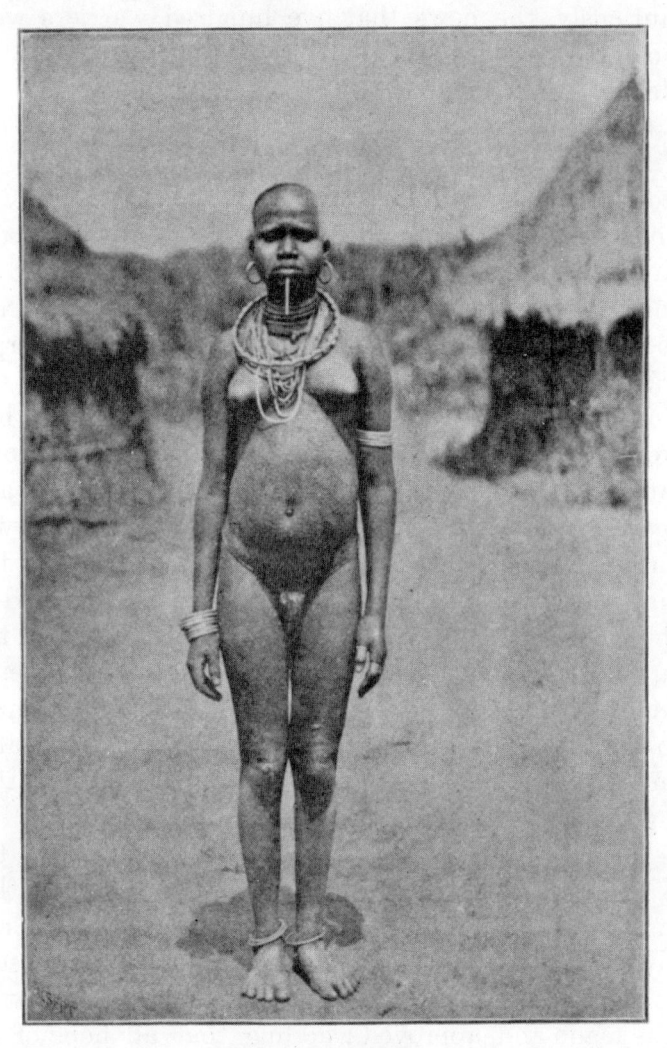

A SHOOLI GIRL.

Umma, chief of the country between Tunguru and Msua, went to congratulate Emin on his escape from the incantations with which Sunga, by order of King

Chua, intended to destroy him and all his soldiers; while Sunga, on the other hand, gave out, most cautiously, the news that five hundred warriors were mustered at Kibiro, and that the peninsula of Magungo was supplied with strong garrisons.

Others asserted that the Wanyoro had crossed the Victoria Nile, and were making arrangements for storming Wadelai, in alliance with the Lango, to whom the king had promised the country of the Shooli. Kolikio, *matungoli* of the chief Boki, related that he knew, from a reliable source, that Guakamatera had been put in chains on account of the outrage perpetrated on Biri and myself; whilst Makiera, the Governor's interpreter, assured us that the king had ordered our arrest and execution in a fit of intoxication; that having recovered consciousness, and hearing that his order had been executed, he was furiously angry. A certain Avanda gave out that the king had given the order against us, on being told of the approach of a hostile body of men towards the lands west of the lake, but had afterwards ordered Guakamatera to send the effects which had been seized to Tunguru, and to announce there the early arrival of an ambassador, as he was convinced he had committed a great error.

The son of chief Sunga, who usually resided at the King of Unyoro's Court, having returned to his father in Equatoria, reported that at the time of Biri's and my expulsion he was at Mruli, and that he was present at the council when the proposal of our assassination was made and approved; adding that all hope of recovering the lost goods and effects must be given up.

"Stanley has arrived," was the news I gave on the 16th, as soon as we were received on board the steamer *Khedive*, and shortly after I informed Emin of the news communicated to me personally by Ireta's envoy about the body of armed men which had been observed on the south-western shores of the Albert Lake. On the morning of January 30, the Governor embarked direct for Msua in order to go from that station to meet the Relief Expedition.

I wished to accompany him, but was prevented from doing so by the unfavourable state of my health, but I was present when he went on board the steamer, greeted by a crowd of officers and employés. He sat down at the stern of the boat, and hearing me repeat a salutation previously unnoticed, he said, "I did not see you; I thought you had not come." I bit my lips, and smiled. His affected indifference was but the continuation of the anger which had possessed him for several days. As I went away, I thought of the advice given and slighted, and of this additional wrong inflicted on me after the many already suffered. On reaching Msua, Emin heard from all sides uncertain, contradictory, and sometimes disquieting news, all of which detracted from the vaunted probity of the King of Unyoro, and prevented his pursuing the projected reconnoissance.

Being convinced of the necessity of repressing the increasing audacity displayed in the tracts adjacent to the eastern shores of the lake, the Governor, on February 6, ordered an expedition into the Magungo territory, on the left shore of the Victoria Nile, and a subsequent attack on the chief Okello, who had openly declared himself in favour of King Chua. However, it was impossible to carry out the first part of the plan, because there was not sufficient water for the navigation of the steamer; but the rebel village of Lur was sacked and burned.

On the 9th February another raid was made upon those lands, in which they captured a number of goats and a quantity of corn. On the 12th Emin asked me by letter to go to Msua, to hold a consultation with him about the intended attack on the salt pits of Kibiro, in order to destroy the source of the wealth of that country; but the fever from which I was suffering compelled me to decline the invitation.

At last, on February 25, 1888, Emin started from Msua to look for the Relief Expedition led by Stanley; but the search was without success. The chiefs of the villages were very reticent in giving information, and some of them even denied altogether the presence of strangers in the adjacent districts. Others who seemed inclined to speak were prevented from doing so by their people, whilst a few asserted that the whites had been seen near Katonzi, but that they had left long ago.

The fatal hand of King Chua, ever raised against us, inspired fear in all, ready as it was to strike us at any moment.

On March 6, 1888, Emin returned to the station of Msua. On the 21st, Babedongo, with a strong body of *banassura*, fell upon the poor districts south of the lake, and laid them waste, because those populations had favourably received the agents of the Government, and given information to the Governor. On the 18th of March, yielding to Emin's urgent request, I went to Msua. He still adhered to the project of attacking Kibiro. However, I succeeded in persuading him, if not to give it up, at least to postpone its execution. I vividly remembered the hospitality and protection bestowed upon me by the chief Kagoro, and the thought of the evil which might befall him grieved me.

The internal condition of the Province had not improved during these last years. Toleration had led to want of discipline, which had been the cause of numerous disorders. The authority of the Governor, weakened by persistent attacks, had been almost annihilated, and the honours still shown him were of a derisive sort.

As far back as the month of April 1886, Major Rehan Aga, of the 1st battalion, invited the Governor to an interview at Kirri, in order to have an understanding about the conduct of the Government.

"Who is the Mudir?" wrote he in his letter. "I cannot receive orders from the Major commanding at Dufilé." He declared himself a faithful subject of the Egyptian Government, adding that he and his subordinates would adhere to the resolution of not leaving the station, but the fear of the Bari, who were not yet subdued, and the probable desertion of the soldiers, who were natives of Makraka, compelled him to quit it.

Rehan Aga died on May 19, 1886, and his unexpected death gave rise to the suspicion that he had been poisoned, which was corroborated by the fact that shortly before his illness he swore on the Koran that he would rather die than go to the south. Ali Effendi, an Egyptian captain, was pointed out as the assassin. It was another misfortune added to those which had so long afflicted the Province, and which caused further excitement in already irritated minds.

Major Hamid Aga was appointed to fill the vacant place. He was an old Soudanese, timid, and of limited intelligence, but beloved by his soldiers for his goodness and honesty in the discharge of his duty, although inclined to severity.

Accompanied by Selim Aga and the doctor, he presented himself to the troops, who unanimously promised him obedience, but demanded the dismissal of Major Hawashi, and that his intercourse with Emin should cease.

"If the Governor wants corn, give us spades and we will cultivate the land for him," the troops said.

Hamid, Selim, and the doctor prepared to return to the Pasha to inform him of the state of affairs, but the soldiers opposed the departure of Ali Effendi.

"The Mudir said he was going to Gondokoro, but instead of that he has fled. Now, if you go, who remains to take care of us? Are we not still the Viceroy's soldiers?"

And prudence required that Captain Ali should remain.

At that time the troops (not yet openly mutinous) could easily have been brought to obedience, had wise concessions been granted and energetic measures taken. I had already written from Juaya to Emin, endeavouring to persuade him to get rid of Hawashi, an intriguer, who had been the first cause of the lamentable condition into which the Province had fallen, and to replace him by a man of more courage and probity; also to arrest and remove Captains Ali Aga and Ghiaden Aga, who were the leaders of the opposition at Rejaf. But Emin turned a deaf ear to my counsel. He did not like to break off the alliance with Hawashi, which he himself had sought, and fear prevented his proceeding energetically against the other two officers. The spectre of open rebellion haunted him, and of all the measures which appeared most opportune he chose the worst. He again pompously gave the order for evacuating the stations, granting authority to punish with death any refusal; the command, however, remained a dead letter, and only served to increase the animosity already existing against him.

Emin thus lost more of his prestige.

A long lull followed this storm. Instead of applying to the Governor when in difficulties, the officers acted in an independent fashion, their only communications being formal documents about accounts, which were conveyed as far as the boundary of the territory over which they held jurisdiction.

Emin, unable to recover the reins of command which had been wrested from him, consoled himself with the hope of a better morrow, to be brought about by unforeseen circumstances. Twelve long months passed without a conciliatory word from the 1st battalion.

Suddenly, in October 1887, a deputation was sent to the Governor with a letter urging him to go to Rejaf, and attend a general assembly there, to arrange about their submission, which they offered on the following conditions:—Removal of Major Hawashi from Dufilé, and appointment of another in his place; removal of Captain Selim Aga for fraudulence in the distribution of the linen acquired in Uganda; grants of promotion similar to those lately bestowed on the 2nd battalion; compulsion of the commanding officer to take up his residence in Rejaf, together with his family, and the appointment of Captain Ali Aga as his adjutant; moreover, that the account department should be reorganised according to law, and the vice-governor, who had been suspended for three years, reinstated.

They concluded by saying they were not unwilling to leave Makraka, and to go south later on, but above all they wished to confer with him free from any pernicious influence, and to show him clearly who were the real disturbers of the peace of the Province.

Emin, trusting in a complete success, hurriedly left Msua on the lake, and went to Wadelai (November 1887), whence, after settling the most urgent affairs, he journeyed to Dufilé, where the display of false zeal and the revelations poured into his ear, damped his ardour. Travelling from station to station, he reached Kirri, and found himself in a snare. Diffident and suspicious, he sent ignorant spies to Rejaf, and thus excited distrust in others. He refused to go there; listened to miserable insinuations, and separated himself from his old soldiers, whom he had called around him. Meanwhile he was expected at Rejaf, and the officers, alarmed by the delay of his arrival, considered themselves in duty bound to satisfy the will of the soldiers, who exclaimed: "Let the Governor be fetched, let him be brought to us"; but another plan prevailed. Ali Aga was to arrest Emin and take him to Gondokoro, where he was to be kept in custody. The latter fled hastily in the night, without escort or effects, and shut himself up in Muggi, ordering that should any soldiers appear on the road to Kirri they were to be repelled by force. At Muggi he received the firman bestowing upon him the title of Pasha, which I had sent from Juaya on December 2; but the public mind was uneasy and bent on disbelieving everything, and Emin withdrew towards the south, gladdened by the triumphal honours conferred upon him along the road, by the faithful of the 2nd battalion. Having reached Dufilé he repealed some severe measures; reinstated the vice-governor and his secretary, and continued his journey towards Wadelai and Tunguru, where he received the news of the misfortune which had befallen me, and was cast down by this additional failure of his expectations. Uncertain and hesitating as to what he should do, he asked by private letter for the despatch of two companies of the 1st battalion, to resist the King of Unyoro, but his request was refused.

In March 1888, the soldiers of Rejaf defeated Befo, chief of the Bari of Belinian. Emboldened by this victory, and enriched by the pillage of cattle, they re-

MAJOR HAWASHI EFFENDI.

garrisoned the places about Makraka which had been abandoned, and established autonomous administration.

On his return to Tunguru, Emin made every effort to

obtain news of the Relief Expedition. The Negroes of Msua asserted that some armed strangers and white men were in the territory of Ndussuma, and it was said that the wife of chief Mpigwa, who was a native of that country, had seen them. Mogo, a bold mountaineer of Msua, well known in the regions adjacent to the lake for his frequent excursions, was despatched in the beginning of April with a letter for Stanley.

On the 20th we heard from Stanley that he was at Nyamsanzi, awaiting the answer to the letter he had given to Mpigwa.

At sunset on April 23, when we were assembled as usual at the Governor's house, musket shots were heard on the road leading from the mountain to the station, causing us to rush out at once. An officer of the British Expedition, bearing a letter from its commander, had arrived the evening before at Msua, where he had stopped, in the expectation of a meeting with Emin Pasha.

On the evening of the 27th, by the dim light of a lamp, Emin read and translated to me and to Hassan the long letter sent by Stanley. It was an Odyssey full of the vicissitudes, sufferings, and misfortunes undergone by the Expedition; of the sickness, starvation, inclemency of the weather, and the difficulties of the route. An immense, impracticable, and uninhabited forest; an almost continual scarcity of provisions had decimated its forces. Compelled by necessity, he had divided it, leaving the main body at Yambuya, and the sick at Fort Bodo; while he, accompanied by Dr. Parke, Mr. Jephson, and 130 armed men, had regained the lake, which had already been visited by him at the end of the preceding December.

Having finished reading this letter, which surprised us more than we had expected, Emin asked my opinion as to what ought to be done under the circumstances, and I candidly said :

"The position in which Stanley has placed himself is not flattering either to his hopes or ours. His communication with the main body of the Expedition has been broken for months. We cannot follow him to join it, on account of the difficulties of the route he has chosen. Such an adventure would be folly ; it would be rushing headlong to perdition. Therefore, it seems more advisable that he should rejoin the main body and return with it to us. This implies a delay of more than eight months, and the chance of our waiting for his return in vain. In my opinion, since the last explorations of Grenfell have proved the Obangi to be our Makua, I think such a route would be a favourable one for the exodus. It lies through countries familiar to us, and well supplied with provisions ; and the natives are friendly. The soldiers would certainly not decline to follow it, Mambettu-land being well known to them all by reputation. I believe that the natives would come forward to supply our needs, because they are accustomed already to see their country crossed by armed strangers, for whom they entertain feelings, if not of sympathy, at least of respect ; therefore my opinion is that we should fulfil the duty of visiting Stanley, and thanking him for his heroic display of perseverance in our favour, that we should assist him with the help, however small, the province can afford, but at the same time inform him of our resolution."

At that time, and under the impression of a new and unforeseen event, Emin thought the advice wise, and said that he agreed with it.

CHAPTER IX.

ARRIVAL OF THE EXPEDITION.

Emin appeals to the philanthropy and humanity of the English people—Stanley is summoned—The road to be followed by the Relief Expedition—There is no other than that of the Congo—Provisions fail—The Expedition separates—A disastrous road—Route proposed by Felkin recommended by Schweinfurth and Junker—Peters on the eastern road—Route by Kibali and the Bomokandi—The 29th of April 1888—Henry Stanley—Hope and joy—Emin is not decided about his departure—I remain with Emin—Stanley refuses to perform an act of courtesy by visiting the station—Emin does not explain the dissensions in the Province—His good faith is not justified—Jephson remains with Emin—Stanley's letter and sword—Stanley's proposals to Emin about the future—Scientific labours bear fruit—An angle of Lake Victoria—The arrival of Stanley increases our weakness—Stanley's error in dividing his Expedition—The post of commander—Departure of Stanley—King Chua does not forget us—Horrible butchery at Kibiro—The arrogance of King Chua does not alter—He knows of our precarious condition—Minds are agitated—A complaint is made to Stanley—Consequent anger and indignation—Measures of excessive rigour—I cannot succeed in restraining Emin's hand—Jephson incredulous as to my experience and knowledge—The fruit of four years' work and observation—Faithful to the Pasha—Advice that I gave Emin.

EMIN had appealed, at the end of 1885, to the philanthropy and humanity of the English people, and not in vain, for the eminently practical genius of that nation, excited by the pathetic and persuasive words of the Rev. Mr. Felkin, for the preservation of Gordon's lieutenant, grasped the idea of the use that might be derived from the generous undertaking. And the English Government, whilst formulating its adhesion to a Relief Expedition of an exclusively national character, availed itself also of the ægis of the Crescent. While effecting the liberation of Emin it clearly saw the possibility of carrying out practical projects for an accession of territory and for the triumph of British supremacy in the region of the Equatorial lakes. Prompt action answered the request for aid, the donations of the benevolent were ready and abundant, and the ivory, shut in by the Soudanese rebellion, charmed the imagination of many.

The enterprise, at once daring and cautious, needed a leader who could be relied on, and Sir William Mackinnon, obtained the co-operation of Stanley. He, with the eminent qualities that distinguish him, overcoming a thousand difficulties, in a short time organised the Expedition, and rejecting various projects as to the road to be taken (after having allowed them to be discussed from mere complaisance), decided on that of the Congo—the glorious scene of his former feats.

The eastern road by Zanzibar was rejected by him through fear of the desertion of the porters and from the probability of causing danger to the missionary stations; the want of water and provisions made the road across the Masai country also unacceptable for the transit of a numerous caravan; and the 200,000 warriors of the Nkole gave an uncomfortable perspective of the route from Usukuma to Karagua and the Albert Lake. He had to reach Emin with arms, ammunition, and merchandise, and he could not guarantee the success of the Expedition by these routes.

The certainty of receiving substantial aid from the King of the Belgians induced him to select the road that crossed the Free State of the Congo. He knew the country; was certain of not having to fight with hostile tribes; and did not fear the desertion of his porters or wounding the susceptibility of the Germans. On that road there were no missionary establishments whose safety might be endangered; and the certainty of arriving in full force was apparent. Such was his belief. The reasons of Felkin, supported by the authoritative words of Schweinfurth and Junker, had no weight with him, and Thompson's opinion as to the way through the Masai had no better success; even Wills, who, though suggesting the road by the Congo, advised reascending the Obangi-Makua, had not the pleasure of seeing his proposition discussed.

Stanley, being the discoverer of the course of the Congo, and the founder of the Free State, bound as he was by agreement with the King of the Belgians, and by ties of sentiment with that country, was induced to take this route by the thought of again seeing the well-known valley, ascertaining its progress, and eventually the errors of administration committed by his successors.

Leaving the Congo, he decided to reascend the Aruwimi, which he had already identified with Schweinfurth's Welle, hoping also to complete explorations in the basin of the great river, for which purpose he had solicited the despatch of fifteen whale-boats from England. Facts, however, proved contrary to the prevision of the leader. The flotilla of the Congo was in a deplorable state; the whale-boats were not sent, and he was obliged to avail himself of the assistance of a steamer of the English mission; the conduct of the members of the caravan kept the natives away from the markets, and the want of provisions put him at a disadvantage from the very first. The difficulties of proceeding rapidly augmented every day, and he found himself constrained to separate from the main body of the Expedition—not yet completely assembled—and speedily direct his steps towards the lake in order to arrive in time to save Emin, who, according to Junker, had not means to defend himself after December.

The route led him across the Great Forest, where

his people were decimated by the hostility of the natives, by hunger, sickness, and desertion; and it was only at the end of one hundred and sixty-five days after his departure from Yambuya that he arrived at Kavalli, near Lake Albert, with little more than one hundred men, and necessity compelled him to erect Fort Bodo, at about ten days' journey from the lake, in order to collect the Zanzibaris scattered along the march. If the Expedition had followed the route proposed by Felkin, and approved by Junker, as more feasible, shorter, and less perilous, it would have gained the lake in a shorter time, and with the forces nearly intact. The return journey to Bagamyo of the column under Stanley effected by this itinerary proves the truth of this assertion. Neither has the reason of the desertions greater value. He suffered far more from these on the Aruwimi than Peters did on the eastern road across the country of the Masai, with means quite as scanty and limited, in a rapidly completed journey that led to Lake Baringo, near the Nile, towards Wadelai, and returning to Uganda by Karagua to the region of Lake Victoria and thence to Zanzibar; so that if Stanley had abandoned the valley of the Aruwimi and taken a northern direction in order to arrive at the valley of the Makua, he could— by traversing the rich countries of the Bomokandi, Kibali, and Makraka—have either descended into the valley of the Nile or reached the source of the Kibali by an unexplored and most interesting route, whence he could have proceeded to Wadelai.

Towards sunset the steamer *Khedive* (April 29, 1888) arrived in the Were roadstead. Stanley was encamped at a little distance, near the village of chief Katonzi. Emin wished to go to him without delay. We went down to the boat, and in less than an hour reached the landing-place; cries of joy, the discharges of rifles, and shaking of hands accompanied us to the tent of the chief of the Expedition, who, cap in hand, saluted us gravely. Our visit was of brief duration, but cordial, and was concluded by the reciprocal drinking of healths in brimming glasses of sparkling champagne.

The following morning Stanley joined us with his Zanzibaris, and we formed a camp at Nsabe, in the territory of Chief Mpigwa.

Emin did his best to supply shoes, linen, tobacco, salt, honey, grain, and sesame to the Expedition, equipped and sent out from Europe to his aid.

The rescuers were rescued, but a painful and uncertain shadow veiled the joy that ought to have been complete and general; and yet Stanley, confiding in his fortune and lucky star, put the question about the return of those who intended to comply with the Viceroy's decree and that of his Minister, Nubar Pasha. Emin subjected his decision to that of the majority of his people, and I, faithful to my promise of assisting him, though desirous of putting an end to our sufferings, declared myself ready to share his future prospects, nor would it have been wise to have arrived at any other decision. A decided separation from Emin would have excited discontent, for already the people who had come with us looked with wonder, eyes wide open and dubious hearts, at this remnant of the Expedition, of which the Governor had sung so many praises, and which he had taught them to consider a fount of comfort. Of what value were thirty cases of Remington cartridges? They had not in the least changed the situation of the Equatorial Province.

Emin profoundly felt the sad impression that must be produced by the description of the miseries suffered.

THE FIRST MEETING OF EMIN WITH STANLEY.

and the difficulties of the road, that the soldiers and Zanzibaris would not have failed to give to our people; and repeatedly addressed entreaties to Stanley, begging him to show himself to the inhabitants, and visit the nearest stations within reach of the steamer.

The employés and soldiers had received no pay for five years; they were partly the refuse of the Egyptian army, but they had resisted the rebellion, had fought for their Sovereign, and there had been few desertions amongst them. Yet Stanley remained firm in his refusal, alleging the shortness of the time, though he afterwards stayed at Nsabe for about a month.

Emin bowed his head with resignation, trusting to chance, not having sufficient energy to force events. I told him many times to unreservedly make known the situation of the Province—the dissensions that troubled it—the reality so opposed to the delusions that passed through the minds and mouths of every one in Europe and Egypt. He promised me that he would do so, but I have reason to believe that he only threw out vague hints at times on these vital matters. To confess his own powerlessness, and censure his own errors, was repugnant to his proud mind.

His nomination to the rank of Pasha, and the admiration and interest shown by the entire world in his favour, ought to have readily silenced every scandal, and given new strength to his prestige.

The chief of the Relief Expedition, complying with the Governor's express desires, at once convened the soldiers and employés to consult them as to their intentions. Those who wished to go to Egypt should assemble at Nsabe and at Nyamsanzi, to await his return from Yambuya with the main body of the Expedition, which had been left there with the provisions.

He recognised the certain and inevitable perils of the route to the Aruwimi, and proposed the one through Karagua and Usukuma (which was rich in supplies) to Zanzibar, thus overcoming his former fears caused by the great fierceness of the numerous warriors of Nkole.

To facilitate preparations for the exodus and compensate Emin, to a certain extent, for his refusal to show himself in the Province, Stanley readily complied with the request made to him by the Governor, that an officer of the Expedition should remain with the latter.

Jephson was selected for this far from easy mission, to fulfil which he was furnished with a letter from the head of the Expedition (Stanley), in which the intentions of the Viceroy and his Ministers were clearly set forth and the position of those who preferred to remain was frankly explained. The letter concluded:

"I send you one of my officers, Mr. Jephson, and give him my sword, to read this message to you from me. I go back to collect my people and goods, and bring them on to the Nyanza, and after a few months I shall come back here to hear what you have to say. If you say, 'Let us go to Egypt,' I will then show you a safe road. If you say, 'We shall not leave this country,' then I will bid you farewell and return to Egypt with my own people."

The future of Emin seemed especially to preoccupy Stanley.

Deferring his decision about his return to Egypt and Europe to the time when he should have concentrated the forces of the Expedition, scattered along the Aruwimi, Stanley suddenly threw a new bait to the excited hopes of the Governor; and one day, endeavouring to persuade Emin of the impossibility of maintaining himself in the Province against the invasion of Mahdism, he gave him a brilliant description of his project of conducting him and his people to the north-east corner of Lake Victoria, that they might dwell there, and by a series of successive stations, established on the road to Mombasa, render himself useful to the British East African Company, which would not hesitate to give fixed employment to him and his followers.

This project, so flattering in appearance, made Emin forget the material and moral difficulties that opposed the realisation of it, and rendered Stanley still more fervent in his efforts to strengthen the British undertaking, and gain for it (if possible) the military force that served under Emin. And Emin, forgetful of the most elementary prudence, boasted of this arrangement to his people, thus engendering, later on, a mistrust in their minds and the fear of being sold and torn away from their brothers in religion. When with firm conviction he hinted at his strong sympathy for the British nation and with great satisfaction praised himself for such faith, he believed that the solution of the difficult problem was near.

"Thus my scientific labours," he used to say, " have borne good fruit. Who would have thought that a bird and a butterfly would have proved so useful to me and my people?"

Stanley finally offered to incorporate the Province of Equatoria with the Congo State, if he were assured of reasonable conditions. Naturally such a proposal was rather in compliance with instructions he had received than from a conviction of the probability of its being feasible. The fate of the Relief Expedition was so eloquent as to render any reply needless.

Emin did not hesitate, and, with due reserve for the rights of the Egyptian Government and the duty that bound him to it, manifested his full adhesion to the project of establishing himself on the Victoria Lake, declaring that that might be effected, both on account of the shortness of the journey and the undoubted consent of his people. He was deceiving himself, and the delusion that it shortly after proved shed bitterness in his heart.

The satisfaction with which Emin related these conversations with Stanley, caused me sad reflection, and I did not cease encouraging my friend to seriously consider the political situation of the Province and to recall the true position of it to his mind.

"Stanley's coming," I added, "augments your weakness instead of increasing your authority. The matters discussed here at the end of the lake, and beyond the Province, between you and Stanley, without witnesses, will excite mistrust and lead to disorders. The Expedition cannot return under eight months, everything being favourable. The enterprise may still fail, and then what way of escape will be left us?"

On May 16, 1888, I took leave of Stanley, and returned to Tunguru.

During the time that Stanley stayed at Nsabe, he gained some insight perhaps into Equatorial affairs, and perceived that they were not in the condition represented to him; but he had not leisure to enter into the matter, anxious as he was about the fate of the principal body of the Expedition that he had left behind at Yambuya. Great was the responsibility he had assumed in breaking up the party. The need of procuring all the porters required for transporting the surplus loads, and to bring back the famous million's worth of ivory that was in the Province, which, as had been discussed and agreed with the Egyptian Government in London, was partly to be devoted to the defraying of the expenses of the Relief, led Stanley to commit this error. Instead of sending an exploring detachment to the lake under an expert and daring officer, and remaining himself behind to direct the more important work, thus securing the triumph of the undertaking, his inordinate desire for doing everything himself, and his ardent wish not to let a crumb of glory fall into the lap of others, impelled Stanley (forgetful of the importance of the charge which had been entrusted to him and not to others) to give summary orders, placing between himself and the principal column an enormous distance, an impenetrable forest, silence and doubt, for long consecutive months.

He decided to return, and assisted by about a hundred porters, supplied by Emin, left Nsabe, May 24.

The region of the lake was acquiring the greatest importance in the course of events in Equatoria; it was to be the road and base for the march to Zanzibar.

The security of the passage and the attitude of the natives were two indispensable conditions for the success of our affairs; but the King of Unyoro was always our bitterest enemy, and he used every effort to keep alive and awaken the animosity of the populations against the soldiers of the Government.

In the early part of May, Babedongo concentrated troops in Muenghe for the purpose of watching over the movements in the camp at Nsabe; one of his spies was arrested in the neighbourhood, and later on put to death at Msua. Boats laden with salt, and conducted by the *banassura* of Wanyoro, were confiscated on the shores of Melindwa; the chiefs Sunga, Boki, Reja, and Okuza were imprisoned, accused of having meditated a massacre of the soldiers and a general rising.

Emin, after having caused Juguro, the chief of the

mountain, to be put to death at Msua, for being suspected of plotting (in conjunction with Melindwa) against the garrison, saw the agitation spread, and, perceiving the insufficiency of partial repression, ordered the burning of Kibiro, in order to destroy the great market which was the pride and wealth of the country of Unyoro.

It was the night of May 30, 1888—the peaceful inhabitants of the village were placidly reposing, ignorant of the dreadful misfortune about to fall on them. The two steamers, knowing nothing, cast anchor in the roadstead, while the soldiers and armed Lur remained cautious and silent; a horrible stillness as of death reigned all round; the men were seen in groups at the corners of the scattered habitations. At a given signal, the drums beat, the trumpets sounded, and flames sprang forth, filling the barren recesses and invading the huts; flight was impossible; everywhere were heard cries, imprecations, and the despairing anguish of the dying; the miserable fugitives were shot down; the country became a scene of extermination; women, children, and infants were seized, stabbed, and cast into the flames by the frenzied assailants. In a short time nothing remained of Kibiro but smoking ashes. Their horrible thirst for blood being appeased, the thievish and drunken gang began to sack the place; goats, salt, and all that had been spared by the flames were stolen and carried off, and the salt-pits devastated.

The soldiery, with festive shouts and military arrogance, triumphantly returned to Msua, drunk with the horrible butchery of women and children.

"I do not thank you," said Emin to the commander of this expedition, " for the zeal you have displayed and the cruelty you have committed."

The glad news reached me at that time that Kagoro,

chief of Kibiro, had escaped the massacre. Fortune so willed it, that a few days before the event he had been called to the king on some business. Pleasant memories and gratitude bound me to him, for succour that he had given me in the time of persecution; I was delighted to be spared the grief of seeing him involved in the massacre.

Nor did the avenging hand rest here; all the villages on the coast of Magungo were assailed and robbed; the territory of Amara and the residence of Ntiabo, the king's wife, were sacked and burnt.

In this manner it was believed that they would conquer the pride and curb the arrogance of King Chua; it caused him to suspend open violence for a while, but he redoubled his intrigues.

He was aware of the disorders that impaired the Equatorial Government, and smiled, well pleased at our weakness; being certain of the support of the natives, he prepared for the time when he would be able to realise his ambitious projects.

The dissensions which had desolated the Province for some time, had little by little alienated the minds of the greater number from loyalty to the superior authority. Some repressions, perhaps not always just and proportionate, had produced a current of wrath, ready to break into open rebellion upon the first opportunity that presented itself. They conspired in secret, solely on account of the isolation that surrounded the little State; fear rendered the malcontents watchful and prudent, and a veil of submissive fidelity concealed the actions of the discontented soldiers of the 1st battalion, who were still decided not to recede from their pretensions.

It was the calm that precedes the gathering together of the tempest clouds.

The appearance of Stanley, instead of hushing complaints and concentrating men's minds on the thought of approaching relief, still further inflamed their latent passions. The unjust sufferings, the uncurbed tyranny, the favours shown to a few dishonest persons, the desire for revenge, were the themes of agitated conversation at the stations, on receiving news of the arrival of the Relief Expedition. Later on, the refusal of Stanley to enter the Province, and ignorance of that which had been arranged at Nsabe, augmented the numbers of the discontented, and opened the way to the strangest conclusions. The supposition that treaties were entered into for the cession of the Province to strangers, very soon appeared a certainty not to be doubted.

During Stanley's stay at Nsabe, Captain Abdul-Waab Effendi, and the clerk Ahmed Mahmoud, the first formerly adjutant and the last secretary to the Governor, presented themselves to the leader of the Expedition, lodging an accusation against Emin, and drawing a very unflattering picture of what had transpired in the Province in the last few years.

Stanley listened to their complaints and counselled them to wait patiently for his return, begging them also to persuade their comrades to concord and obedience, and to turn their attention to carefully preparing for the departure to Egypt. He, prudently and with much sense, thought it would not be wise to speak to the Governor about the denunciation he had received, lest it should cause fresh complications, and interfere with military discipline.

Hardly was Stanley gone, when Emin heard of this circumstance, and was so full of anger and indignation that he could not pass over the matter; wounded to the quick by the confidences made to the leader of the

Expedition, self-love moved him to an infraction of military discipline.

Emin arrived at Tunguru, June 3, 1888, with a gloomy countenance and heavy heart; he had been informed of the discontent that was spreading amongst the soldiers and employés, and supported by the wicked counsels and unwise deeds of Major Hawashi Effendi, and he consented to a secret inquiry intended to strike at the mutineers and malcontents. It was a list of proscription, in which the major, by yielding to private hatred, sealed his evil labour of so many years.

I had attentively followed the spirit of general discontent that afflicted the Province for some time, and had several times persuaded the Governor to adopt a more conciliatory policy, that might avail to maintain the crumbling edifice in tolerable condition till the time of our departure. Rigorous measures that in former times would have been of use in consolidating authority, had then no probability of success, in consequence of the general alienation of the people's minds. This course was naturally repugnant to Emin, but force of circumstances exacted it, because he had himself brought on the situation by his own actions; but once more, instead of accepting my prudent counsel, given in a cordial spirit of friendship, he gave himself up to a policy of repression and rigour, supported by the heated encouragement of Jephson, who, relying on the principle—not denied by any one—that energy produces salutary effects, even advised that the two culprits who had complained to Stanley against their own Governor, should suffer the extreme penalty. He did not know the political condition of the Province, nor did present circumstances lead him to modify the ideal that had been engraved on his heart and mind in England, where he had heard the praises of the prisoners in Equatoria sung. However, a lighter sentence was passed : the captain was reduced to the rank of second lieutenant, the secretary was put in irons, several of the other officers were reduced in rank, and the Vice-Governor, Osman Latif, was deprived of his office.

On the morning of June 6 the steamer *Nyanza* was ready to start, and only waited the consignment of the mail; I resolved to try once more to turn Emin from his impolitic deliberations and excessive severity; I went and spoke to him, but by way of reply he accused me of trying to rule him and usurp his privileges; I bowed, saluting him, and returned to my house.

Mr. Jephson, seeing how I acted after the last incident, and that I did not frequent Emin's house as was my wont, came to see me, and reproaching me gently for my want of respect to the head of the Government, begged me to resume our old relations, as, in his opinion, Emin had been quite right in exercising his full authority.

I smiled, understanding that he had interpreted my mode of acting as a defence of punished individuals, and endeavoured to make him comprehend that the affairs of the country and public tranquillity were getting worse and worse, and that Emin by his actions was hastening its ruin; on his part, he shook his head with an incredulous air, and, smiling, showed his surprise at hearing me utter words so little in Emin's favour, whom all Europe considered a scientist, administrator, and soldier.

"One day you will do me justice, Mr. Jephson," I said; "I am the friend of Emin, and it is precisely on account of this friendship that I have never concealed the truth from him. And now, even to you who have a difficult and delicate mission to fulfil, I think it right to make known my opinion on the affairs of the

Province." I did not, however, allow myself to be persuaded to give in to Emin, and kept from his presence.

On June 23, Jephson, accompanied by the Governor, presented himself to the assembled troops of the Presidency of Tunguru, to question them as to their intentions with regard to Stanley's proposal, presented in the name of the Viceroy of Egypt.

The voting did not result in any explicit declaration, but was ambiguous, covered with a thousand protests of servile hypocrisy; "faithful to the Pasha, we will do exactly what he may decide to do," was the refrain repeated from line to line and man to man.

The officers and employés, interrogated by Jephson apart in his own house, expressed still more emphatically their devotion and respect, and confirmed and repeated to satiety their declarations of esteem for their Governor.

But when discussing the situation among themselves these were the subjects which inflamed their minds: The road was difficult—full of dangers for children—without means of subsistence; there was the danger of being sold to the English—the Pasha was so intimate and friendly with them; and not only in Tunguru station were these ideas commented upon, but they rapidly spread everywhere. Rigorous measures had roused people's minds, everything was looked upon with suspicion and judged with despair and anger; but Emin and Jephson, ignorant of the hurricane that was gathering, decided to proceed in the work of scrutiny, and their departure from Wadelai was fixed for the 26th. Struck by their careless serenity, I charged Vita Hassan, in my name, to advise Emin to suspend all discussions concerning our departure, for the present, and to say that I wished him to wait a little, so that the public mind might be relieved from its present agitation and be brought to look at matters in their proper light; adding that if Jephson persisted in continuing the work of inquiry at the stations, Emin should allow him to do it, but that he ought not to move from Wadelai; I only feared for him—there was no danger for Jephson : a guest would certainly be treated with respect.

CHAPTER X.

EMIN'S ARREST.

An old slave of the Baggara—Beginning of the rebellion—A despot and a drunkard—Captain Fatelmula—The Pasha at Dufilé—Opposition of the soldiers of Kirri—Insult to the Governor—The station of Muggi and Abdallah Menze—Threatening attitude of the soldiers at Laboré—Return to Dufilé—Prisoners of the rebels—Ahmed Dinkani—Resignation of Emin—I hold the knife by the handle—I receive the sad news—I resolve to go to Emin—Conduct of the rebels at Tunguru—The news of Stanley's return and its subsequent contradiction—At Wadelai—Agreement amongst the Egyptians—My arrival at Dufilé—Permission to remain with Emin—Interview with Emin and Vita Hassan—A sitting of the revolutionary assembly—Surprise prepared by the factions—Dismissal of Emin Pasha—I advise Emin to sign his name—The new Governor—Violence against Major Hawashi—Fear of Stanley's return—My sympathy for Emin—Proposed transportation of the prisoners—I oppose the insane proposal—"I'll have him put in chains"—Search of the Governor's house and that of the doctor—Little Ferida—The commander of Msua retires to the mountains—The Mahdists in Rejaf waters—Horrible massacre—The three dervishes and Omar Saleh's letter—Emin's advice—They want war—Imprisonment maintained—Selim Matera and Solyman persuaded by me—Defeat of the troops—Emin and Hassan are enabled to settle at Wadelai—Departure from Dufilé.

No sooner had Emin left Tunguru than the commander of the garrison, a certain Solyman Aga, a Nubian (formerly a Baggara slave), a man of narrow mind but quick in action, openly threw off the mask, and, having called together the officers and officials of that station, preached resistance to the Christians, uttering the grossest insults against them.

In his fits of savagery and drunkenness he did not forget me. His injunction to me to shut myself up in my house, was accompanied by these arrogant and cowardly words : " If he will not obey, I will have him thrashed," which he uttered in presence of his timid followers. Astonished, I endured this insolence without retorting, but next day I went to his quarters with a letter for the Pasha, requesting that it should be despatched without delay. Perhaps he was astonished at my indifference, and probably repented of his disgraceful conduct, but anyhow, a few days after, he excused himself through one of his confidants. Nor did he confine himself to advising his soldiers and subordinates, but endeavoured to extend the fire of rebellion. He sent messengers to Fatelmula Aga, one of his compatriots and a captain of the Fatiko garrison, asking him to become his ally for the sake of their common safety, to prevent, by his co-operation, the evils which the Pasha was about to let loose on the Province, and lastly to assume a discretional power over the northern stations, while he intended to keep under those of Tunguru, Msua, and Wadelai. The seditious appeal was responded to (secretly at first) by disaffected and eager men; but the incessant and most cunning organisation of the conspiracy could be inferred from the frequent journeys of messengers, and from Aga's unusual activity with his officers and employés. He acted as absolute master; and woe to him who attempted to oppose his uncurbed will. Reason, justice, civility, and freedom were trodden under foot. The soldiers themselves were indignant on account of the unjust and inhuman acts perpetrated, and the Donagla were even in fear of their lives. The station became dull and lonely; only the colossal figure of the despot could be seen at the door of the military office, often shaking with excessive rage, which became ferocious when it was excited by abundant libations.

During the night a loud beating of drums, sounds of fifes and gunshots, were signs of the orgies which the

THE EGYPTIAN STATION AT KIRRI.

commander and his worthy friends enjoyed. The conspiracy, arranged by Soudanese roughness, assisted by Egyptian malice, soon attained its aim. Low passions as well as just resentment allied with each other on account of the conditions which weighed so painfully on every mind; and this alliance led to victory. The whole body of officers and officials was acted upon as if a magic wand had been brought into play, and the commander, Fatelmula Aga, was clever enough to succeed in assuming the part of main exponent of the planned revolt.

Emin and Jephson ignored the machinations which were in course of organisation, and were deaf to the advice already given by me that they should use moderation and political prudence. They reckoned the homage proffered by a deputation of the 1st battalion, sent from Dufilé for the purpose, as a triumph; and, having been cheered and comforted by the welcome reception arranged by Major Hawashi, they decided to proceed at once towards the stations of the north and to initiate there the consultations about the evacuation of the Province.

The soldiers at Kirri unanimously answered the question put to them; they all approved of the proposal of departing for Egypt; thus giving an example of respectful obedience, perhaps without depth of conviction; but at any rate it was necessary to act prudently and moderately, that is to say, the exodus should have been carried out with discipline and with a sense of fitness in regard to the object in view. Unfortunately, precipitation and the hobby of acting authoritatively everywhere, even in this case, in which the Khedive had granted freedom of choice to every one, caused the good intentions exhibited at first, to be followed by evil results. Emin ordered the ammunition to be sent to the Dufilé storehouse, but the soldiers opposed it to a man; mistrust seized their minds, they found that they were no longer free to act as they would, but compelled to submit immediately, under the penalty, if they did not obey, of being abandoned, with their families, to the mercy of the natives and external enemies.

Emin ought to have been aware of the irritable and suspicious temper of Negro soldiers, His yielding to them was doubly fatal, for he was powerless to enforce his personal authority, and was obliged to endure insults, to the detriment of his prestige. Stanley's letter and the sword displayed by Jephson were considered as contrivances to uphold falsehood.

"Treason is manifest, but to defeat it, is not difficult if we are united." Such were the words uttered in all the garrisons, and the plots which had been kept secret by the few immediately became the will of the majority. Nor could anything better be expected from the soldiers of the Rejaf station, for the danger of Emin being arrested and imprisoned at Gondokoro was now very much greater than in December 1887. The deputation of officers who had come forward in order to calm the public mind, kept silent for several days, and such silence was considered as a sign of hostility. Emin and Jephson agreed to retire to Muggi.

There another attempt was made, through the brave captain, Abdallah Menze, who, they hoped, would be able to increase the public feeling of confidence in the Government; and that by his example public excitement would subside and calm be restored in the minds of the soldiers. These, out of respect for their commander, remained faithful to discipline, consented to the proposal of abandoning the country in order to return to Egypt, and offered no resistance to the transport of nineteen boxes of ammunition from their magazine to that of Dufilé.

No message was received. The officers of Rejaf and Bedden remained stubbornly silent, whilst the soldiers of Kirri persisted in their determination. No news came as to the course of arrangements in the southern

EMIN AND THE MUTINEERS.

stations; only a few messengers from Laboré succeeded in eluding the vigilance of the guards. After fourteen days of miserable uncertainty, the Governor resigned himself to the idea of returning.

On August 13, 1888, the troops of Laboré were arrayed in the village square. Jephson, accompanied by Emin and several officers, read Stanley's proclamation, which was translated into Arabic by the Governor himself, and he requested the soldiers to declare their opinion on the matter. An unusual whispering, an ill-disguised restlessness, agitated the ranks, but no one dared to utter a word. Then at last a soldier, with a provoking and resolute countenance, gun in hand, made his way through the ranks, and, addressing the Governor, declared that they were willing to depart, but that the date should not be fixed till after the harvest. Jephson replied through the Pasha, peremptorily requesting them to let him know their intentions the next morning. Then the soldier, assuming an arrogant tone, said that was not the way to treat the Government troops; that the order must be false, since the Viceroy would have commanded and not begged them to do so; he would have led them to safety, and not abandoned them to their own will. Emin, indignant at these audacious words, threw himself upon the soldier, took hold of him by the nape of the neck, and ordered the commander to disarm and arrest him.

The scene occurred with the rapidity of lightning; the soldiers rose as one man and, breaking the ranks, formed a group, aiming their loaded rifles at the Governor, who had drawn his sword in order to reduce the rebellious private to obedience. The timely intervention of some of the officers prevented a catastrophe. The troops retired, taking possession of the magazine where the arms were kept, and refused to perform their usual night duty at the Governor's residence.

Next morning, Emin went to Khor Ayu, and there received information from the major in command at Dufilé, about the dangers that were accumulating in the Province. Later on, he received another communication, soliciting his return to avoid serious disasters.

On August 19, Emin, Jephson, and Vita Hassan entered Dufilé by the northern gate. The streets of the place were deserted; not one single person came to meet them, and a gloomy silence prevailed everywhere. They entered the residence, but their leaving it again was prevented by the sudden appearance of a picket of soldiers, who placed themselves at the entrance, as a guard. The Governor and the doctor were prisoners, but Jephson was not included in the odious measure, being considered a guest.

There had been no delay in organising an energetic mutiny: the painful incidents at Kirri and Laboré had united all minds in a single purpose, and the irresolution shown by the Governor in the protracted and useless halt at Muggi had facilitated the spread of the insurrection.

Fatelmula Aga, assisted by Ahmed Dinkani, left his residence at Fabo; a few days previously he had occupied Dufilé station, arrested the major in command, and proclaimed himself the saviour of the Province, which was going to ruin through the bad administration and recent intrigues of its ruler. The venture found the minds of the people disposed to approve it; and a provisional Government was installed without opposition.

Emin, not uttering a word of protest nor attempting to defend his outraged dignity, bowed his head resignedly and accepted imprisonment. Unhappy man! He would not listen to me, and when Hassan communicated my prayer to him (not to leave Wadelai), he answered: " I have no cause to be afraid now; I hold the knife by the handle and am accompanied by an Englishman"; but the latter in that painful occurrence could only show his friendly feelings by sharing the bitterness of the outrage inflicted on him.

At about 3 p.m. on September 9, the steamer *Khedive* entered the bay of Tunguru. An unusual bustle enlivened the soldiers of the garrison, who, having put on their dress uniforms, were drawn up by the landing-place. A short time after, Jephson came to my residence and sorrowfully related the sad events with which he was associated. I should have reproached him, although in friendly terms, for not having given due consideration to my words as to the doubtful condition of the Province, but a genuine pity overruled all my feelings, and I promised my full support, encouraging him with hopes of a brighter future.

The news had greatly afflicted, but not disheartened me. I was a sincere friend of Emin and Vita, and had always been frank in my opinions and actions. I had several times disapproved of the mode of government adopted; still, I felt bound to devote all my energy, not only to the improvement of their sad condition, but also to the reinstatement of its rightful owner, even by the very men who had assailed it.

The work which I intended to do was facilitated by an order of the provisional Government at Dufilé, in which the commander of Tunguru was directed to pay every attention to me and my attendants; moreover, I was invited to Dufilé, if I wished to have an interview with Emin, and to be present at the sittings of the assembly which was to meet there.

On their arrival at Tunguru the newcomers took possession of the Government storehouses, and minutely examined the doctor's house, with an odious rigour, which I could scarcely restrain; and their excesses went so far as to cast suspicion upon Captain Solyman Aga, who was thus rewarded for having been one of the first to strike the spark that kindled the conflagration.

The commission, composed of six officers and employés, presided over by Ahmed Dinkani, explained to the assembled soldiers the history of the insurrectional movement for the safety of the Province and for the defence of the principles of justice, which they considered ought to shine with immaculate splendour in the Viceroy's territories.

"The Mudir," added the Captain, "has outraged the Province for five long years by acts of despotism, injustice, violence, and extortion, and has favoured people according to his own caprice, to the detriment of others who had better claims, and now, as a culmination of the ignominy, he conspires to sell it to the British, but the hour for reclaiming the rights of the Viceroy has arrived. We have cast off the yoke and proclaimed a new Government which will mean the realisation of order and justice for everybody." And the crowd applauded, but more for the change, which opened the way to individual licence, than on account of sincere conviction.

On September 13, 1888, the commission went to Msua, and, after some opposition from the commander, abstracted thirty boxes of Remington cartridges from the magazine, which Stanley had deposited there, causing them to be taken to Dufilé. A vague rumour was current at Dufile that the Stanley Expedition had reached the southern regions of the Albert Lake, in consequence of which Jephson had obtained permission to accompany the commission entrusted with the organisation of the provincial garrison, to Tunguru and Msua. But on reaching Tunguru I persuaded Jephson not to go to Msua, because the news was absolutely without foundation; but I wished I had not said so, for, as soon as the steamer had started, that clever young man was tormented by the doubt of not having fulfilled his duty, and could not rest. I suffered for his pangs, not, however, because I thought that the assertion expressed by me might have been reconsidered, for I was sure of what I had said, but from an easily conceivable sympathy; and when the steamer returned I was extremely happy to hear that the inaccuracy of the news was confirmed.

The commission, after having completed the inventory of the Government storehouses and supplied the public service with a fresh organisation and trusted men, departed for Wadelai. There the employés were concentrated in great numbers, especially the Egyptians, because the place was the seat of the Government, and also because those who had abandoned their posts to avoid the tyranny of the commanders of the distant stations sought refuge under the protection of the chief of the Province.

We landed at Wadelai on the 18th, and a general council, consisting of Egyptian officers and employés, was appointed for the same evening, with the object of confirming the success of the insurrectional movement and of concocting a programme for presentation at the general assembly which was to meet at Dufilé. The Egyptians tried to take advantage of it, in order to secure, if possible, a preponderating influence in the resolutions, and, turning the moderate suggestions of the Soudanese to their own profit (being no longer in fear), they endeavoured with all their power to extinguish every sentiment of moderation. At this council a list of charges against the Governor was compiled. The men, who were easily affected by personal animosity, displayed more than usual excitement, and the worst characters, assuming a deceitful appearance of loyalty, obtained the confidence of the majority and the mandate to defend their violated rights.

After a two days' voyage, in company with an inebriated, disorderly, and imprudently vociferating crowd, as jubilant as if they were going to a banquet, Jephson and I joyfully welcomed the arrival of our steamer at Dufilé. My companion went to his lodgings in the house where the Pasha was residing, and I, to the great astonishment of the former, went to Fatelmula's house, who was the provisional chief of the new Government. I knew later on that Jephson could not refrain from pointing out where I went to Emin, and that the latter was deeply wounded by my proceeding. However, I was bound to do so. It was an indispensable step, in order to begin work in favour of my friend. I did not act in this manner because I had lost the sense of my own dignity, but because calm reflection proved to me that it was the best means of performing the friendly duty I had undertaken; and if the course of events had compelled me to give up European customs to such an extent that my life might have been thought incomprehensible, still I can certainly say that my courage never wavered, that my mind was constantly bent on my purpose, and that I did not care to indulge in vain pride, either in reason or out of reason, as others did.

I easily obtained permission from Fatelmula to fix my abode at the Governor's house, and to take part in the meetings of the assembly called to decide on the destinies of the Province.

I was painfully affected on presenting myself to Emin by his stretching out his hand to me, and saying, "I wish I had listened to your advice."

"Let us not speak of the past," said I, "but of the present. Have courage; we will struggle. I have come here to do anything in my power for your safety.

Let us hope; have confidence in me, and you will see that we shall defeat our enemies."

I could say no more, for my mind was oppressed by anxious thought. I wondered that Emin, the man of superior intelligence, the scientist so much admired in Europe, should be a prisoner at the mercy of an ignorant and frantic rabble. Nor did I salute and encourage good Vita Hassan with less affection, who, as a friend devoted to his chief, had fallen with him.

When the military party began agitating for a change in the conduct of the affairs of the Province, they did not intend extending it as far as overthrowing the Government. Its object was only to remove all pernicious influences, and supply the Governor with a council, which was to share his responsibility. But this did not suit the majority of the Egyptian intriguers, who had concentrated their forces in their meeting at Wadelai; and, being also strong from the superiority of their education, they promoted an administrative inquiry, as well as the impeachment of the Governor, the doctor, and the major of the 2nd battalion.

The general assembly was opened September 24, 1888, with a programme of this kind. The reasons which had suggested severe measures against the Governor and the two officers, his associates, were explained, and the proposal of appointing a military commission was accepted, in order to report on the best means to secure respect for the law, individual rights, and personal safety. But during the night a meeting was convened at the house of Captain Ali Giabur, an audacious Soudanese, with an evil disposition, hostile to the feelings of moderation shown by Fatelmula, the head of the provisional Government; and it was resolved to act by surprise, and wrest, by intimidation, a vote from the assembly for a radical change in the constitution of the Government.

Next morning three notorious conspirators, Sabri and Taib (civil employés), and Mustapha Ahmed (a military officer), aided by Ali Giabur and his friends, read to the few members of the assembly called in, the impeachment and consequent decree of dismissal of Emin Pasha from the Governorship of the Province, as well as that of the doctor, and of the suspension from his rank of the major, which the meeting was requested to approve and confirm. There were only a few curt and timid remarks. Some feeble opposition was repressed by threats, and in a short time all the officers and clerks present at Dufilé being successively called upon, the hateful and arbitrary act was approved and sealed by them. The evil counsellors proudly withdrew to their houses, with the conviction of having saved the country and performed a memorable act of justice, while the nervous, few in number, were perhaps sorry; but they felt their conscience delivered from the incubus of responsibility weighing upon them, and concealed their cowardice with the excuse of numerical impotence.

The decree of dismissal was communicated to the Governor by a letter bearing the signature of the Government agent, Major Hamid, who was unanimously raised to the rank of Lieutenant-Colonel by the assembly, and at the same time the Governor was informed of the order for his detention and that of the doctor and major.

I advised Emin to affix his signature to the document sent to him, and to any other paper of the sort which might subsequently be sent him.

Before my arrival at Dufilé he had signed an order which restored some officers and employés, previously dismissed by him, to their posts; another concerning some changes in the administration of the Province and finally a third, directing the commanders of Wadelai, Tunguru, and Msua to send their superfluous ammunition to the central magazine at Dufilé.

There was not sufficient reason, therefore, for considering himself deposed by the request made to him, since it was not a new one, and I was astonished that Jephson should have felt pained on that occasion, as if an indecorous precedent had been set. The violence resorted to before was still in full sway when the last occurrence happened, and to submit to it was only the repetition of a policy previously practised.

The new Governor, old and weak in intellect, did not exert any influence over the public administration, which was despotically directed, according to the will of Captain Ali Giabur. This man had brought seventy soldiers with him, picked from the scum of the barracks; these acted as masters at Dufilé, and were always ready to forcibly support the directions of their chief. There was soon a display of their violence, for one fine morning Major Hawashi's house was invaded by the soldiers, his goods seized, and himself roughly handled and assaulted. He was hated in the Province for his extortions, incessant injustice, and intolerable arrogance; was considered an evil adviser of the Government, and had become the target of public contempt since he had fallen from power. His cowardly tears excited laughter instead of compassion. He was suspected of possessing a considerable amount of money; and the men in office spared neither threats nor molestations to discover it. His domestics were imprisoned and flogged, and part of the money was found, but he obstinately persisted in his denial, and preferred suffering every abuse, notwithstanding my advice to yield to his persecutors in order to end a disgusting scene, which might have resulted tragically.

The probability of Stanley's sudden return aroused the minds of the rebels, and his mission in the name of the Government of Cairo was acknowledged in a public sitting; where it was resolved that the question of the evacuation of the Province and the return to Egypt, were to be treated directly with him; but the most guilty amongst the rebels were not entirely satisfied with the resolution, thus publicly voted, and they entered into a secret understanding with one another, in order to prevent Stanley from being informed of the last change of the Government, and to secure the ammunition sent by the Viceroy. They, moreover, agreed to send the three prisoners to the northern stations, to prevent their escape.

Soon after my arrival at Dufilé, I took advantage of the invitation sent to me, and did not fail to be present at all the public convocations, in which discussions were going on about the imprisoned men and the further changes which it might be advisable to introduce into the methods of administration; and whenever I found an opportunity, I always blamed the rebels' insane work and advised them to take better counsels. Their resolutions were always put down in writing and were legalised by the seal of the Government Commission. It was not difficult to obtain a full knowledge of them from the clerks. Although the rebels knew that I was Emin's friend and cordially interested in his favour, they never forbade me interfering with their meetings, because, they said, they were doing nothing wrong, and wished their deeds to be made known to the Khedive, whom they considered their supreme judge.

I constantly frequented the houses of the officers and

the most influential employés, and was even sometimes accompanied by Jephson. I discoursed with them, without exciting suspicion, about the excessive severity which was being practised and also the projected relegation of the prisoners; but with those who were most prudent and cautious I went a step further, and tried hard to prove that the system with which the country was being ruled was a false one. I even ventured to try and lay the foundation of a counter-revolution, which had become indispensable on account of the violent despotism of those who misruled; and if my words had not always an immediate effect, at least they softened the hearts of many and made them reflect.

Very early on September 28, 1888, Major Selim Matera secretly sent me the information that a council of the leading men was on the point of meeting at Captain Fatelmula's house, with the object of settling the draft of a decree for the relegation of Emin, Hassan, and Hawashi, which on that day was to be submitted to the approbation of the assembly. I sent one of my boys to Captain Fatelmula, begging to be admitted to that council, and, as he did not object, I went to his house, and found about a dozen of Emin's most determined enemies there. That stormy and sometimes violent meeting lasted from 7 A.M. to about 1 P.M. I explained reasons, pointed out inevitable dangers, appealed to feelings of humanity, and I silenced most of the conspirators, isolated the most violent, and gained a victory by wresting the promise of suspending every act of hostility from them.

But, being always afraid of finding myself suddenly confronted by treachery, I went with Major Selim to see the Lieutenant-Colonel, and persuaded him to promise his absolute opposition, and that of his friends, to the hateful measure. In case of failure and as a last resource, I sent my faithful boy, Oakil, to some sergeants and soldiers, with whom a secret understanding had already been arranged, and who were unsuspected by the rebels, in order to request them to be ready to fight in defence of Emin, if they saw him forcibly carried away from Dufilé on the road to the north.

On my return home I found Emin very restless; he was anxious about me. Osman Latif had sent a message requesting him to recommend moderation and prudence to me, because Captain Ali Giabur, on my leaving Fatelmula's house, had exclaimed, "If that man comes again and speaks to me in that manner I'll have him put in chains."

"Do not be afraid, Pasha," said I, "I hope that our affairs will take a favourable turn; and with regard to Ali Giabur, believe me, he will carefully avoid declaring himself against me. I do not wish you to listen to the excessive prudence of Osman Latif; he is a cowardly man."

The commission entrusted with the examination of the accounts of the public administration (presided over by the chief auditor, who had been suspended by Emin) had finished its work and arrived at the conclusion that a search of Emin and the doctor's houses was advisable, in order to ascertain whether the missing despatches, cloth, percussion caps, and ammunition were concealed there. This heinous proposal was approved at once; the news was transmitted to the interested parties, and I obtained recognition as the representative of both.

On October 8, half-an-hour after the arrival of the steamer at Wadelai, the Pasha's house was surrounded by soldiers, and the search began. The most private places were looked into; boxes, hampers, and receptacles of every description were overhauled, and the things supposed to be objectionable were set aside; coarse language was freely uttered, jesting and questioning, but I endeavoured to remain serious and as conciliatory as possible. When the operation was completed I received a copy of the report of the search, signed by the delegates.

Emin's daughter, little Ferida, came to me several times that day, weeping, both on account of the prolonged absence of her father and the harshness of the proceedings. I reassured the dear child, who on my leaving made me promise that I would soon return with her parent, and fortunately after a short time I was able to do so.

On the 14th the delegates proceeded to search the doctor's house at Tunguru, and here everything was seized, furniture as well as provisions, without any mercy; their arrogance even extended to flogging the servants. The confiscated goods were deposited in the storehouse, in order to be transferred to Dufilé.

The reluctance of the commander of Msua station to comply with the order of the new Government, had compelled the latter to bring the unwilling officer to obedience, and resort to violence if necessary. With this object, the officers departed from Tunguru, and took the road to Msua, where, to their great astonishment, they found that the commander had gone to the mountains for corn. Being resolved to wait for him they thought of turning time to account by pillaging everything that was in the station—goats, salt, skins, oil, and tobacco—but a peremptory order required their immediate return to Dufilé, where they arrived on October 30, 1888.

The news was worse than sad; it was terrible.

Three steamers coming from Khartoum had suddenly appeared before Rejaf; the soldiers disembarked from them had assailed and taken the station, after a short resistance, during which three officers and three employés had fallen while heroically defending the entrance to the fort. A horrible slaughter of men, women, and children, without a single exception, had occurred; the victors revelling in the blood of their victims.

On their appearance the Arabs had sent a letter of intimation to Emin by three dervishes, in which Omar Saleh, a Mahdist officer, related the story of his master's deeds, and after promising a general pardon as well as efficient protection, he requested a surrender, declaring that he had been sent to take all the faithful from the Province, which was a country of infidels, to unite them with their brethren the Mohammedans. The rebels, terrified by this letter, applied to Emin for advice, and he, declining every responsibility, declared his opinion as to what was best to be done, namely, that a victory in the northern stations seemed to him difficult, whilst surrender meant certain death; therefore, there was no other alternative than to go south and make a strong defence of Tunguru. But the news of the massacre of Rejaf roused the minds of the officers, and the provisional Governor, together with the soldiers of the 1st battalion, and reinforcements taken from the stations, took the road to Muggi, with the intention of concentrating a certain part of the forces at Makraka, and then of attacking the Arabs entrenched at Rejaf.

Under these new and extremely critical circumstances, resistance being considered impossible by the majority, it was resolved to send at once the noncombatants and the soldiers' families to the southern stations, and simultaneously a written message was sent to the Governor, exhorting him to abandon the idea of avenging the victims of Rejaf, and to order a concentration of troops at Dufilé instead. The hope, of course, arose that, considering the dangers which terrified the Province, all those who were threatened by the Arab invasion would put aside their foolish rivalry, and direct all their efforts to the same supreme object—that of the common safety. But it was a delusion : Ali Giabur and the officers of the 1st battalion, who were on the point of starting northwards, to fight the Mahdists, maintained the arrest of Emin, the doctor, and the major, entrusting the responsibility of their custody to Captain Fatelmula, with general acquiescence, especially that of the Egyptians, who were delighted to continue their tyranny and licence.

The progress of the Mahdist invasion was quite certain, but the success of our soldiers in opposing them, very doubtful. Dufilé was in near and inevitable danger. I resumed the negotiations momentarily suspended, hoping to get, if not an unconditional liberation, at least a mitigation of Emin's confinement and that of his companions. To begin with, I requested their transfer to Wadelai. After having sounded the officers separately, I availed myself of the co-operation of the less perverse of them, and clearly and openly declared that the relegation of the prisoners to a place entirely safe from a sudden attack of the invaders was a homage to the principle of humanity.

The major's removal to Wadelai was allowed, but as to the Pasha and doctor, Captain Fatelmula told me that, though he was not averse to the proposal, he would require the consent of the Regent, who was with the troops at Kirri. The cheerfulness which formerly made us happy in the evening, decreased from day to day, and we often looked at one another in silence. Emin and Hassan had lost all hope of liberation; Jephson often deplored that he was not in a favourable place for at once hearing of Stanley's arrival; and, on my part, though hopeful of achieving the so much longed for object, I was afraid that mournful events might suddenly happen amongst us, before I had attained it.

Turning the discontent which began to prevail amongst the soldiers to advantage, I urged Selim Matera and Captain Solyman, and was fortunate enough to persuade them, that for humanity's sake, and also for preserving their own responsibility, they ought to allow the removal of Emin and the doctor to prevent a grief (which after all was not desired) from saddening to a much greater extent the already pitiful story of their captivity. It was agreed to assemble a council of officers only, considering that the Province was already in a state of war. At dusk, on November 15, 1888, we received melancholy news from the north: the troops under the Lieutenant-Colonel had been defeated by the Mahdists in the neighbourhood of Rejaf; the soldiers had fled in all directions; the commander, a major, three captains, and a clerk had fallen in the fight.

The news rapidly spread amongst the soldiers; the imminence of danger and lack of discipline of the troops, made every one shudder.

Next morning Major Selim Matera assumed the supreme command without opposition, and his first act was to keep the promise he had already given. Having called together the officers, he proposed that the Pasha, together with the doctor, should be sent to Wadelai, which was approved, the news being communicated to the civil functionaries *pro forma*.

At noon a commission of officers announced their approval of the measures to Emin Pasha, and the guard at the entrance of the house was removed. On the morning of the next day, that is, November 17, Emin, with military honours and a salvo of artillery, boarded the steamer which was to convey us to Wadelai.

CHAPTER XI.

CROCODILE HUNTING.

Bows and kissing of the hand—The crocodile hunter—The Bari of Bedden —The Dinka's whistling—The clerk Taib—A difficult position must not be attacked openly—Proposed abandonment of Wadelai—Yussuf Fahmi's mother-in-law—At Fagongo—Arrival of the steamer *Khedive*— Mahdists' discomfiture at Dufilé—Injunctions to the Pasha to return to Wadelai—Emin's refusal—Major Selim Matera's letter—Mahdist dollars— Evacuation of Dufilé—Captain Solyman—His death—Emin's fears—I do not agree with him—Lieutenant Saleh—Indignant revolutionists—The two factions—Execution of chief Sunga—His corpse on the shore—Kolikio and Katto—King Chua madly enraged—A slaughtered child—A black bullock and a girl twelve years old—The Lur of the mountain—Boki is dead—Funeral ceremonies—Proclamation of the successor—Raids of the Unyoro—Emin an ornithologist—Jephson a hunter—Emin will not leave Tunguru—Stanley's return—His letter to Jephson—Emin left to himself— Jephson and Emin write to the chief of the troops at Wadelai—Jephson's departure—I advise Emin to take time—What an imprudence would cost us.

ON the arrival of the steamer at Wadelai the people rushed to the landing and showed their satisfaction by loud and prolonged cheers. It was a triumph due to the victor. The authorities, clothed in white, bowing before the Pasha, kissing his hand, and murmuring words of thanks, joined the procession. Saluted by the troops who lined the road, and by discharges of artillery, Emin, more astonished than affected at such expressions of respect and affection, went to his residence, where he was compelled to receive the homage of officers and employés. After the cheering ceased, and while I was going up the hill to the station very slowly, owing to a pain in one of my legs, which I had suffered from since the last days of my stay in Dufilé, I met the good Hassan, the superstitious Turk, the provider of amulets for protection from lions and crocodiles. He began a long panegyric on the Pasha, with which he loudly mixed vulgar insults to the Dufilé agitators.

"Do you know, Hassan," I said, in order to interrupt his speech, which was not agreeable to me, "that the crocodile which bit off the leg of Mahmoud Tiki-Tiki, the clerk, has been captured and killed?"

"I heard of it, and was very glad."

"It was caught by the courageous Bari of Bedden."

"Clever fellows, they did it by some secret which I do not know, nevertheless I would undertake to do the same."

He then repeated to me an endless category of impossible sorceries, to which I listened in silence till we reached the top of the hill, where I wished him good-bye.

"I am in a hurry," said I. "Good-bye, I am going to the Pasha's. We shall have plenty of time to talk, as I shall stay some time at Wadelai."

Mahmoud-Ahmed, nicknamed Tiki-Tiki on account of his short stature, was an Egyptian, who acted as secretary to the commander of the Kirri station. When the revolution began in the Province he went to Dufilé on some official business, where, one morning, whilst he was bathing in the river, a crocodile assailed and dragged him amongst the papyri and grass.

The Bari people hunt these voracious amphibia, and a few days after this misfortune they were gratified by the capture of a very large crocodile, inside of which was found the leg of its victim.

The island of Bedden is inhabited by a small tribe of Bari, whose traditional prerogative is to hunt crocodiles. They feed exclusively on the flesh and

CROCODILE HUNTING. 195

eggs of the animal, and by ancient custom enjoy exemption from paying tribute, and from serving as soldiers to the native chiefs or to the Government of the Province. They never practise their art without the previous consent of the chief of the locality.

The way in which they always succeed in their enterprise is surprising. The hunters, properly posted on the banks of the river, gesticulating and throwing

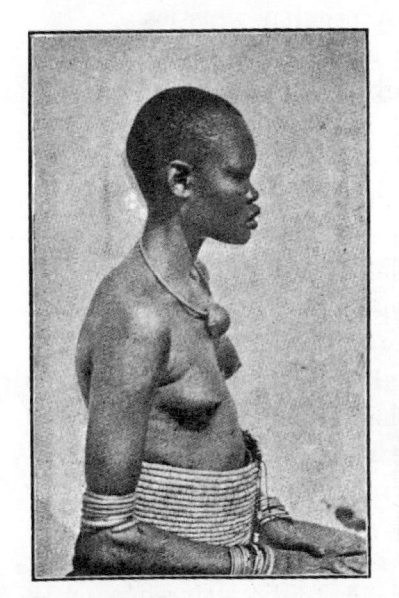

BARI WOMEN.

grain on the water, pronounce, with a loud voice, and in monotonous rhythm, the words appropriate to the ceremony. The crocodile, endowed with very sharp sight, leaves its hiding-place and gradually approaches the shore, at first timidly showing its nose, then its head. Some of the hunters then get cautiously into the river, and, approaching the creature at its sides, rapidly throw a rope with a noose over its head and round its neck. Immediately all precipitate themselves into the river, and, without giving their prey time to resist, they drag him out of the water and kill him on the shore.

I was told that ten crocodiles had been captured in this manner at Dufilé, and two at Wadelai. Whatever the impression that the hunters make upon the reptile may be, it is certain that they attract its attention, and prevent its perceiving the approaching danger.

There are also among the Dinka individuals able to draw snakes to their feet by peculiar whistles.

At the head of the disaffected people at Wadelai was an Arab named Taib, of a bad but resolute character, who at that time held the office of secretary to the commander of the station. He had taken a leading part in the rebellion of the Province, and had managed to make others accept his counsels, which were inspired by a spirit of intolerance and fanaticism.

He was one of the most dangerous men at that period, and it was necessary to place him in a position in which he would not be able to influence the course of affairs. Therefore, I had asked for and obtained from the commander of the Province in Dufilé an order for his dismissal and his arrest, which was put in force at once, but the scoundrel, at a banquet given by his friends and relatives, laid his right hand on the Koran, and solemnly, as a man about to die, uttered a curse devoting Emin, Hassan, Jephson, Marco the Greek merchant, and myself to death. So great an honour certainly deserved more than the passing notice we bestowed on it. To be away from Dufilé meant freedom for us. Wadelai was the first halt on the road to Kavalli on the lake; it was no longer impossible to overtake the Relief Expedition. I used to say, " A situation made difficult by restrained passions must not be attacked openly, but one must rather study, with prudence, how to turn matters to one's own

A BARI VILLAGE.

advantage, and to be always on the look out and know how to seize propitious opportunities, which never fail to present themselves."

All questions, owing to the Oriental character, present themselves in a pompous form, and, divested of this false appearance, spontaneously show their vulnerable side. Difficulties at first perceived fade away, the cowardice of boasters is always defeated by the patient steadfastness of a strong mind. A good intelligence department, moderation towards adversaries, and actions that are able to inspire and maintain the confidence of friends, will always rule men and events.

No steamer arrived, and no news from Dufilé. Thus we reached the 4th of December 1888.

During that night Lieutenant Amat arrived from Bora, a Shooli village on the right bank of the Nile, where he had been staying several days on a journey for the requisition of corn. He related how the chief of the tribe had urged him to go to Wadelai because Fabo* had been assailed and taken by the Mahdi's hordes, who, with the assistance of the natives, were even now surrounding Dufilé.

The funeral bell was tolling. Most probably Dufilé had already fallen into the hands of the enemy, and, availing himself of the two steamers, he might appear before Wadelai much sooner than we wished. The station was not sufficiently fortified for defence against a serious attack ; the surrounding land was not suited for successful combats ; the storehouses were deficient in corn ; water had to be brought from the river ; there was no choice : we had to give up every idea of resistance and march to Tunguru, keeping on the heights.

* A new station at two days' journey from Dufilé, where the garrison of Fatiko (abandoned on account of the King of Unyoro's hostilities) was concentrated.

The proposal of retreat was confusedly voted, with the usual unwilling and stupid protestations of sacrifice from those who (as it always happens) would have been the first to set the example of flight.

The iron boat was sunk after having been made unfit for use. The ammunition of the magazine was distributed among the soldiers, whilst the furniture and provisions that could not be carried away were abandoned. Early in the morning of the next day the exodus began, without order or discipline. About nine o'clock a rumour spread through the long column of soldiers that the boats bearing the Government flag had arrived at Wadelai. The column stopped, soldiers and many officials returned, while we encamped near a torrent, and next morning left for Fagongo, not far from the Nile. During the night some boys were sent to search for the old, sick mother-in-law of a clerk named Yussuf Fahmi, who had been forsaken by the servants accompanying her, but only her corpse was found; she had been stabbed with lances by the Lur natives.

The steamer *Khedive* was signalled by some armed youths of the vanguard, and shortly after she stopped in an inlet of the river near the village. An officer landed, who told us that the Mahdists, assisted by the natives of Muggi and Laboré, had been fighting for three days against Dufilé, and had entered the station from whence they had formerly been driven away.

On the 28th of November 1888, they had been compelled to take a hasty flight, leaving on the ground many dead and wounded, The officer added that a detachment of soldiers had pursued them, killing all who lingered behind.

Owing, however, to the almost complete exhaustion of ammunition, the abandonment of Dufilé and the mustering of the troops at Wadelai was decided upon.

The officer then requested the Pasha to comply with the order, of which he was the bearer, to return to Wadelai, where the reorganisation of the Government of the Province would be discussed at a general assembly. A long and animated discussion ensued, at the conclusion of which the officer yielded to the firm resolution of Emin to proceed to Tunguru, and consented to make for the lake.

The following letter from the commanding officer at Dufilé to Emin sums up the movements of the Mahdists and their operations against Dufilé :—

"To His Excellency Mohammed Emin Pasha, Governor-General of the Equatorial Province.

"The garrisons of Muggi and Laboré were concentrated at this station on the 18th of November, as well as a few soldiers of the 1st battalion; in all, one hundred and twenty men. On the morning of the 24th, I sent Lieutenant Bachit Aga Mohammed to reconnoitre the locality occupied by the Mahdists, and at about eleven o'clock A.M. I received a message from him informing me that the enemy were encamped near the river Tin, at three hours and a half journey from Dufilé. In the evening when he returned to the station he confirmed the news.

"During the night a letter from Omar Saleh, the commander of the Mahdi's troops, was delivered to me, in which he called on us to surrender and lay down our arms. In the same letter he informed us of the death of Hamed Aga Mohammed, commander of our soldiers, of Captains Abd-el-Waab, Ali Aga, Salem Effendi Halaf, and of secretary Hassan Effendi Latif, in the fight near Rejaf. He ended his letter thus :—

"'If you do not surrender at once, I will come and make you.'

" We did not think it advisable to answer this epistle, but committed it to the flames.

" The enemy appeared in the neighbourhood of this station on the morning of the 25th inst., and at about four o'clock P.M., notified his arrival by a letter, that was burnt by the soldiers of the outer guard, in which he said that they would compel us to surrender.

" About nine o'clock on the morning of the 26th, the Mahdists opened fire on the station and continued until three o'clock P.M., when they were driven away by a company of soldiers, who made a sortie and inflicted on them a loss of twelve killed and several wounded. Thank God, our troops did not sustain any damage.

" During the night of the 27th, our enemies attacked the station with a brisk and intense fire, to which at about four o'clock A.M. I replied. At daybreak, the assailants made a rush on the part towards the gardens, and succeeded in penetrating into the station, and attacking the steamers, killing Mohammed Ali el Nagiar, captain of the *Nyanza*, the engineer Ali Ahmed, Mergian Derar the pilot, and Faragialla Moru the stoker; all these died on the *Khedive*.

" On account of this serious assault, part of our soldiers were detached from the fight towards the north side, and, under the command of Captain Bachit Aga Bargut, faced the audacious invaders. The fight lasted till eight A.M., when the enemy, discomfited on all sides, slackened his fire and shortly afterwards retreated. We counted 210 dead, but there were certainly many more killed, besides the great number of wounded who were carried away by their comrades.

" Eleven flags fell into our hands, among which was the chief's, a silken one; we seized also a great number of Remingtons and muzzle-loaders, a number of swords and lances, and one prisoner.

" The soldiers were rejoiced at their victory, which was celebrated with military honours paid to the Vice-regal flag.

" Thursday passed without any event, the enemies limiting their action to demonstrations with a few shots.

" At seven o'clock P.M. of the same day, the soldiers arrived from Fabo station ; an hour later, a Bari negro, previously captured by the Mahdists, but who had succeeded in escaping, came to tell us that, owing to their heavy losses, the enemies were retiring towards Rejaf.

" At dawn on Friday morning, a message from Lieutenant Abd-el-Bein Aga Shialai informed us of the flight of the Mahdists during the night, news which was confirmed at nine o'clock by a soldier who had remained at Laboré.

" I ordered the soldiers from Fabo to cross the river in the boat, and go to the last camp occupied by the Mahdi's troops, where they found many killed and wounded rebels, who are to be added to the figures already given. Our soldiers returned here (after having killed all the wounded Mahdists) with several cases of ammunition left by the enemies in their camp.

" In the night of the 30th, a soldier, the servant of the late Major Rehan Aga Ibrahim, arrived ; on being questioned, he told us that he had come with the expedition from Khartoum, and that all that we had already been told was true. He added that the enemies' force was lessened, and that they could not attempt a new assault. Later on I sent some of the dragomen of the station as far as the torrent Abd-el-Aziz, where they found some bags containing clothes, and the bayonet of a Remington rifle.

FACSIMILE OF SELIM MATERA'S LETTER.

LETTER FROM DUFILÉ. 203

FACSIMILE OF SELIM MATERA'S LETTER.

"Fatelmula, a soldier belonging to the Muggi garrison, who had been made prisoner by the Mahdists at the Rejaf fight, has returned to the station.

"He relates that the Mahdi's troops were in great despair, and hurried on their march. Their number did not exceed 150, of which from time to time some fell on the road. In their retreat they had set fire to the Government stations of Ayu, Laboré, and Muggi.

"I send this letter, as is my duty, to inform your Excellency of these events, and you will highly honour me by reading it.

"Major SELIM MATERA.

"*December* 2, 1888.

"P.S.—The chief clerks and the Cadi are among the dead."

In the booty taken from the camp of the assailants and from the dead, our Dufilé soldiers found, besides a great quantity of garments, leather bags in the shape of belts filled with silver coins. Amongst many *medjidie* dollars, a few coins struck at Khartoum by the Mahdi's Government were found. These, which were of the ordinary size of a dollar, had on one side : " Struck at Omdurman, III year;" and on the other side : " Current coin, Mohammed Ahmed, the Mahdi, year 1304."* Fear lends wings, therefore the evacuation of Dufilé was speedily effected ; quite an unusual thing with the people of the Province. Families were first collected at Wadelai, whence they were sent by degrees to Tunguru and Msua. The removal was accomplished without grave inconvenience, but it was deplorable that the

---

* Durub fi um Omdurman, senet talata; Macbul Mohammed Ahmed el Mahdi, Senet 1304.

DEATH OF CAPTAIN SOLYMAN.

granaries of the stations were without wheat, which, under the circumstances, was more than ever needed.

On the 16th of December 1888, Captain Solyman was carried to Tunguru, seriously wounded in his right leg during the battle at Dufilé.

Report said that the bullet which wounded him did not come from the enemy's rifles—his soldiers hated him for his overbearing and arbitrary acts, and their justice is often cruel.

Emin, with his characteristic professional charity, attended him, but science and care were of no avail;

COINS OF THE MAHDI.

the unlucky man died on the night of the 29th, without the comfort of seeing regret felt for him; and leaving very few affectionate remembrances.

On the evening of his death, Emin, coming from the house, whither I had accompanied him for his usual visit, told me that his patient's end was imminent.

" Are you going to trouble your mind about that?" said I.

" Yes, for two reasons; the first being that, as I have attended him, evil-minded people will accuse me of having caused his death; the second reason is, that we are about to lose a man who might have been useful to us in our circumstances, especially on Stanley's arrival."

"I understand the first of your reasons. As to the loss we are going to sustain, I am not of your opinion; on the contrary, I consider his misfortune will be to our advantage. I am inclined to call his a providential death. This man, with his violent character—with neither respect nor consideration for anybody—would be a serious impediment on the day when Stanley's arrival will compel our prompt departure for Kavalli. Do not forget that he was one of the first to rebel."

"But he repented, and made himself useful to us at Dufilé."

"It is true. But he did so only because he was compelled by Selim Matera and myself, when we made him understand the isolation to which his friend Fatelmula would probably be reduced."

"Well, why should he now change his mind?"

"For the sole reason that the perils which formerly alarmed the factious have disappeared; the war has ended with a victory, and the Government of the rebels claims the merit of it. Besides, I will say further, that he would never have been induced to return to Egypt, and therefore would not have allowed you to go, lest you should ask the Viceroy to avenge the insults you have suffered."

"But in his place we shall have an officer selected from amongst my worst enemies."

"Let us hope not; and endeavour to prevent it. Selim Matera will do us this favour also."

And in fact Lieutenant Saleh, whom everybody used to call "the madman," from his eccentricity, but who was, after all, a good-hearted man and a good soldier, full of respect for the Pasha, was appointed commander of the Tunguru station. Amongst the victims of this war was Captain Ahmed Assuti, who died at Wadelai from his wounds, lamented for his military qualities. He was struck by a bullet whilst heroically fighting for the defence of Dufilé ; he would not, however, withdraw from the battle-field until a second wound in his head disabled him.

The insurrectional committee would not recognise the authority of Major Selim Matera, who was therefore compelled to confine Major Hawashi at Wadelai, instead of at Tunguru, as previously arranged.

The dismissal of the Governor was approved and confirmed at a meeting, when, to the reasons already brought forward at the general assembly at Dufilé in September, there was added the accusation of his opprobrious abandonment of Wadelai station, and the destruction of those magazines. Consequently, a petition was signed by nine officers and officials, in which the chief of the Province was requested to order that Emin Pasha should be put in chains, and brought before the Khedivial tribunals, and that the doctor, Jephson, Marco, and myself should be hanged for having incited the troops to abandon Wadelai, on purpose to cause the ruin of the soldiers who were at Dufile. They claimed also that judgments should not be pronounced according to law, but should be given by religious authority, and that successions and guardianships should be ruled in accordance with the sacred principles of the Koran. Major Selim opposed these wild pretensions, and attempted to put a stop to the want of discipline and licentiousness that daily assumed greater proportions. He suggested that, when Dufilé had been abandoned and burnt down, a general assembly at Wadelai should discuss the definitive constitution of the country, and the departure for Egypt of those willing to leave the Province. But the germs of discord troubled all minds. The wisest among them joined the Major, and if they did not desire that Emin should return to power, they were at least firm in the opinion that the country ought to be abandoned. This party was formed by the majority of the officers, and by a good number of Egyptian and Coptic clerks.

The opposition party was composed of a few Egyptian and Soudanese officers, some clerks and many Donagla, with Captain Fatelmula at their head. Those who were most compromised in the rebellion were firm in their resolution not to leave the Province.

The insurrection of the month of August had hastened the ruin of the Province, which had been for several years in a disorderly and dangerous condition. Nothing was to be hoped from a wise and moderate form of government; everything depended on fortune and its favours.

On July 16, 1888, the chief Sunga, who had been in prison for a long time, accused of being in secret intelligence with the King of Unyoro to the injury of the Government of the Province, was put to death and his body thrown into the lake. Sunga's relatives and the whole tribe of Lur were much grieved at being deprived of the corpse of the "great rain-maker," to whom they decreed solemn funeral honours. The sacrifices performed, and the occult practices suggested by the superstition of the people on that occasion, were crowned with success; and it was believed to be a miracle when, three days after death, and in consequence of a storm that made the lake rough, the waves deposited the corpse on the shore, by the road that the water-carriers in attendance at his former house usually followed.

Great and solemn were the honours paid him, and his venerated name increased the hatred of the people for the foreign domination, which weighed upon the country tyrannically, and caused all hopes to turn to the powerful King of Unyoro. About this time Kolikio and Katto, of the Boki people, were denounced by their own chief, as secret agents of King Chua. He did so to save himself from certain condemnation. They were accused, brought to Wadelai, and there barbarously put to death. The king was very angry at the offence thus given to him, and meditated vengeance, incited by his mother, who venerated Sunga as a friend of her late husband; he was urged on also by the Madundi, offended at Chua's betrayal by Boki, their fellow-countryman. His never extinguished hatred for the Egyptian domination increased, and again engaged his attention. Once more watching the dissensions about to blaze forth in Wadelai, and the imminent division of the military forces starting for the south, he counted his allies, alarmed the timid, encouraged the perplexed, mustered his soldiers, and waited, trusting in his star, which his father's spirit promised him would shine with a new light. One of the ritual customs of the populations on the coast of the Albert Lake, is that every enterprise must be preceded by human sacrifices, both to ensure its success and as a defiance to the adversary they mean to strike. In the night of the 9th of January 1889, a child was immolated and left on the boundary of the chief Boki's dwelling, and on the following night a black bullock and a girl, twelve years old, were killed (by cutting their throats), and buried on the confines of the territory of Attikende, Sunga's successor, near the Tunguru military station. The news of the funereal augury was at once spread over the country, and reached the mountains. The chiefs Okello, Boki, and Attikende were sadly impressed by them. The mountaineers of Okuza revolted and surrounded the troops, who were making a raid there for wheat, under the orders of Lieutenant Saleh. But Attikende, vigilant for his own safety, immediately brought the news of the impending disaster. A reinforcement of soldiers was despatched, and, rushing on the assailants, liberated the officer from his dangerous position, and spread discouragement and fear among the mountaineers.

The morning of the 20th found Boki dead, and his friends ascribed his pitiful end to the inexorable hand of the King of Unyoro. Thirsting for revenge, the relatives of the deceased bound an eastern Magungo, whom they found in the village, with ropes, and after having declared him a sorcerer, on the strength of some magical proofs, beat him to death.

Boki's death was not made known until the third day, as prescribed by their customs. The chiefs of the neighbouring territories and his friends assemble at his house to present condolences as to a sick person. In the meantime the corpse has been tightly wrapped up in cloth made of bark, and then put into an ox-skin sack. This package is then exposed to the heat and smoke of a continual and even fire, in order to dry the bag and its contents. Should the bad smell be too strong, the bag may be enclosed in a second, third, and fourth skin, but their number must not exceed ten, as prescribed by the custom of the country. After a certain number of days, varying in accordance with the political condition of the country, the prince's death is solemnly announced. The ceremony of tears and shrieks then begins, which is prolonged to satiety, and finally they proceed to bury the corpse. The son who succeeds the deceased in power, immolates an ox on the grave, with his own hand, and his tears being then dried, he seats himself on a palanquin, and amidst shouts of joy is proclaimed chief of the country and carried to his abode. The festivals of the ascension to power have a longer or shorter duration, according to the importance of the principality and the quantity of beer and provisions devoted to consumption.

Such are the customary funeral ceremonies of princes of secondary importance in the countries bordering on the Albert Lake, differing from the honours paid to a king, whose much grander and more solemn ceremonies are accompanied by the infamous and atrocious custom of burying the living in the grave and immolating human victims.

Not long after Boki's death the country was devastated by the hordes of King Chua, who set fire to the chief's residence, and carried many women and children into slavery. A great many soldiers hastened to the spot from Wadelai to check the boldness of the invaders, but, owing to their delay in coming, the assailants had already retreated to the opposite side of the Nile when the troops arrived.

The bands from Unyoro also announced their presence by frequent raids in the southern regions of the lake. Babedongo invaded the Katonzi country, and, having seized a large booty of oxen and women, took up his position at Kieya. The King of Unyoro prepared for a decisive battle, and, like a clever guerilla, kept up agitation, and spread alarm at intervals in the several regions near the lake, until the day on which the departure of some of the garrison troops should have weakened the Government, and made the country an easy prey to his ambition; thus fulfilling the plans of conquest dreamed of for so many years.

Emin was again devoting himself to his favourite pursuit of ornithological collections, which, although much admired and praised in Europe, contributed to give rise to discouraging opinions about his care for the public administration. But he was then free from any responsibility, and could give his whole time to study—a pleasant relief from the troubles of his heart and mind. Jephson had become a sportsman, and was so delighted with the prey that he gathered every day, that he forgot the safety of his legs, which were covered with numerous wounds, the stings of insects.

Occasionally the proposal to leave Tunguru for Msua was discussed and energetically sustained by Jephson, especially after Shukri, the commanding officer at Msua, had made the generous offer (perhaps beyond his power) to send the porters and escort of soldiers required for our removal. But Emin repeatedly and emphatically declared his intention not to move till Stanley arrived. Perhaps the reason that influenced him was a just one; both from the uncertainty of the return of the Expedition, and from his natural repugnance to present himself at Msua deprived, though wrongly, of all power and authority. Emin despatched Mogo to chief Mpigwa with letters for Stanley, and shortly afterwards he (Mogo) sent the news of Stanley's presence in the country. On the 26th of January 1889, letters from the commander of the Relief Expedition for Emin and Jephson reached Tunguru. Stanley's terms were harsh. He allowed us twenty days to join him, with the warning that at the end of that time he would start for the south. He gave a most painful description of the condition in which he had found the rear column; and the errors of others as well as his own, he, in dictatorial style, threw back upon our poor persons.

I quote what follows from Stanley's letter to Jephson, which I copy from his work, *Emin Pasha: The Rebellion at the Equator*, p. 389, by A. J. Mounteney-Jephson.

We separated from the Pasha on the 23rd May last, with the understanding that in about two months you, with or without the Pasha, would start for Fort Bodo with sufficient porters to take the goods at the fort and convey them to the Nyanza.

* * * * * *

We somewhat doubted if his affairs would permit the Pasha's absence, but we were assured you would not remain inactive.

It was also understood that the Pasha would erect a small station on Nyamsassie Island as a provision depot, in order that our Expedition might find means of subsistence on arrival at the lake.

Eight months have elapsed and not one single promise has been performed.

* * * * * *

The rear column, which on our departure from Yambuya numbered 271 all told, was a mere wreck. Major Barttelot was dead, had been shot with a gun by one of Tippoo Tib's Manyuema, on the morning of the 21st of July. Mr. Jameson had departed on the 23rd July for Stanley Falls, and a letter dated August 12th, five days before my arrival at Banalya, states that he was about descending the Congo river for Bangala; but the couriers who brought his letter to us stoutly asserted his last intentions were to go down to Banana Point. Mr. Herbert Ward had been sent to Bangala, and finally to St. Paulo de Loanda. He had returned and reached Bangala with letters, instructions from the committee, but was detained there by order of Major Barttelot.

Mr. John Rose Troup had been invalided home in June 1888. So no one was left with the wreck of the rear column except William Bonny, who is now with me in this camp.

One hundred Soudanese, Zanzibaris, and Somalies had been buried at Yambuya; thirty-three men were left at Yambuya, helpless and dying, and fourteen of these died later on; twenty-six deserted.

So that when I saw Bonny and his people, the rear column, Zanzibaris, Somalies, and Soudanese, numbered 102, all told, out of 271, and only one officer out of five! Besides this deplorable record, the condition of the stores was just as bad. Out of 660 loads—65lb. each—there remained only 230 loads, of 65lb. weight. All my personal clothing, except hats, boots, one flannel jacket, a cap, and three pairs of drawers, had been sent down to Bangala because rumour had stated I was dead, and the advance party gone to the dogs; a remnant of thirty, however, had managed to escape to Ujiji!!!

* * * * * *

The difficulties I met at Banalya are repeated to-day near the Albert Lake, and nothing can save us now from being overwhelmed by them but a calm and clear decision. If I had hesitated at Banalya very likely I should still be there waiting for Jameson and Ward, with my own men dying by dozens from sheer inanition.

* * * * * *

Are the Pasha, Casati, and yourself to share the same fate? If you are still victims of indecision, then a long good-night to you all; but while I retain my senses, I must save my Expedition. You may be saved also if you are wise.

* * * * * *

The first instalment of relief was handed to Emin Pasha on or about May 1st, 1888. The second final instalment of relief is at this camp with us, ready for delivery at any place the Pasha designates, or to any person charged by the Pasha to receive it. If the Pasha fails to receive it, or to decide what shall be done with it, I must then decide briefly what I must do.

Our second object in coming here was to receive such at our camp as were disposed to leave Africa; our Expedition has no further business in these regions, and will at once retire.

Try and understand what all this means. Try and see the utter and final abandonment of all further relief, and the bitter end and fate of those obstinate and misguided people who decline assistance when tendered to them. From May 1, 1888, to January 1889, are nine months—so long a time to consider a simple proposition of leaving Africa or staying here!

Therefore in the official and formal letters accompanying this explanatory note to you, I designate Kavalli's village as the rendezvous where I am willing to receive those desirous of leaving Africa, subject, of course, to any new light thrown upon the complication by a personal interview, or a second letter from you.

And now I address myself to you personally. If you consider yourself still a member of the Expedition, subject to my orders, then, upon receipt of this letter you will at once leave for Kavalli's, with such of my men, Binza, and the three Soudanese, as are willing to obey you, and bring me the final decision of Emin Pasha and Signor Casati respecting their personal intentions.

* * * * * *

I understand that the Pasha has been deposed, and is a prisoner. Who, then, is to communicate with me respecting what has to be done? I have no authority to receive communications from officers' mutineers. It was Emin Pasha and his people I was supposed to relieve. If Emin Pasha were dead, then to his lawful successor in authority. Emin Pasha being alive, I can receive no communications from any other person unless he be designated by the Pasha. Therefore, the Pasha, if he be unable to come in person to me at Kavalli's with a sufficient escort of faithful men, or be able to appoint some person authorised to receive this relief, it will remain for me to destroy the ammunition so laboriously brought here, and return home.

You must understand that my people are only porters. They have performed their contract with me with a fidelity unexampled; and having brought the boat and goods here, their duty is ended. You have been pleased to destroy the boat, and have injured us irreparably by doing so.

I presume the two cases of Winchester ammunition left with the Pasha are lost also.

I ought to mention also that the people at the Ituri ferry camp are almost all sick, and will be unable to move for at least a month.

And also I have brought with me about 100 Manyema, with 42 of whom I have contracted to pay a tusk of ivory to each for 42 loads they have brought here for Emin Pasha.

Therefore, to satisfy them I require 42 tusks of ivory to pay them. Please consider how this can be done to their satisfaction.

Finally, if the Pasha's people are desirous of leaving this part of Africa, and settle in some country not far remote from here, or anywhere bordering the Nyanza (Victoria), or along the route to Zanzibar, I am perfectly ready to assist, besides escorting those who wish to go home to Cairo safely. But I must have clear and definite assertions, followed by promptitude, according to such orders as I shall give for effecting this purpose; or a clear and definite refusal, as we cannot stay here all our lives awaiting people who seem to be not very clear as to what they wish.

I describe in Jephson's own words the impression made upon us by the above letters, and by another addressed to Emin, an exclusively official one:

We had been looking for Stanley's arrival, and were hoping if the worst came to the worst he would, with his augmented strength, be able to extricate Emin by force, if necessary; but instead of being strengthened he had a tale to tell of deaths and disaster only.

The chief of the Expedition, anxious ab miserable condition to which the rear colur reduced, both with regard to men and provisions, and forgetful of the primary reason, proclaimed *urbi et orbi*, of Emin's liberation, declared that it was impossible for him to achieve it; sent an ultimatum of limited time, not very courteously worded, and certain that Emin would go to him, should a ray of hope shine, amidst such misfortunes, speculated on Emin's sad condition. He recalled Jephson, and abandoned Emin to himself, either because he would not or could not risk anything for his safety.

Jephson wrote a letter to the head of the provisional Government, rather to inform him that he had been commissioned to bring forty-two elephant tusks than to announce Stanley's arrival. Emin in an epistle to Major Selim Matera sent the news of Stanley's arrival, and, whilst requesting that steamers might be sent to convey him to Were, advised him to send a deputation of officers to Stanley, and positively declared that, for the moment and till the arrival of the officers from Wadelai, he should not leave Tunguru.

On January 28, 1889, after having overcome some difficulties made by the steamer's crew, Jephson left for Msua. Next morning he was greatly surprised to find that the *Khedive* had left for Tunguru, and he was, therefore, obliged to cross the lake to Were, in a native boat, procured by the commander of the station. He had left us with the firm conviction that we should never meet again. To the last moment he had insisted on Emin accompanying him; but this time I was gratified to see my advice accepted " that no inconsiderate step should be taken," but that the course of events should be watched; that firmness and confidence should rule every action, and that the word he had given, that he would not move until he had conferred with the officers who were to arrive from Wadelai must be kept. "It will be a matter of a few days, but I promise you to take the Pasha to Stanley," I said to Jephson, at his departure. It is certain that, had we accepted the strange proposal of leaving with Jephson, the Pasha's departure would have been prevented at any cost, and that Jephson would have never dared to disobey Stanley's imperious order. As to myself, it is true that nobody would have opposed my departure, as I was only a visitor in the Province, but Emin's position having been made more difficult I should have considered myself bound not to take advantage of my independence. Then through a culpable imprudence and hasty resolution, the way of our ulterior redemption would have been closed for ever. In order to avoid being driven to ruin, it was important for us to choose a wise and prudent mode of action, that would lead to the accomplishment of our wishes. The advice of the great poet was a light and guide to us:

"'Grapple that,'
Said he, 'but first make proofs if it be such
As will sustain thee.'"—DANTE, *Inferno*, Canto 24.

CHAPTER XII.

STANLEY'S MANIFESTO.

News of the arrival of Stanley—Departure from Wadelai—Nomination of a commission to be sent to the head of the Expedition—Refusal of Emin Pasha—New perils—The means of avoiding them—Proposal accepted by Emin—The opinion of the officers of the Province asked—Departure for Msua—New intrigues—Emin concedes a pardon and amnesty—Selim Bey—The voyage to Were—Osman Latif—His equivocal conduct—He throws himself into the river—" You should have left this carrion to be drowned!"—Always the same—Counsels given to Emin—Emin shares my opinion—Emin goes to Stanley's camp—William Bonny—Danger of being assailed by the troops of the King of Unyoro—Bonny sent "not to fight, but to bring over the luggage"—Return of Emin to Were—Colonel Fatelmula and his menaces—Impression of the officers after their visit to Stanley—Letter from Stanley to the officers at Wadelai—Advice given to Emin—Difficulties of the situation—Flight of soldiers and servants—Departure of Vita Hassan—The road from Were to Buguera—Arrival at the encampmment of the Relief Expedition.

THE news of the arrival of Stanley did not excite much animation in the discussions at the camp of Wadelai. Officers and employés, soldiers and servants, were all prostrated by the violent shock that the recent invasion had given to the strength of the Government. They had conquered the enemy, but the victory had absorbed all the resources of defence of which the country could still dispose. It had also increased the boldness of the natives, always ready to profit by the recent weakness of the conquerors, and to enter into open warfare against them. The desire to return to Egypt, and the want of ammunition, however, united the two opposing factions in one sole interest. Those who had decided to leave, no less than those to whom the idea of leaving the country was not pleasing, hailed with joy the return of the Relief Expedition.

There arose, however, a difficulty: that of entering into communication with Stanley. But this also disappeared when the Pasha spontaneously offered to become, in a certain manner, their intermediary in the relations that must take place. Fully assured of finding no obstacles to the execution of their programme, the most influential men did not delay in agreeing to the nomination of a commission, composed of six officers, who were ordered to assemble at Tunguru, and proceed to Stanley's camp under the ægis of Emin Pasha.

But when Major Selim Matera waited on Emin to beseech him to assist the representatives of the Province and to facilitate their intercourse with Stanley, the Pasha resolutely refused to accede to their request. Appointed to the Government of the Province by the Viceroy, he could not wrong his own dignity, and injure the authority of the legitimate Government, by thus recognising the work of rebellion, and still less could he lend himself to the office of an irresponsible interpreter, as they foolishly asked him to become. In face of such an unexpected refusal, the officers were at a loss to whom to apply. They knew that if they presented themselves in Stanley's camp alone they would not be admitted to confer with the leader of the Expedition. Disputes were renewed with vigour, void of sense and result. The greater number agreed to give up the project; some seemed disposed instead to excite public opinion against the Pasha for interfering with their incontestable rights to the help sent by the Viceroy. The submission of the first, and the possible success of the intrigues of the latter and more daring, gave cause to fear that new complications might arrive which it was most desirable to avoid, so that the much longed for hope of escape might not be lost.

If Emin, in his humiliated condition, caused by the rebellion of his officials, secretly nourished any desire to avenge his injuries, he was unable to carry it out from want of energy and courage; and he also retained for his followers, from habit as well as tenderness of sentiment, a good deal of affection.

To profit by this state of the Pasha's mind, and make him cut the Gordian knot, did not appear to me difficult, nor did I judge it to be improper, could we arrange matters so as not to offend either his susceptibility or his dignity.

I explained my idea frankly to Emin. I pointed out to him the new perils to which we might be exposed, and the vain hope of any probable aid from Stanley, and concluded that the only expedient presenting any hope of success was that he should resume the reins of government. Although not confident of success, but impelled by a sense of ambition to reinstate himself in his former office, he seemed disposed to direct prudent efforts to the purpose. It was not difficult to find adherents to the proposal, especially amongst those who intended to abandon Equatoria and return to Egypt. But when the project was presented to the assembly for discussion, the usual reservations and doubts arose again, and it was decided that the officers and employés residing at Wadelai should be consulted about it. Delay was advised and accepted; but whilst awaiting their reply, considering the limited period conceded by the chief of the Expedition, it was decided to start for Msua. This was a step in the right direction, and we hailed the decision with joy.

In that furthermost station of Equatoria were assembled the greater part of the families of the officers and civil employés, especially Egyptian, who had gone there on abandoning Dufilé. These were desirous of profiting by the invitation of the Viceroy to go to Egypt, and lamented the delay that was interposed to their departure, rendered necessary as it was by the scarcity of food, which was quite inadequate to the wants of the great number of persons in that little station.

In agreement with Major Selim Matera, a man of moderate mind and serious disposition, it was proposed, in a numerous and influential assembly, that the project postponed at Tunguru should be slightly modified in presence of the pressing necessity of no longer delaying to send a deputation to Stanley's camp, and that those who had decided to return to Egypt (realising the duty of being united under the orders of their Governor) should humble themselves to ask his pardon for the deplorable actions of which the Province had been for many months the theatre, and pray him to resume his former functions as the only legitimate representative of his Highness the Viceroy.

There were no discussions, and the act was approved and signed by all who were at the station. It was therefore settled that a copy of the resolution should be sent to Tunguru and Wadelai, requesting at the same time the adhesion of all those who intended to profit by the invitation sent by the Khedive. On the 9th of February 1889, Emin resumed the direction of affairs. He raised Selim Matera to the rank of lieutenant-colonel, appointing him Vice-Governor, and decreed other promotions as the recompense of the acts of valour of the officers who had fought at Dufilé.

Having then given the principal orders for evacuating the stations, Emin, some officers, and I embarked in the steamer direct for Were.

Osman Latif, recently promoted to the rank of

OSMAN LATIF.

major, was commanded to hasten the arrival of the

people at Msua, and subsequently to despatch them to the camp of concentration. This man had come into the Province about the end of 1882 as Vice-Governor. He had great experience in intrigues, and for about twenty years had held various offices under the administration of the Soudan—putting into his actions an apparent good nature and exaggerated respect, as well as a hypocritical appearance of religion. In consequence of a dispute occurring at Dufilé between himself and that commander, Emin had dismissed him from his office, and he had only lately been reinstated. During the imprisonment of Emin, Osman Latif's conduct—faithful to his principles—had been equivocal; while suggesting odious measures, without, having the courage to declare them openly in the assembly, he stealthily sent news and advice to the Pasha, thus seeking to win his friendship, and that of Jephson, in order to get from both, in due time, favourable declarations of his honesty and loyalty to the Government at Cairo. But there was a person who was aware of his double game, and reproached him bitterly for it, denouncing his deceitful conduct.

The rogue, at once perceiving the gravity of the situation, and pretending to be driven mad by the infamous calumny, was seized with a wild impulse to throw himself into the river. Some humane persons took him out, still trembling with convulsions, and brought him into the presence of the chief of the rebels, who said, in a tone of irony and contempt, "You should have left this carrion to be drowned. What was the use of saving him?" I was afterwards assured that Osman would not have been drowned, even had he remained all day in the river, for at the place he had selected, and where he threw himself on his knees, the water only reached his chin. Later on he said to

Fatelmula that he had the public good in view when feigning friendship for the Pasha, and he said just the same to Emin, when speaking of his suspected sympathy with the rebels; also in the duty entrusted to him at Msua by the Governor Osman Latif did all he could to retard the regular work of concentration.

During the journey, which lasted two days, being obliged to pass the night in a village of Lur, Emin and I had several long conversations on the line of conduct that it would be best to adopt. We were agreed as to the mode of judging of the situation, and our conclusions coincided. Nor could it have been otherwise, because they arose from facts which, being misrepresented, as they were later on, were ascribed either to a former programme, unknown to me, or to sudden fears, unsupported by cool reasoning.

The departure from the Province, and consequently our certain liberation, was a work for which we were not indebted to the Relief Expedition. The attainment of its aim had embittered the minds of the discontented in Equatoria; that is to say, of those who were firm in their decision not to move. It was, therefore, the duty of the Governor, and a debt of gratitude to Lieutenant-Colonel Selim Matera, and towards all who had, by the act of Msua, contributed to a good result, to take care of those men and their companions who intended to return to Egypt.

Emin also, by reason of his office, had to try with all his strength to satisfy the wishes of the Government at Cairo, and to watch over its interests.

To ensure the full execution of this task, it was necessary for the Governor to preserve his own independence until the caravan of his subordinates was organised for the journey. The situation of Were, on the shore of the lake—admirably adapted both for the calling of the steamers and for keeping up constant communication with the camp of the Relief Expedition at Kavalli—was pointed out as best fitted for the arrangements. Besides these essential reasons, there was another which merited serious consideration. It related to the character that public opinion attributed to Stanley, which would have made it difficult for him and Emin to agree. It was to be supposed that the chief of the Relief Expedition, according to the promises made to the Viceroy, would have postponed his departure until all were ready ; but in the event of his deciding to hasten the return, the number of guns that should have been available, and the ammunition which was to have been handed over by Stanley, would have been sufficient to protect the column in its long journey, and guarantee the necessary supply of food.

The mustering ordered by the Governor, assisted by his officers and employés, would have silenced the inevitable mistrust and friction arising from their direct dependence on European officers, speaking another language and accustomed to another style of discipline.

Our column once formed, the Governor could easily settle everything about the march to the coast with the chief of the Expedition.

These were our ideas of the situation, and, fully possessed by them, Emin and his officers started for Buguera on February 16, 1889, to visit Stanley. Four days later another plan would probably have been proposed and substituted for that chosen by Emin. On February 20, Mr. William Bonny arrived at the camp of Were, with thirty Zanzibaris and sixty-four native porters, to assist the Pasha's people in their removal to the camp at Buguera. Katonzi, chief of

Magala, who in the month of May of the previous year had concluded a friendly alliance with the Government, cemented by the exchange of blood brotherhood between himself and Captain Shukri, came in the night to tell me that Babedongo and Ireta, noted chiefs of the King of Unyoro, were near us at Kieya on a marauding expedition. They had already ravaged and devastated a large tract of country, and might shortly storm our camp.

The news might be exaggerated, but, as King Chua hated us, the tale was credible. A surprise would have been injurious, for we had but twenty guns and a limited supply of ammunition in the camp. I then went to Mr. Bonny, who had announced his intention of leaving the following morning, and, having told him of the information just received, I begged him to remain with us until I could send a letter to Emin at Stanley's camp, as the delay would allow the two steamers to arrive from Msua, whose position would be critical if we were found retreating to the hills, before superior numbers. With calm, icy serenity, Mr. Bonny declined to grant my request; talked of his responsibility, and said he could not take the liberty of altering the orders of his chief, who had sent him, "not to fight, but to bring over the luggage." I said no more, and he left early next morning. Two days later, Captain Nelson said I should have been wise had I compelled him to remain.

On February 22, 1889, Emin returned and told me of the compact made between Stanley and himself, he having said nothing of his own plans, as he had intended.

On the 26th, he again joined Stanley at Buguera, carrying with him the news that the party of rebels in Wadelai led by Captain Fatelmula, indignant at the weakness of Selim Bey and his comrades, had deposed him from the command of the Province in favour of Captain Fatelmula, whom they had further promoted to the rank of colonel. A court-martial had been held, which not only confirmed the deposition of the Pasha, but pronounced sentence of death against him and me.

Our officers were much pleased with their reception by Stanley. They had gone to his camp expecting to be severely reprimanded because of the late disturbances in the Province, but he had been perfectly cordial and courteous. He had confided to their care a written manifesto, addressed to all officers and employés in Wadelai. It ran as follows :—

SALAAMS ! The officers, Selim Bey and others, having requested Mr. Stanley to await the arrival of their friends from Wadelai, Mr. Stanley causes his answer to be written down in order to prevent misunderstanding. Mr. Stanley and his officers having been specially sent by the Khedive as guides to show the road to such people as desired to leave the Equatorial Province for Cairo, cannot do otherwise than consent to give such reasonable time as may be required for the assembling of all people willing to depart with him.

It must, however, be positively understood that all men proposing to depart with Mr. Stanley must provide their own means of carriage for themselves, their families, and baggage. No exception can be made, except for the Pasha, Captain Casati, and the Greek merchant named Marco, the two last being strangers, and not in the Egyptian service.

Therefore, all officers and men proposing to depart from this country with Mr. Stanley will be careful to provide such animals and porters as they may need for the transport of their children and goods.

They will also be careful not to burden themselves with superfluous articles: arms, clothing, ammunition, cooking pots, and provisions being the only necessaries needed.

The reserve ammunition which has been brought from Egypt for the service of the Pasha and his people, is of course at the disposition of the Pasha only, according to the orders of his Highness the Khedive.

Mr. Stanley wishes it to be distinctly understood that he is responsible only for finding the right road, and for provisioning all the people according to the nature of the country.

Mr. Stanley, however, holds himself in honour bound to do all in his power for the comfort, safety, and welfare of Emin Pasha and his people, and to assist his friends in all things to the best of his ability.

On the arrival of this answer before the officers at Wadelai, the officers responsible for the direction of the people will do well to hold a general council, and consider this answer before moving. Such people as believe in their hearts that they have the courage and means to depart from the Equatorial Province will prepare to proceed to this camp as directed by the Pasha. Such people as are doubtful of their power and ability to move will act as the superiors of the party will decide. Mr. Stanley, in the meanwhile will form an advance camp to make ready for the reception of such people as are going out.

HENRY M. STANLEY,
Commanding the Relief Expedition.

AT KAVALLI'S,
February 19th, 1889.

Selim Bey told me the drift of this letter. I was astonished at the paragraph concerning the time allowed, well worded, but not so clear and intelligible as the people to whom it was addressed and circumstances required it to be. The Pasha was the person directly responsible for executing the Viceroy's orders, and the way in which his authority and interference were spoken of irritated me the more, because through me, and afterwards personally when he left for Buguera, the Pasha advised the Lieut.-Colonel not to look too closely into the division of the ammunition in Wadelai between those who wished to leave and those who remained with Fatelmula. The same day Selim Bey left for Wadelai, determined to stand no more of Fatelmula's interference. I exhorted him to urge forward the soldiers and their families. He wished me good-bye, and I told him I hoped to see him again; but I did so merely out of politeness.

CASATI WITH HIS NEGRO CHILD, VITA HASSAN, AND DR. JUNKER.

In the Province, Selim was beset with difficulties, and the camp at Were was constantly disturbed by repeated requests to move forward to Buguera ; and this took so many men that on the arrival of a steamer the getting in of fuel became a work of time and toil. The Pasha's stay in Stanley's camp was regarded as a virtual abandonment of his subjects. Food was becoming scarce, and, worst of all, there was neither order nor organisation anywhere, so that no one knew whether the promises made would ever be carried out.

The monotony of our sojourn was broken by the disappearance one night of a few of our soldiers and servants. Some fled because they wished to join their absent families, and some because of the scarcity of provisions. Five of them were killed in trying to pass through Melindwa (by night) on the road which skirts the lake.

The Negro has a singular nature. He usually has no thought for the morrow, is inured to privations, and impassive in danger. Woe if he thinks ! The moment he does so he sees visions, panic seizes upon him, trouble annihilates him, he seeks safety in flight, and rushes on to his own destruction.

I remained at Were until I could send my friend Vita Hassan to the camp at Buguera, as his position amongst the Egyptian malcontents was insecure after what had happened at Dufilé, where he was looked upon as a loyal adherent of Emin's. Hassan left on March 1, and I followed next day. The road from our camp at Were, following a westerly direction, for three hours' march leads over a grassy plain, broken only by a few clumps of mimosa bushes, and is not crossed by any important stream, but is watered by the innumerable windings of the Niebetembe, flowing from the mountains at the end of the plain.

The banks of this small river once passed, the ground gradually rises, and two hours' climbing conducts us to a magnificently wide terrace, which commands a view over the lake to the wooded shores of Nyamsanzi and Nsabe on the western side, whilst away to the east is the mighty mountain wall enclosing Muenghe and the district of Baganghese. The narrow road, with its perpetual windings, looks sharp and steep, seen from behind the hills, but it is not really so.

We spent the night as well as we could on this wide terrace, only suffering from the heavy dews and cold. Rising early, we pressed forward next morning, our nerves tingling with the enjoyment of the pure bracing air. Then the road again became steep, and for an hour we had fatiguing climbing, after which a series of gentle undulations brought us to Buguera. About ten o'clock on the 3rd of March 1889, I entered my tent in the camp of the Relief Expedition, and became henceforward but a unit in the crowd.

CHAPTER XIII.

DEPARTURE OF THE EXPEDITION.

Waterparting between the Aruwimi and the Albert Lake—The plateau of Buguera—Flora and fauna—The chimpanzee—Catching with nets—Drunk in the trap—A chimpanzee drummer—The Walegga, Wahuma, and Vavra—The Mount Virika—The camp of Buguera—Service of the camp—Transports from Were—Refusal of the Zanzibaris—Stanley *Bulamatari*—His character—Robbers rewarded—The departure is fixed—Even Captain Fatelmula wishes to go to Egpyt—Conversation with Stanley—The officers complain—The Koran peeps out—Samadia—How to cure headache—A letter of recommendation to a Wahuma—The torture of the *tabatt—Bismillah il Rahman*—Final evacuation of the camp of Were—Stanley's fears—Emin's hesitation—The 5th of April—"I leave you to God"—The assembly—"As sure as my name is Stanley"—Rigorous watch—Those who leave—Omar the Shillook—Well-distributed bastinado—Abandonment and burning of the camp of Buguera—The river Tarara—Mpinga and Mazamboni—Flight of sixty-nine soldiers and servants—Council of inquiry—Mild sentence—Necessity of procuring porters—Stanley seriously ill—Fever and rheumatism—A furious hurricane—Chests of ammunition buried—Flight of servants—Arrest of Rehan—Summary judgment—The body thrown among grass.

THE plateau of Buguera, which has an altitude of about 3691 feet (1125 metres), is formed by a slightly undulating grassy surface, broken here and there by currents flowing from the waterparting of the Albert Lake and the river Aruwimi. This tortuous line runs without a break, and almost unnoticed, except on the western slope, where it is intersected by small rivulets, forming the river Deki, which flows to the Ituri.

On the eastern side, on the contrary, after a short space of flat ground, the slope suddenly changes its character, and the drainage, falling into the Niabetembe, is carried to the lake.

The plants found here are numerous and varied, uniting those of the highest altitudes, such as the *Trifolium intermedium*, the *Cardamine hirsuta*, the *Helicrysum angustifolium*, belonging to the European region, and the *Protea acaulis* and the *Spermania Africana*, of the southern countries of Africa. To complete the rich family, a beautiful specimen of the fern-tree, an *egathea*, may be admired upon an arid little hill, reminding one of dear and distant countries.

The fauna also includes a very diversified family of animals, especially of birds; to a kind of pigeon hitherto only found in countries of great elevation, one may add the *anthus* and the cuckoo, which come from Europe, and a species of *nettarinia*, which generally prefers the plains.

The woods which bound the plateau, at a few hours' distance, are inhabited by a colony of chimpanzees, which rush about and plunder the rich fields of Indian millet and bananas.

We amused ourselves for several days by sending some young and expert Soudanese hunters to try to kill or capture some, but the cautious chimpanzee, making a slow and prudent retreat, always deluded our hopes, disappearing in the dense parts of the forest. To surprise a family of those monkeys and take one alive, the Western Sandehs, on a favourable opportunity, spread the nets generally used for capturing gazelles and antelopes. At dusk they disturb the silent abode of the chimpanzees with loud cries and the barking of dogs; terrified by the unexpected assault, the animals run away in a disorderly and precipitate manner, and fall into the nets, which entangle their limbs. The struggle with the furious prisoners is more dangerous than ever, their muscular strength and agility giving them an almost certain chance of escape. The adults, wounded

AN APE PARADISE.

with knives, and the little ones, powerless after the long struggle, form the trophies of the hunters.

It is said that the Walegga are in the habit, on dark nights, of placing large jars of foaming beer at the foot of the trees where a family of chimpanzees live. At dawn the gluttonous animals pounce upon the desired beverage and, after many quarrels, the stronger and more fortunate plunge their heads into the jars and empty them. Staggering and intoxicated, they fall into a deep sleep, and their apparently lifeless bodies lie scattered about upon the scene of their orgies. The wary hunters, who up to this point have watched the wild gaiety of their prey, come out of their hiding-places, and securely tie the limbs of the poor drunkards, who soon after awaken to the loss of their liberty.

Captain Shukri, commander of the station at Msua, told me that, during an excursion into the mountains of the Lendu (a name given to the Walegga by the eastern populations), he was obliged to pitch his camp in a dense wood. Upon rising the next morning, he saw to his great surprise that a drum had been taken from near where the guns were stacked. The general opinion was that some daring native had stolen it, but after proceeding a short distance, they heard the sound of the beating of a drum from the top of a tree. An old chimpanzee was discovered with a drum-stick in his hand, imitating the beating of the instrument, which, unobserved, he had witnessed the day before. Gunshots, menacing shouts, throwing of darts, did not avail to recover it, for the monkey, leaping, with herculean strength, from branch to branch and from plant to plant, and still tightly holding his precious spoil, was lost to the sight of the soldiers, and probably joined his own companions.

The original population of the country, in remote

times, was the Walegga, who, being driven out by the Wahuma coming from Unyoro, took refuge in the mountains. The Wahuma are considered in the country as of noble caste, and are the true masters of the soil, having the Vavra as their subjects and as agricultural labourers.

The latter come from countries situated in the West; their front teeth are filed and painted, their ears are pierced, and the women have a piece of round wood stuck through the upper lip. They live entirely upon agricultural produce, and are forbidden to possess cattle, which are the exclusive property of the nobles.

The conquering tribe of the Wahuma is not governed by a single chief, but divided under several, according to the groups forming the great family. Thus Kavalli commands the Waviasi, Mpigwa the Wavivaghi, Sagara the Wavisu, and Katonzi the Wavitu; the latter being the most aristocratic part of the tribe. The chief of the Wavitu, by right of custom, has the prerogative of the investiture of new chiefs in the single branches.

The climate of Buguera is healthy, and the air salubrious. The wind blows periodically from the east, rising and subsiding with the sun. The mean temperature does not descend below 16° Centigrade. Frequent and abundant rains refresh the soil.

Looking towards the horizon, which extends along a vast line of heights stretching from south to southeast, attention is attracted by a great mass of greyish-white cindery clouds, which, suspended in the air, enfold the highest crests of the chain. The aqueous vapour, dissipated and rarefied at intervals, just when it seems inclined to withdraw the veil and satisfy the desire of the eye, suddenly becomes denser, as if jealous of its guardianship.

It was the afternoon of the 30th of April 1889 ; the air was calm, and the sky clear ; all eyes were turned to the south ; clouds which obscured the great mountains, moving with increased rapidity, broke up and rose ; the sun darted its vivid rays, and through a clear and limpid atmosphere there appeared the crest of the Virika or Ruwenzori, the great mountain of the Vakongio. The top and sides, clothed in white, showed that it was a snow-clad mountain. Its height is gigantic, and, although the distance is considerable, its Alpine form was distinctly visible. It is the Varikampanga, of which the people of Unyoro say that no one who has attempted the mysteries of its ascent has ever returned. Cold, and horrible monsters are supposed to rule over it. As if offended by the intensity of our scrutiny, the protecting clouds resumed their usual office, leaving us with a keener desire than ever to solve the mystery.

One entered the camp of mobilisation by the southern gate, and at the end of an ample square the Egyptian flag floated on the top of a high pole. A large hut, with a sloping roof, and opening on one side, formed the office of the commander of the Expedition. On each side of it were the tents of the British officers, and those which were used for the magazines. The two long sides which enclosed the square were formed by a series of huts of uniform size, symmetrically arranged, and were the dwellings used by the officers and employés. A second group of huts, placed at a convenient distance from the former, was occupied by the soldiers and minor officials. The camp was enclosed by the huts of the Zanzibari and the Manyuema of the Expedition.

The guards of the camp were the Zanzibaris, under the command of a British officer. The daily distribution of food was limited to those composing the Expedition; the distribution of animal food to the people of the Pasha was effected weekly. The rules for the government of the camp, the authority over everybody and everything, emanated from Stanley and his officers. The Pasha had but an apparent authority. Stanley touched him in his most tender point by saying, with some slight irony, that he was the man who must make the scientific observations during the journey.

As Stanley had promised, the transport of the effects of the camp of Were to Buguera was performed (from February 14) by Zanzibaris, assisted by the natives. Of course, the fatiguing journey from the lake to the plateau could not be agreeable to the porters. Their discontent was increased by continual invectives thrown at them in a tone of contempt as Government men—invectives which ended by taking away that reciprocal respect which it was a paramount duty to preserve, for the sake of order and discipline. It is true that, by every report, the officers and employés, especially the Egyptians, were not distinguished by their morality. But this should not have surprised the members of the Expedition, who had still fresh in their memory the outrages of which Egypt had been the theatre during the rebellion of Arabi Pasha. The revolt which had broken out in Equatoria against Emin ought still less to have constituted a motive for the harsh treatment of those who had complied with the wishes of the Viceroy, and to whom Stanley had pledged himself as leader on their return.

The morning of the 10th of March 1889, the troops who should have gone to the lake on their usual service did so with murmurs, and only the intervention of Stanley could make them go. But when a little way from the encampment the most daring obstinately refused to proceed, and Captain Nelson thought it better to send back the whole company.

Repression was prompt and immediate. The principal instigators were disarmed, flogged, and put under arrest. And when justice had been done, and Stanley ordered their departure for the lake, no one made any further opposition. Not a word was spoken. The punishment was inflicted in a bold, frank, confident manner; and to one of the guilty men, who in a frightened, faint voice, answered the call, he said in a grave voice, while the blows rained down :

" My name is Stanley Bulamatari (the stone-breaker), and not only Ibrahim, like yours."

Stanley is a man remarkable for strength of character, resolution, promptness of thought, and iron will. Jealous of his own authority, he does not tolerate exterior influences, nor ask advice. Difficulties do not deter him, disasters do not dismay him. With an extraordinary readiness of mind he improvises means, and draws himself out of a difficulty; absolute and severe in the execution of his duty, he is not always prudent, or free from hasty and erroneous judgments. Irresolution and hesitation irritate him, disturbing his accustomed gravity; his countenance being usually serious. Reserved, laconic, and not very sociable, he does not awaken sympathy; but on closer acquaintance he is found very agreeable, from the frankness of his manner, his brilliant conversation, and his gentlemanly courtesy.

During the night of the 23rd of March 1889, an alarm was raised. Some natives, allured by a few fine heifers (stolen in raids from a tribe which had had the audacity to attack the body of the Expedition in its march towards the lake), had stealthily penetrated into the camp, but not cautiously enough to elude the vigilance of the sentries. Two of the band were arrested, and next morning brought into the presence of Stanley.

" You have come for meat, at a great risk," he said. " I will make you a present of two goats, but remember, and do not forget to tell your friends, that if a similar attempt is repeated, the culprits shall, without fail, be hung on a tree."

The delay in the arrival of news from Wadelai occasioned various comments. Stanley, who only waited to start until the health of some of his Zanzibaris was restored, had fixed the date of his departure, as he had originally decided in his own mind when he caused the letters to be written to the officials of Wadelai, conceding to them a *reasonable* time.

Stanley had already proposed to Emin that the departure should take place on the 25th of March, and the latter had agreed to it. He afterwards put off the time until the 10th of April, and Emin accepted the new arrangement. Mr. Jephson told me of the decision arrived at, on the 14th of March, and to him I frankly observed that it would be impossible to collect the people, so as to depart in twenty-five days.

" The assembling them for departure requires a long time. We are in the Soudan, my dear Jephson ; fixing such an early date is as much as to say that many of them are to be abandoned."

I spoke of it afterwards to Emin, who, however, constantly said that he wished to await the arrival of his men, and was ready to separate himself from the Expedition, should it set out before they were all assembled.

But on the 25th a letter arrived bearing the signature of thirty-six officers, and announcing in concise terms (without the display of either presumption or servility) their unanimous wish to return to Egypt. The names of Fatelmula and other rebels, that figured in the letter, caused alarm ; the people regarded it as a snare, and in a council held by Stanley, in the presence of the Pasha, it was voted necessary to hasten the departure ; to abandon the people of Wadelai, to evacuate Were, and to send ammunition to Niangabo, a territory subject to the chief Mazamboni.

Captain Nelson alone maintained that the Pasha could not agree to a sudden departure, without failing in his duty, and opposed it ; but Stanley willed it, and the 10th of April was accepted by Emin as the date, with a formal pledge.

I was only informed of this resolution on the following day, and then by the chief of the Expedition himself ; I heard of Captain Nelson's objections later on.

In the afternoon, Stanley came to my abode, and briefly represented to me the vicissitudes which were leading the British Expedition to ruin, and its present critical position. He enumerated the negotiations which had taken place between him and the Governor, deploring the carelessness and slowness with which Emin's people proceeded, who every day declared their intention of starting, and yet delayed their arrival. He concluded by expressing his doubts as to the intentions of the Wadelai officers, since Emin himself was rather suspicious. Was it his duty, he asked me at last, to protect the body of the Expedition under his orders from every possible danger ? Should not Emin, in the face of such risk, think of his own safety ? Was Emin expected to sacrifice himself for people who had vilified and imprisoned him ?

" Frankness for frankness," I replied, " he had the full right to expect the fulfilment of agreements, freely and reciprocally contracted, and that it was his duty to watch over the welfare of the Expedition entrusted to him." As to the duties and obligations of the Governor, I differed from him, and considered Emin bound by the act of submission which he had accepted on the 8th of February, at Msua.

I concluded by saying it was a question of moral opinion. The Pasha might, perhaps, look at it in a different light.

Stanley then sent a message to Emin, begging him to come to us, and when he arrived repeated to him the last questions asked me. The Pasha decided that he was not obliged to keep the pledge accepted at Msua, and that he had only accepted it as a means of opening a way to get out of the Province.

"You see," said Stanley to me, "that the Pasha speaks as I expected. Now, what do you say to it?"

"I have nothing to say," was my reply. "I do not change my opinion. No one can prevent your acting according to your own will."

The joy of those who were in the camp at the news of the decision voted by their companions of Wadelai was of short duration. The idea of their early departure filled them with grief, which they did not attempt to conceal. Not being in the habit of frequenting public meetings, and having led a retired life for some time, far from the excitement of discussions and the danger of opposing other people's opinions, one day the wish struck me to know the impression made on the officers by the last decision, more to satisfy my curiosity than from any interest I could possibly take in them. Fortune favoured me before I tempted her, and the morning after the conversation with Stanley, four of the officers came to pay me a visit.

"So we are to leave Kavalli without waiting for our companions from Wadelai?" said one of them.

"If they choose to come, they can overtake us in a few days," I replied to Lieutenant Ali Shambruk.

"It is impossible to do so in such a short time. The steamers cannot carry so many people," said he.

"They can come by the route which skirts the lake. There is a large body of them, and they are well armed. Have they cause to fear the Melindwa and the Lur?"

"That is true, I admit; but when the soldiers learn the decision adopted by Stanley and the Pasha they will be agitated by various opinions, and the departure, thereby deferred, will be suspended and then abandoned. Unprovided as our brethren are with ammunition, they will one day become an easy prey to our enemies of Khartoum, who have sworn our destruction, and more carnage will be added to the disasters already suffered. The scene will be horrible, like the end of the world. Who could describe that disastrous, frightful day? 'They shall be dispersed like locusts.'"

"There you are, Ali, with your Koran, and uttering lamentations you do not feel, and maxims you do not practise. Speak on, and I will answer you."

"He who knows the secrets of heaven and earth gave us the Koran, and he is indulgent and merciful. But how is it that the Pasha, who has assured us of so many things, and made us great promises, does not care for us any longer?"

"How can you be sure he has forgotten you?" I asked.

"We can infer it from his behaviour. He said he would take us all to Egypt, and then he starts with the smallest number. From the time we came to this camp he has deprived us of his favour. He has forgotten the beautiful saying of the Book: 'The believer who has practised benevolence will find a refuge in the garden of delights.'"

"Why do you allow yourself to become so depressed since Stanley, as well as the Pasha, has the goodness to assist you, and do everything to attain your end? One thing is undeniable: should the soldiers from Wadelai not hasten their arrival, we shall be obliged to proceed on account of the famine which threatens us here."

"You are right. A few wicked people have ruined the Province. At Msua we confessed our error, and implored that it should be forgiven and forgotten. And will he not pardon us? God pardons in His indulgence and mercy, and exacts from each one according to his abilities."

"Not only has he pardoned you, but he has your fate at heart. Certainly he cannot see with satisfaction the little care your brethren have displayed in answering the call made to them. Besides, he was obliged to give a definitive answer," I said.

"Lieutenant Ali has told you a good deal, but something still remains to be said on the subject," added Osman, the Vice-Governor. "Will you allow me to tell you what is in my mind? I do not pretend to give advice to the Pasha, nor to influence his decisions in the slightest manner, but the rank with which I am invested compels me to warn him of an event which is about to happen."

"Speak, if you will, Osman, but I must tell you I do not mean to meddle in your troubles," I said.

"You are the friend of the Pasha, and after you have heard me I believe you will be inclined to think that I am right, and will communicate the matter to him, for his benefit as well as our own. You know I have not ventured to speak to him for some time as I used in former years," said Osman.

"Speak, speak; but for goodness' sake do not give me another lesson from the Koran. I know that you cannot engage in a serious discussion without pointing your argument with verses from the prophet. But spare me as much as possible."

"You are joking with me, as usual. But it does not matter; I am not offended."

"Bravo! Bravo! but fear not; time, as it passes, leads us to reflection. I am listening to you."

"Do not interrupt me, or destroy the thread of my ideas. 'By the *war horses* which run swiftly *to the battle* with a panting noise; and by those which strike fire, by dashing their hoofs against the stones; and by those which make a sudden incursion *on the enemy* early in the morning, and therein raise dust, and therein pass through the midst of the *adverse* troops; verily man *is* ungrateful unto his Lord.'* Fatelmula and the other Wadelai mean treason—for they are people of ungrateful heart and perverse mind. They wish to come and fight us to take possession of the ammunition. It is necessary to prevent this guilty design, to warn the Pasha, and advise an early flight."

"Dear Vice-Governor, this is not my business, but yours. I would never charge myself with such advice; and allow me to tell you that the accusation you insinuate is grave, and must be corroborated by clear evidence. You know, as we all do, that there is so much discord among the people in Wadelai, that any treason, even scarcely meditated, would come to our knowledge. And if, as there is no doubt, some bear malice and brood revenge, leave their punishment

* Koran, chap. c. (Sale's translation).

to God. The wickedness of such beings will not hurt us in the least."

"Just so; and God Himself has promised it in His law with the words: 'Verily, if the hypocrites, and those in whose hearts is an infirmity, and they who raise disturbances in Medina, do not desist, we will surely stir thee up against them *to chastise them*. Henceforth they shall not *be suffered* to dwell near thee therein, except for a little *time, and* being accursed. Wherever they are found they shall be taken, and killed with a *general* slaughter, *according to* the sentence of God concerning those who have been before; and thou shalt not find any change in the sentence of God.'"*

"Well, Osman, but remember that in the same chapter—it is suggested to me by Captain Ibrahim Hellem—it is said: 'And they who shall injure the true believers of either sex, without their deserving it, shall surely bear the *guilt* of calumny, and a manifest injustice.'" *

The man stood silent. He had spoken in fear of the arrival of the officers from Wadelai. The tranquillity which he now enjoyed would be disturbed, if they came, by reason of the long series of his former deceits. Osman Latif, now in Cairo, has forgotten his habit of delivering ascetic lectures; at that time he used to recite, with sacrilegious imposture, a thousand and seventeen times a day the chapter *Samadia*, that is, "The declaration of God's unity," which runs thus: "*God* is one God; the eternal God: he begetteth not, neither is he begotten: and there is not any one like unto Him." †

To the faithful, who daily practise this herculean

* Koran, chap. xxxiii.   † Koran, chap. cxii.

labour of prayer, it is given to behold in their dreams the seat assigned to them in Paradise.

Major Hawashi and Captain Ibrahim Hellem were alarmed at the thought that the decision taken might do them harm; since many of those with us would return to Wadelai. I encouraged them, entreated them to tranquillise their minds, and to have confidence in their Governor.

Captain Ibrahim Hellem enjoyed a great reputation for curing headaches. His cure was performed by the hand. It consisted in binding the head with a ribbon, and tightening it with a drumstick and an iron key, until the measure of the perimeter reached its supposed natural dimension. "The space measured from the point of the nose to the nape of the neck in its normal condition," said he, "should correspond exactly to that round the head. But each time that the pain attacks this region, there is an enlargement, and cure is obtained by reducing it to its normal size; the remedy would not be successful if the knot which secured the ribbon was not tied with the left hand."

He was most desirous of seeing again his native country, which he had left as an officer; but his wishes unfortunately were not fulfilled. Footsore and dragging himself along in pain, he followed the caravan by long marches. But, one day, his strength failing him, he was left behind at Kitega, in the territory of Nkole, with the sole comfort of a letter to that chief, in the following terms :—

"I, Governor-General of the Equatorial Province, Mohammed Emin Pasha, leave here Captain Ibrahim Effendi Hellem, also Captain Abdul-Wahd Effendi, and Ibrahim Effendi Tahir, a clerk, on account of sickness

"I order you to give them the necessary nutriment

and should a caravan pass which touches at the English mission of Mr. Mackay, send them by it."

The chief into whose care those unfortunate men were given, and who was to execute the written orders, was a Wahuma, in whose fields we had gathered provisions without paying for them.

The strange remedy I have just mentioned reminds me of the torture called by the Arabs *tabatt*, which was abolished in Egypt by the Viceroy Ismail Pasha. Two bamboo canes applied to the temples are tied tightly at their extremities, both behind and before, with a cord. The agony of the torture is caused by beating the anterior point of the apparatus with a small stick. The slowness of the shock and the trembling which it occasions produces such acute pain that it causes the victim to fall senseless. This infamous mode of torture was applied to three Dervishes who had carried Omar Saleh's letter (the commander of the Mahdi's forces); but those intrepid fanatics, rather than reveal what had been confided to them, with eyes bursting out of their sockets and trembling limbs, continued faintly murmuring, "*Bismillah il Rahman, il Rahim, il hamd Ila Rab il Alamin.*"* They were then barbarously beaten to death with clubs by the infuriated soldiery, when the Mahdist horde threatened Dufilé.

In order to execute the plan which had been definitely decided upon by Stanley, Captain Nelson left the camp on the morning of March 29, 1889, with orders that all who were then at the camp of Were were to leave for Buguera. Stanley and the British officers considered that their most important and only mission was the liberation of Emin. Being anxious

* In the name of God; God is merciful. Thanks be to God; God is omnipotent.

about the condition of Equatoria after the late events that had disturbed it, they had determined to abandon the soldiers to their fate, and return.

Suspicion and mistrust were roused in Stanley's mind by some Egyptian officers, the chief amongst whom was Osman Latif, who continually insisted on the dangers that would be created by the arrival of the Wadelai people in the camp.

According to him, they had conspired to ruin the Expedition, to arrest the Pasha, and to commit any crimes, if necessary, in order to obtain the ammunition which was at Buguera.

Osman Latif was supported in this infamous work by Major Hawashi's suggestions, who, being aware of the general hatred that he had aroused in a few years, through arbitrary abuse of power, shuddered at the mere thought of contact with his numerous victims during the journey. The reports of Stanley's faithful servant, Saleh, entirely supported Osman's insinuations, being inspired by a certain Ahmed, a wretched creature of abject habits and a vile mind.

The grief of Emin's followers at seeing their companions abandoned, the murmurs at the delusion they had been under, and their openly declared intention of returning to Wadelai, were represented as pretences for carrying out guilty designs and wicked intentions.

Emin hesitated. On the one hand, he seemed desirous of placing some distance between himself and the people of Wadelai; on the other, a certain amount of shame overcame him on account of his diminished authority, on finding himself at the mercy of the British, and obliged to follow them as a trophy of victory. He did not dare to lend an ear to his people's complaints, as he was afraid of causing trouble by personally inquiring into the state of their minds.

He received petitions and sent advices through an intermediary, but thus, instead of simplifying difficulties, he complicated them.

Stanley was indignant. The information he received made him doubtful as to the Pasha's intentions, and a few angry words about the latter betrayed his impatience. The news that the evacuation of Wadelai was about to become an accomplished fact stung him to the quick ; he determined to put an end to further delay. The cunning excuses, ambiguous expressions, and predictions of inevitable danger had strangely impressed him, prone as he always was to suspicion.

On the morning of April 5, 1889, after giving some directions, he went to Emin's house, and, making him promise not to repeat a word of what he was going to say, he told him distinctly that an attempt had been made during the night to steal some guns from the huts of the Zanzibaris.

"A conspiracy is going on here against me," said he ; "plots are being concocted against the Expedition. I know that a refusal will be made to the resolution of departure."

"I do not know," replied the Pasha ; "to what you allude. I do not think that any one would be so wicked as to dare act as you have been made believe."

"Do not let us evade the question, Pasha; that is not my habit. I have two proposals to make to you ; it is for you to choose, and that without delay. To-morrow morning I mean to make the round of my Zanzibaris and to tell them of our immediate departure. In case of any resistance or attempt at refusal, I am prepared to use force, and then start with you and the few who remain faithful to you. Should these strong measures not suit you, then I propose that you should start with a trustworthy escort at once, unknown to every one; I would soon rejoin you. Choose, Pasha; decide."

"I cannot accede to your proposals. The first I will not discuss; as for the second, you will understand that I cannot abandon Casati, Vita, and Marco."

"Do not think of them. As soon as I have encamped in a favourable position, I shall come and take them (by force if necessary) from the hands of the Egyptians."

"But I do not think there will be any necessity for employing such means. We shall depart on the 10th."

Stanley's anger rose to its highest pitch. He stamped his foot upon the ground and said in a convulsed voice:

". . . ! I leave you to God, and the blood which will now flow must fall upon your own head!"

He rushed out and whistled the signal of alarm, and entered his tent, leaving it again almost immediately, gun in hand and his cartridge pouch on his belt.

The Zanzibaris assembled in the square, part occupying the exit of the camp; the tents were taken down, exposing heaps of merchandise and cases of ammunition. From the door of my house I could observe an unusual bustle of armed men. I thought it meant a drill to prepare them for the approaching departure. I asked some of the passers by, but none knew the reason of the commotion. I sent my boy to ask Emin, and he quickly returned telling me that the Pasha was making preparations for an immediate departure.

I went to see the Pasha; he was pale with rage and indignation.

"We are going," said he to me with a trembling voice. "To-day, for the first time in my life, I have been covered with insults. Stanley has passed every limit of courtesy, but I have promised not to speak, so can say no more."

The Pasha was under the incubus of dreading to see the first of the proposals made to him carried out at any moment. In the meantime, Emin's officers, employés, soldiers, and servants were assembled in the square, stupefied by the great agitation—a sure sign of some calamity. Emin and I arrived at last.

"If you have the courage, point your guns at my breast," cried Stanley, addressing them. "I am here alone and unarmed."

Blind fury made him forget that he held a Winchester rifle in his hand, and that there was a wall of about a hundred armed Zanzibaris behind him.

"My orders alone are to be obeyed here, and whoever resists I will kill him with this gun, and trample him under my feet. Whoever intends to start and follow me, let him pass to this side."

In a moment every one moved, and all was changed; the terrible conspirators became as quiet as lambs. The reputed chiefs of the opposition, being called into Stanley's presence, were ordered to be disarmed and cast into prison.

"Will you start with me?" he said.

"Yes," they all answered.

"Will you obey my orders implicitly?"

"Yes, we promise," they hastened to say, simultaneously.

"I will conduct you to safety and will supply your needs during the journey. You have my promise; but I warn you that, as sure as my name is Stanley, I shall not tolerate any renewal of the disturbances of Dufilé or Wadelai. Bear in mind that the departure is irrevocably fixed for the 10th."

From that day the encampment had the appearance

A QUARREL IN THE CAMP.

of a village which had been placed under martial law. The guards were doubled, patrols were continually on the move during the night, all were forbidden to leave their dwellings under pain of being placed under arrest. Those present in camp, inscribed after a general muster, were 350 people of the Relief Expedition, of whom 294 were armed; and 570 from the Province of Equatoria.

An inspection of the arms belonging to these, made by Stanley, which Emin declined to witness, gave the numerical result of only 40 guns!

Differing in origin, language, and customs, the Soudanese and Zanzibaris, who composed the caravan, apparently maintained cordial intercourse among themselves; but in reality it was preserved only by the innate thoughtlessness of the Negro race, not by any other sentiment, and they were ever on the look out for any circumstance which might cause an outburst of their latent mutual jealousy.

One morning it happened that some thoughtless Zanzibaris, standing near the river which bounded the camp, spoke disrespectfully of the wife of a certain Omar (commander of the soldiers) who had joined the Expedition at Cairo.

The Shillook, a strong, passionate man, armed with a knotted club, was about to avenge the offence; but scarcely had he fallen upon the insolent offenders than he was surrounded by a number of their friends. He did not lose his presence of mind; whirling his club he inflicted some crushing blows on them, which laid low three of the most daring, and wounded one of them rather seriously in the head.

The news of the unequal contest spread throughout the camp like lightning; and soldiers and servants, quickly arming themselves with sticks, rushed to the spot to defend their countrymen. The affair was becoming serious, when Stanley fortunately appeared and put an end to the quarrel.

At daybreak on April 10, 1889, the well-known whistle was heard; the signal for departure. Stanley kept his word; the caravan fell into marching order, and at seven o'clock began to move, leaving behind it a dense black column of smoke and the crackling flames of the burning camp. The road ran in a south-westerly direction, over grassy hills, with few trees, separated from one another by streams flowing into the Ituri. The monotonous aspect in the small valleys was only broken by some palm-trees. The country is inhabited by agricultural labourers and shepherds, who dwell in the villages of Sagwa and Mbuti or in huts scattered on the slopes of the hills. The fields are cultivated with Indian millet, sweet potatoes (*Batata edulis*), and beans.

The march proceeded with tolerable regularity, considering that the majority were unaccustomed to such fatigue, and that there were so many children. At one o'clock we arrived at Katenta, the residence of Mpinga, chief of the tribe of Wahuma Wavitu. During the night heavy rain and strong wind inconvenienced the less favoured ones who were encamped in the open, outside the village.

On April 12, 1889, with the assistance of a limited number of porters, supplied by Mpinga, who, during the march, threw down their loads and fled, we covered, in about six hours, the ten miles which separated us from Niangabo, the residence of chief Mazamboni, where we encamped, near the shore of the river Tarara, close to the mountain.

The first part of the road is a plain covered with grass and bushes, but after passing the river near the village of Miro, there are high plateaux, cultivated with Indian millet, bananas, sweet potatoes, and beans, scattered here and there, with villages and numbers of huts. The frequent rivulets, with sandy beds and slightly sloping banks, contain good and limpid water. The country is rich in cattle; the population is of the Wahuma Vgiviga tribe.

The measures adopted by Stanley to suppress the disaffection which prevailed in the camp at Buguera, the burning of the village upon his departure, the persuasion that they were abandoning the people of Wadelai, had excited anger and grief in the minds of the soldiers and servants. However, they gave no expression to them as long as they were at Buguera, for fear of incurring punishment; but once at Niangabo, relying upon the long distance which separated that place from Were, they determined to return, and the very evening of our arrival sixty-nine soldiers and servants, eluding the vigilance of the sentries, took to flight. The fact alarmed the officers, and one of the most zealous, being told that others intended to follow their example, informed Emin, who, on purpose to stop the fatal current, acted without delay. That same evening, although it was late, he assembled his people and warned them of their danger; disarmed several soldiers and servants whom he suspected, among the latter being four of his own household.

On the following morning, April 27, 1889, the officers met in council, and, assisted by Lieutenant Stairs, began an inquiry into the plot which threatened the integrity and safety of the caravan. The tribunal laboured patiently for several hours. They interrogated, investigated, and threatened, and at last, about 2 p.m., found that four of the Pasha's servants, a Negro, formerly in the service of a noncommissioned officer who was dead, and two others who were employed at a clerk's house, had combined to escape to Wadelai. They had been alarmed and led astray by the accounts which a certain Rehan (a youth whom Stanley had taken with him upon his return after the first meeting with Emin) had given of the sufferings endured on the road to Yambuya; but the youth had disappeared during the night, consequently it was impossible to make him a scapegoat. The meeting adjourned for two hours, and was then resumed to discuss the punishments which ought to be inflicted upon the seven intending deserters. After having successively proposed and abandoned shooting, imprisonment in chains, extra hard work on the march, or to be handed over to the missionaries, it was decided at sunset that they should receive a few strokes with the lash. Six hours' work had softened the judges' hearts. The scarcity of porters for service on the journey, and the improbability of procuring assistance from the native chiefs, made it advisable, however grievous it might be, to use force in a country where the rule of paid service could not be applied. Necessity has its own laws, and the preservation of one's life is a law of Nature. We had to employ force to retain it.

Several raids with this object were attempted; they met with but little success, owing to orders having been given to prevent the capture of Negroes being attended by fatal results. One of these excursions was made in a north-westerly direction, four hours' journey from Niangabo, in the territory of the Jongolo, inhabited by Vavra, under chief Ndinda, whose authority extended over the villages of Tendiabro, Nsabaco, Muninga, Muicu, and Manzoca. The country is crossed by a river of some importance, the Mbagungue, which flows into the Ituri. In the adjacent country of Kumbiere, there was a colony of Wahuma, whose chief was called Kise.

NEGROES WARMING THEMSELVES BY THE FIRE.

A few days after our arrival at Niangabo, Stanley was taken seriously ill. The care taken of him by good Dr. Parke, added to that of Emin, soon overcame the violence of the attack, but his weakness was so great that it prevented a speedy renewal of the journey. We therefore had to prolong our stay at Niangabo, and, owing to the scarcity of provisions, we were obliged to resort to compulsory requisitions, which were usually made on the property of chiefs who did not recognise the authority of Mazamboni. In these raids Stanley strictly forbade the use of violence, maltreatment of the natives, and the stealing of bullocks and goats; corn, bananas, beans, tobacco, and poultry were the only kind of food they were permitted to take.

Frequent rains and the unfavourable condition of the place, daily increased the number of those attacked by fever and rheumatism. The neighbourhood was searched in order to find a healthier locality, but scarcity of water proved to be the obstacle to our selecting a place for encampment which offered more favourable surroundings; and, as if our daily troubles did not suffice, on the evening of April 30, 1889, a hurricane from the east burst over the camp, accompanied by thunder and lightning, and torrents of rain. Most of the huts were overturned and destroyed. The morning found us shivering with cold, and crouching in the spots least exposed to the fury of the tempest.

The cases of ammunition which Stanley had received in Egypt for consignment to the Government of Equatoria, and which had been saved from the misfortunes that had befallen the Expedition, amounted to sixty-two. In view of the perils which he imagined he might encounter at the hands of the soldiers of the Province, he had not chosen to give any to the people of Wadelai; and Emin, who had always yielded to Stanley's wishes, had not dared to mention them for fear of awaking fresh quarrels, even when it was decided to abandon the soldiers of Wadelai, to which he had assented ; it must have pained him to know that they were unprovided with the means of defence, and thrown on the mercy of the Mahdists and natives.

The absolute impossibility of procuring porters there, obliged the chief of the Expedition to abandon some of the cases of ammunition, and he simply ordered that those exceeding the number of available porters should be buried, and Lieutenant Stairs saw that this was done with great precaution during the night of the 29th.

The flight of the servants did not cease, but, in spite of the watchfulness which was exercised, proceeded at intervals.

The officers, alarmed at the condition to which they were reduced by these desertions, went to Stanley, begging him to allow them to send an armed expedition to Were to try and arrest the fugitives. He complied with their request, and also consented that thirty armed Zanzibaris should go with the Egyptian soldiers under the command of Captain Shukri. Early on May 1, 1889, they returned from the lake, bringing with them nine of the fugitives, among whom was Rehan, the youth who had roused the fears of his friends by relating to them his sufferings on the road of the Aruwimi.

The exceedingly lenient sentence which had been pronounced on the 27th did not please Stanley, and, to avert the danger of its repetition, it was thought necessary to strengthen his authority by an act of terror which would put an end to all further attempts at injuring the compactness of the caravan.

Having assembled the Zanzibaris, he appeared before them, followed by the English officers, and ordered

EXECUTION OF A DESERTER.

DEATH OF REHAN.

Rehan to be brought forward, declaring that he deserved to be condemned to death. Although he had already received the sanction of his officers, he asked the approval of the Zanzibaris, which was clamorously given.

Young Rehan was hanged to a tree, and his body exposed till the next day as a salutary example. It was then cut down, thrown amongst the grass, and left as food for the hyenas and vultures.

CHAPTER XIV.

THE VIRIKA MOUNTAINS.

Marching order of the caravan—Toil—Diseases—Hard treatment—Slighted complaints—The little Amina—Departure from Niangabo—At Joddo—Selim Bey's letter—The reply—At Buhogo—The attack of King Chua's *banassura*—The brave Oakil killed on the battle-field—Unlucky youth!—His tomb—The land before us—Western route—The study of the White Mountains—The Semliki river—Crossing of the stream—The Wamba country—The Bassua—At the foot of the Virika—Sanitary conditions of the caravan—Clerk Wassif—A horrible thing to relate—Fighting the Manyema—Lieutenant Stairs's exploration—Karalla, a servant, killed by the Vakongio with their lances—New victims—Stanley arms the servants to guard the caravan—Discontent augments—Exit from the forest—The Usongora—The sun shines on the Virika peaks—Lake Ruitan—The salt lake—King Chua's power—Salt trade—At Amkongo—Attack by the soldiers of the King of Unyoro—Return to Unyampaka—Moral and material conditions of the caravan—Abundance of food—Routes from Unyampaka—Selection of the route through Nkole.

THE formation of the caravan for the journey had been determined in the following order :—

The march was opened by Stanley, preceded by a vanguard of Zanzibaris with native guides; the company under Jephson's command followed; then Emin with his people, escorted by another company. The families of the officials, servants, carriers, and the Manyema, enrolled at Yambuya, were in the rear. The long column was protected by a company who served as the rear-guard, under the alternate command of Captain Nelson and Lieutenant Stairs.

The march began at sunrise, and was continued until eleven o'clock A.M., without halts. Generally in that lapse of time, and often before it ended, the head of the caravan had reached the place where we were to pass the night; but the greater part of the people—the porters especially—used to drop in by groups, or singly, so that the camp could not be said to be complete till three or four in the afternoon. The nature of the route—the difficulties of mountain passes—the slackening of the pace—and the necessity of short stoppages for the porters to rest—soon lengthened the column, in which long intervals were to be seen, breaking the compactness of the march. Later, either on account of the continual fatigues or the hardship of the route, frequent cases of fever occurred in the ranks, and many, especially the Egyptians, were afflicted with painful sores on their feet. The assiduous cares of Dr. Parke, always ready and courteous, were not sufficient to meet the requirements; sick people from time to time begged for some days' rest; the Pasha used to advise them to apply to Stanley, and he, in his turn (wishing to decline any responsibility towards people who were not under his direct authority) asked Emin for advice—whose decision always was that, a few days being insufficient to ensure recovery, the best thing to do was to continue the journey. And those poor suffering creatures dragged themselves along, cursing in their heart the moment in which they had listened to the promising offer of relief.

It was a daily occurrence for people to fall and be abandoned on the road, or to go astray; and every day the losses we sustained increased the labour of the survivors. The employés frequently complained of having been insulted, while servants showed the marks of strokes of the stick which had been inflicted upon them, and, lamenting, threw their loads in the grass. The British officers alleged their duty of attending to the speed of the march, of urging on the stragglers, and their right to use coercive means against the indifference and insolence of warned offenders. To this painful daily occurrence was added the disdainful and insulting behaviour of the Zanzibaris, who also believed themselves authorised to assume the character of liberators and to commit any act of oppression they pleased.

Complaints made to Stanley were not always unattended to, but, on account of his prejudiced mind, he generally limited himself to mere recommendations, and never took any preventive measure. Emin, for a mere show of authority, used to order the cases to be most minutely investigated.

In the allotment of carriers, Stanley favoured me with three Manyema, one of whom I gave up that he might carry the little Amina.

This girl was born in Juaya, in Unyoro, of a woman then in my service. I took great interest in her, from a charitable feeling, as well as in opposition to the wishes of some people, who would have rejoiced at the abandonment of both mother and child. Two years afterwards latent malevolence succeeded in obtaining a sentence in accordance with the Koran, by which the guardianship of the little one devolved on the Government, as it could not be entrusted to a Christian.

I took no notice of the strange order, but continued my protection to the child, thus enabling her and her mother to overcome the hardships of the journey and be saved.

On May 8, we left the camp of Niangabo, and followed westwards the outskirts of the range of mountains rising behind us; we then turned to the south, on slightly elevated spurs of the chain, and reached Joddo, a territory inhabited by the Walegga and ruled by chief Kabonga.

We were there overtaken by Ayoub, a clerk, who

brought a letter from Selim Bey. In it, after having

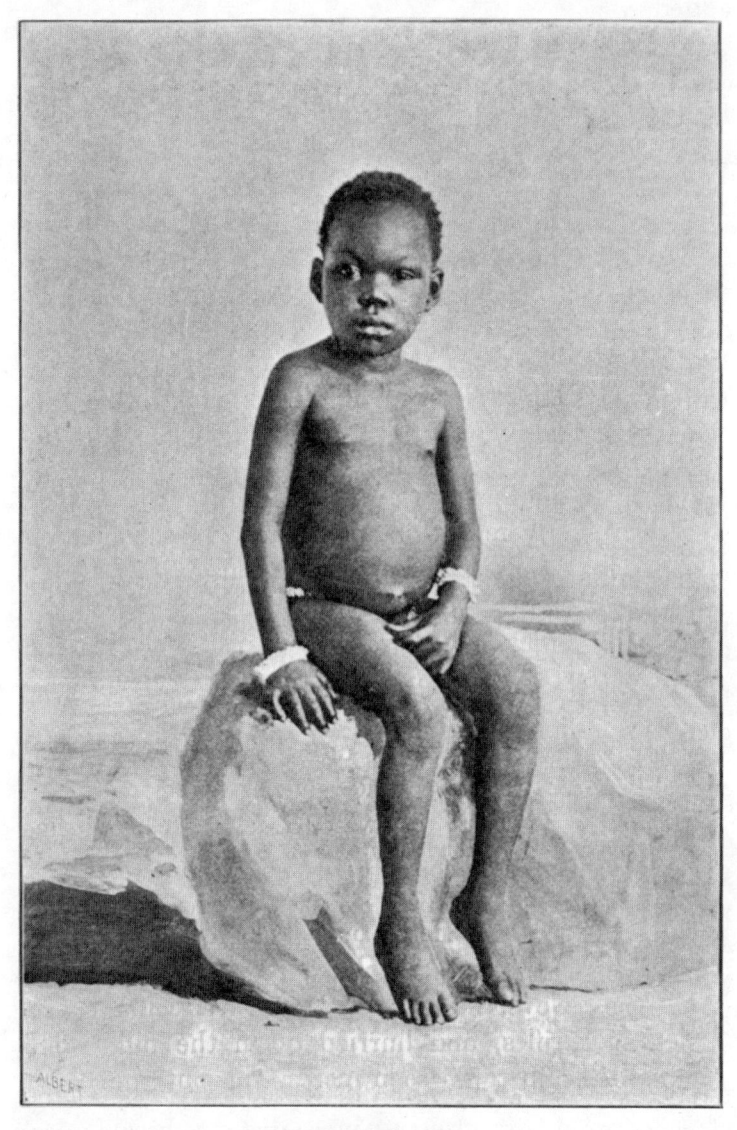

LITTLE AMINA.

announced the concentration at Msua of the soldiers

and officials who intended to leave the country, he added :—

We have no ammunition, having been obliged to leave almost all of it to the soldiers who have remained at Wadelai with Captain Fatelmula; the natives may overwhelm us during the journey; pray stop and wait for us. If you do not, and a misfortune happens, Pasha, you will have to account for it before God.

The abandonment of those who begged for help was decided on, nevertheless. A letter was written to them, alleging the impossibility of waiting, and begging them to hasten their arrival, as the caravan would stop several days at Mount Virika, and also at Lake Ruitan. By steep and fatiguing slopes, ascending continually to higher altitudes, and passing through Bujungue and Vochumbe, we arrived at Buhogo, May 11, on the line of waterparting between the Ituri and Semliki rivers. It is peopled by Walegga, who, as a matter of habit, do not live in large villages, but in groups of huts by families. The country is rich in Indian millet, bananas, and beans; colocynth is much cultivated in fields, and there grows also a kind of tobacco, much appreciated for its flavour.

We were on the confines of Mboga's territory, at a short distance from our deadly enemy; the *banassura* of the King of Unyoro awaited us. One hour had scarcely elapsed after our arrival when we heard repeated reports of guns close to our camp. The alarm was given, but only a few young men responded to it, the greater part of the people having gone in search of provisions. Nevertheless those few youths courageously seized their rifles, and hurried down the hill. The number of combatants soon increased; but the sound of shots, gradually growing more distant, became less frequent, and at last ceased. At sunset four young Soudanese ascended the hill, carrying a corpse, that of my brave boy, Oakil, who had been shot in the forehead. Having started among the first, he began with them the combat which ended in the enemy's defeat ; but in the rush of pursuit, and with his youthful contempt for danger, he did not perceive the deadly gun aimed at him from behind a rock. His distressed friends showed their grief for his loss with the respect due to heroism.

In the camp, regret was general, for he had known how to acquire the esteem and affection of all. Unhappy youth ! Picked up by Gessi, and entrusted by him to my care when he left for Khartoum, he had grown up at my side, and had been a faithful and affectionate companion in my excursions.

At the time of his death he was about sixteen years of age. He had become a fine, tall, agile fellow—intelligent, loyal, and brave. In the Mege country, when a child, he had given proofs of the firmness of his character when I had to suffer from Azanga's vexations. In after-times, during the troubles we underwent in Unyoro, he did not belie his good qualities. A good hunter, a diligent keeper of everything that was in the house, untiring on the march, with a knowledge of dialects, which he easily learned, he had rendered great and continual services to me. His grave was dug close to a group of wild date and palm trees ; it was carefully filled up and covered in order to prevent its discovery by King Chua's soldiers, who, having perhaps recognised the fallen boy, might have attempted to carry his head to our old persecutor.

On the following morning, when I was shown the spot where he had been killed, and saw the blood-stained ground, I felt much grieved. My remembrance of him is still vivid, both from affection and gratitude.

The configuration of the land extending before us was

no longer doubtful. The river flowing in the valley was the Semliki; embanked between mountains, it forms the connecting link of Lakes Ruitan and Albert, as the good Kategora had told me, in Unyoro. Beyond the river the mountains rise to the height of the Virika, in a comparatively small space. It was obvious, therefore, that, if we crossed the river into the territory of Mboga, we should put ourselves on the way to a difficult region, on account of the numerous spurs of the range of mountains, the many rivers enclosed in the deep valleys, and the woody nature of the country.

The western range did not present such obstacles, either in the altitude of the peaks of its lesser chains, or from the nature of the soil, mostly covered by grass and without forests of any extent.

Had we, therefore, pursued our march through the Walegga land, we should have been able to cross the river Semliki at a more southern point in the Usongora district, and by a less uncomfortable route, without being exposed to the danger of attacks from the *banassura* of Unyoro. But at Kavalli, when the white summits of the mountain excited curiosity and the desire for observation, the ascent of the Virika was discussed as an essential point for the choice of the route to be followed. Afterwards, when the danger was perceived of the caravan being overtaken by Selim Bey and his soldiers, this itinerary was preferred.

"When I shall have put between me and them," said Stanley, "such a series of obstacles, the Expedition will have no longer any cause for fear."

We therefore went down to the Semliki, where the gunshots of our implacable enemies received us, and on May 17, 1889, they daringly attempted an assault on the camp.

The river, which is named Malemba at its outflow

from Lake Ruitan, is called Ngazi all through the Naunga country, and has the name of Semliki when it falls into Lake Albert. At Wamba, where the caravan ferried it, it is 200 feet wide (60 metres) and 10 feet deep (3 metres). The passage was made in boats seized from the natives.

The spot is picturesque. The flowing river forms an ample curve; on its eastern bank the land gradually rises from a swamp; on the western side a grove of *Cucifera thebaica* contrasts with the dark thick forest of Katanda, which covers the hilly land.

We entered the Wamba country; the natives fled at our approach. In the thick of the forest we came across villages of pigmies, with huts in the shape of skull caps. In some of them we saw smaller ones, the size of a hamper, destined for the use of children. These little people, called Bassua by the Walegga, from time to time annoyed our people with their arrows, on their way to fetch water; but they were paid off for their audacity by three of the most daring being shot. At this point the road runs through swampy woods; the ground then rises little by little, and on the sixth day of our march, when we reached the village of Vugorama, on the borders of the Wamba region, we were 575 feet (175 metres) above the level of the Semliki river. On May 28, 1889, we were still in the forest. The road was fatiguing, with steep ascents and precipitous declivities; there were rivers with violent currents and very cold waters; and, as we could not get a guide, we were compelled to make great circuits in order to look for an exit. On the 5th of June we reached the Msucali village, in the country of the Vakongio, which is situated on a narrow elongated neck of land, at the foot of the high peak of the Virika, flanked by horrible precipices. We were at an altitude of 3513 feet (1071 metres) above the level of the sea. Our sufferings were very great; the number of people with sore feet and legs was on the increase; the fatigue of the march prostrated many; the clerk Wassif died on the road. An Egyptian soldier, Hamidan, seized with fever and unable to march on, was maltreated by the Zanzibaris of the rear-guard. Blinded by anger and pain, he threw his own child away into the grass—an infamous deed, that no one prevented by taking up the innocent creature. Near Bwasse, by mistake, a serious fight was begun against a column of Manyema searching for ivory. When the two parties recognised each other there were six of ours wounded, and of the supposed enemies one killed and five wounded. On the night of the 8th of June, the Vacongio, having stealthily approached our camp, killed, with their lances, Karalla, one of Emin's servants, who, relying upon the tranquillity in which the natives had left us, and quite certain of his safety, fell asleep at a distance, out of sight of the guard.

On the same day Lieutenant Stairs returned from exploring the Virika peaks. Dense woods, intricate and inaccessible precipices, prevented him from reaching a higher point than 10,683 feet (3256 metres) above the level of the sea. He brought back with him some plants gathered on the mountain, among which were the *Erica arborea* and a *Vaccinium*. The great mountain, therefore, still holds its mystery, and the several conjectures existing about it make it desirable that a scientific exploration should rend the veil. The hopes conceived at Kavalli failed.

From plateau to plateau, and still in the forest, we arrived, on the 10th of June, at the small village of Saura, where the natives greeted us with arrows. Of these men one was killed and several captured; the chief then hastened to submit to us. As on the 11th, Mabù, a Soudanese, was abandoned on the road, so on the 12th Havari, an Egyptian, was forsaken at the camp, being unable to pursue the journey owing to large sores on his feet and legs.

Stanley was informed at Muchora of the presence in Usongora of many of King Chua's *banassura*. As a precaution against attacks along the road, he ordered all servants, armed with guns, to join the rear-guard with the Zanzibaris and the Manyema. This arrangement caused great resentment in the people of the caravan, who wanted their own servants for the carriage of their effects and children and to attend to their own sick.

Emin, when he saw himself deprived of six armed servants, went to complain about it to Stanley, who received him brusquely, and threw upon him the responsibility for the misfortunes which at every place befell the Expedition.

The Pasha withdrew, and Stanley, as if to give vent to his anger, ordered Hassan, Marco the Greek, and the clerk Basili to be arrested and brought before him by an escort of soldiers, for non-compliance with the orders received; hence threats, shouts, and fresh discontent arose.

On the 14th we left the Ukongio territory, and with it the forest. Before us lay a vast plain rich in vegetation, and enlivened by frequent villages. Boundless to the south, the plain was cut on the west by the course of the Semliki, beyond which rises the range of the Walegga mountains. It is the Usongora district, the region of the Ruitan Lake. We all felt happier, as the lake was our long-wished-for aim, where we should have a rest. Leaving the mountains, we descended the spurs of the range, and, winding round the curve of the hills, we reached Kiambali, inhabited by the Wahuma people. But the difficult and wearisome road, broken by the rocks and stones of the mountain, demanded its victims in the persons of a clerk, an Egyptian soldier, and some women and children, who fell exhausted, never to return among us.

Who cared for them ?

Helplessness may compel abandonment, but does not diminish its horrors. Sad events of the kind were so frequent that people grew indifferent to them, and the strong ones saluted with joy the sun already gilding the white crests of the Virika, shining in the far distance.

On the 17th we reached Katua, at 2920 feet (890 metres) above the level of the sea, and from thence beheld one of the branches of Lake Ruitan.

The surrounding country is covered with short grass, and scattered about are many trees of *Euphorbia candelabra*. The lake has two small and hilly islands at a short distance apart; its waters are very much like those of the Albert Lake in colour and taste. It is 82 feet (25 metres) below the altitude of Katua.

The small lake Kio, not far off towards the north, has salt waters of a carmine red colour; its circumference is about $2\frac{1}{2}$ miles (4 kilometres), and is situated about 147 feet (45 metres) below Katua.

Beautiful saline crystals are to be found in the deposit of the water, and are the object of an active trade in the country and surrounding lands. The shores, which rise several feet above the surface of the water, are covered with plants, *Euphorbia candelabra* and *Palma Phœnix*. The possession of so rich a country has always been jealously desired by the neighbouring potentates, the Kings of Uganda, Unyoro, and Nkole. King Chua's *banassura* have often tried to settle in the region of the

ATTACKED BY BANASSURA.

lake, but have always been driven away by the troops of Uganda. Owing to the sad condition of King Muanga's domains, caused by internal dissensions, the King of Unyoro was enabled easily to consolidate his dominion over Toru, Mruli, and Usongora. He also tried to make the Nkole country tributary, but, after having been discomfited several times, he gave up the idea, and confined himself to raids for cattle. A large trade in salt is carried on in the territory, and is extended as far as Kitaguenda, Uganda, Nkole, and Mporuru, where this product finds an easy sale.

The boats being insufficient to ferry the whole caravan over the lake (June 20), we were obliged to reach the eastern shore by reascending to the north-east in order to avoid the extensive swamps and marshy ground. We journeyed over an ample plain, arid and without water, where no trees grew, except a few *Euphorbia* and *Mimosa*. Only near cowsheds are found pools of water; they have a greenish surface, are disgusting to the palate, and are met at a certain distance from each other as far as Amkongo, a village on the eastern branch of the lake, opposite the Irangara Island. That tiresome march was prolonged to a length of about $18\frac{1}{2}$ miles (30 kilometres).

In order to go from the Unyampaka territory to the eastern shore of the second branch of the lake, we had to pass through the Mruli and Toru districts, under the direct domination of King Chua, whose troops laid ambushes for the column in three different places. The attack on the 22nd of June, at the passage of the river Unyamwambi, had it been vigorously carried out, might have been fatal to the caravan.

Whilst we were issuing from the Kitindi forest, on the 26th, the *banassura* attempted to divide the column, but they were repulsed by the timely coming up and energetic counteraction of Captain Shukri with the Soudanese of the rear-guard. This attack proved of no consequence whatever.

On the 28th of the same month the King of Unyoro's soldiers assailed us at our exit from their territory on the Ruroi river, but the result was as harmless as a salute. On the 29th of June we passed through a strip of Unyampaka's territory, and crossed over the river Roali, about 66 feet (20 metres) wide, with a rapid torrent amongst rocks and stones, and arrived at Bukorongo, on the eastern coast of the Ruitan, on the first day of July 1889.

The lake here is imposing from the depth and extent of its mass of water. The shore is gaily dotted over with villages and huts, surrounded by groves of banana-trees, with fields of maize and beans. The Wahuma people possess plenty of cows and goats. The journey from Kavalli to the eastern shore of Lake Ruitan was completed in thirty-five days' march. Neither the roughness of the countries crossed, nor the harsh treatment received, had destroyed the faith of the members of the caravan as to their eventual return. Though held in small account, and subjected to grievous exactions of all kinds, they met everything with apathy and indifference. The sanitary condition of the caravan was very bad. Most of the people, without distinction of sex or age, were afflicted with ulcerations and sores on their feet and legs. The route taken for the study of the geological formation and physical structure of the Virika had caused them (deprived of the means required for the protection of health) the inconvenience of following the wildest and most arduous road of the region.

Fortune willed, however, that circumstances should be favourable to us, and we had a supply of food

ARRIVAL AT LAKE RUITAN.

beyond our requirements. In the open spaces of the forest, cultivated with bananas, maize, and colocynth, we easily obtained an abundant and constant supply of sustenance, as the natives generally fled on our arrival.

We then emerged from the gloom of the forest and went down the hills sloping to the lake, bright with crops of wheat and leguminous plants, which satisfied all our wants.

From Unyampaka three routes lead to Zanzibar: the first runs through the Usimba and Kitaguenda countries, following the mountain path by which it descends to Uganda; the second goes through the Nkole country; the third borders the lake and the Nkole territory, and enters the Ruanda district. Stanley, who once feared the 200,000 warriors in the gorges of the Nkole, now chose that very route without hesitation or discussion.

CHAPTER XV.

FROM LAKE RUITAN TO LAKE VICTORIA.

The Nkole State—Conformation of the region—Wahuma and Wichinesi—King Ntali—A shepherd, not a king—Fear of strangers—" I will not flee, but wait for you"—Negotiations started in Unyoro—Hospitality granted to Uganda Christians—Mtesa driven away—Slaughters—Either circumcision or death—Karema—Persecutions against Christians—Muanza christened at the French Mission—A difficult path—The Mpogo swamp—The king's concessions to the caravan—Disorderly conduct of soldiers and Zanzibaris at Ruganda—Fight to rescue a woman—The king's son visits the camp—Murder of a Manyema and of a woman—The river Kagera—A girl carried away by a leopard—The mineral waters of Ntagata—Karagua's country—King Ndàgora a vassal of the King of Uganda—Carried in a hammock—Death by cold on the way to Batenga—The Urigi Lake—Fatelmula, a soldier, abandoned to the Mtara people's revenge—His horrible death—Requisitions end—Provisions are bought—Fatal effects of manioc—An Akka's flight—The Victoria Lake—At the British Mission—Mackay.

THE region surrounded by the kingdom of Uganda, the country of Ruanda, and the Kagera river forms the Nkole State, under the dominion of King Ntali. The territory consists of the group of heights which, sloping from the main range of the so-called Mountains of the Moon, go down as far as the Karagua, towards the Victoria Lake. The high mountains, some of which have an altitude of about 6500 feet (2000 metres), protect the country from the danger of invasions and raids. Narrow gorges, rocks, difficult paths, mountain pastures, want of water and trees, give a wild aspect to the territory, which, only in the farthest slopes and in the valleys, is brightened by cultivations of Indian millet, sweet potatoes, peas, manioc, and banana groves.

The tobacco of the country has a good repute for the quality of its leaves, its delicate scent, and for the diligent preparation it undergoes.

The original part of the population is formed by the Wichinesi, who were conquered by a strong tribe of Wahuma, called Wagassara. These are now employed in agriculture, and live in the country as a class of slaves, whilst the Wagassara possess great numbers of cattle, especially oxen, remarkable for the extraordinary length of their horns.

Ntali, the lord of Nkole, is a shepherd rather than a warrior, who does not leave his mountains to attack the neighbouring tribes and make raids in their countries; but whilst he keeps on good terms with the potentates at his borders, he is a jealous keeper of the gates of his kingdom.

He had business intercourse with the Arab merchants for the purchase of arms and cloth, but he would never allow them to travel over his dominions. He sends his people to the Karagua and Uganda markets with ivory for the necessary purchases, and occasionally he allows caravans to stop at the boundaries of his country.

Challenged by King Chua, he had recourse to arms, fought against the troops of the latter, and conquered them; but he did not avail himself of his victory to settle down as an autocrat in the basin of Lake Ruitan. To Muanga, who, with youthful boldness, asked him for a tribute of cattle, he answered: "You have plenty of soldiers; if you have courage enough, come. I will not flee, but wait for you."

In Unyoro, when I was negotiating for the selection of a route for our correspondence, the hopes we entertained of sending it through Nkole would have been successful, if King Chua's jealousy had not put a stop to the discussion by suddenly sending away Nguro, King Ntali's envoy.

When we crossed his country, we were given proof of his hospitality to Christians, fugitives from Uganda. Muanga had inaugurated his reign by persecuting the neophytes of the British missionaries. The peace (the benefits of which were enjoyed during the last years of Mtesa's government) was abruptly disturbed ; Muanga condemned hundreds of people to be burnt alive, and spread terror and desolation over his country. Mr. Mackay, the chief of the British Mission, was soon pointed out by the Arabs as an enemy of the king and kingdom, and suffered odious vexations and ill-treatment. He was exiled, but arrested shortly afterwards as a runaway. The horrible insult was inflicted on him of witnessing the spectacle of the death of a youth, a convert, of whom he was particularly fond.

The Zanzibar Mohammedans did not stop their nefarious persecution, and obtained from the insane king the expulsion of all missionaries, either of the Catholic or Protestant Church—and their audacity went so far as to suggest to the king that he should eradicate and extinguish in blood the dawning idea of Christianity existing amongst the various castes of the population.

The persuasions of those fanatics would have been complied with had not the king become aware of the danger he had unadvisedly placed himself in, and attempted to master the current which dragged him in its vortex.

He promised the Arabs friendship and protection, but in the meantime secretly plotted against them, and was forsaken by all. The Arabs, wishing for absolute power in the country, and jealous of a supremacy which the frivolous nature of the king might have suddenly made void, allied themselves with the converts to the new religion against their common enemy, trusting in the hatred which persecution had excited in the people. Hence revolution ensued; Katikiro, the Prime Minister, and the most dangerous and influential persons were put to death; King Muanga scarcely managed to escape to a small island in the Victoria Lake, whilst Kavira, his younger brother, was triumphantly proclaimed king of freed Uganda.

The excitement of victory subsided after its celebration with orgies and bloodshed. The new king, advised by friends upon whom the ruin of the country weighed heavily, turned to gentler counsels, and, feeling ashamed of foreign influence, spoke words of peace and brotherhood to his subjects.

The Arabs, who were powerful both as regards arms and friends, could not tolerate his breach of the treaty, and, threatening the king with the menace: "Either circumcision or death!" besieged his abode. The king replied with an emphatical refusal, and appealed to his people, who made fun of him and left him to the revenge of the fanatics. He and forty of his faithful friends met death in the flames of the piles of wood set on fire around his residence.

Having run the risk of seeing their work destroyed, the Arabs grew prudent, and after having put to death all the other members of the royal family, kept and revered Karema, a timid and inexperienced lad, as a mere puppet of a king. Under his reign persecution and pyres were again resorted to, with daily victims. Those among the persecuted ones who were able to leave the country found safety in Nkole.

Meanwhile Muanga, with a few of his household, repaired to Usukuma, where he begged protection from the missionaries; and the murderer of Hannington, the ferocious persecutor of Christians, the Nero of Uganda, was pompously christened at the Catholic Mission, and, if not praised, was certainly protected and forgiven. Roman Catholic and Protestant missionaries recognised him as the King of Uganda, and exerted themselves in in his favour.

On the 9th of July, Stanley, on being welcomed by a deputation of Christian rebels, when entering the Kitega village, encouraged them in their hopes, and promised to protect them and interest himself in their

FORDING THE MPOGO SWAMP.

cause, thus smoothing the way to a settlement for an eventual protectorate over the whole kingdom of Uganda.

At Jikombi (July 4, 1889), having left the lake, the route traverses high mountains, and is difficult, owing to the steep and stony nature of the soil, as well as to the narrow and tortuous paths. Here and there it slopes from the heights down to the valley, and then runs for a long distance through cultivated grounds and villages, surrounded by groves of banana-trees; but soon the path goes up steep and tiring hills again. Necessary rest did not compensate for the fatigues of the march, as the cold temperature of the nights prevented our sleeping, and compelled us to sit by the fire, owing to want of proper shelter.

On the 12th of July we journeyed on a less hard road; we left the range of mountains, which runs southward, and made for the south-east, over smaller spurs, whence, descending from terrace to terrace, we could from time to time discern a large plain covered by a thick vegetation of papyrus, the sight of which had filled our minds with joy when on the mountains. It was the Mpogo swamp, a basin of black mud, formed by the Ruizi river, which expands as it flows into the valley, and inundates it, its bulk of waters being increased by the streams flowing from the neighbouring mountains. We crossed the narrow ford in single file, grasping the papyrus tufts and falling occasionally over one another when the one in advance made a false step, thus covering ourselves with mire. With shouts of anger and ironical jokes, we dragged ourselves along for some distance before we reached a wide stream, where any attempt to protect ourselves was of no avail, as there was not a bush, or anything to catch hold of; we were in the water up to our chins.

The scene changed; the travellers, no longer in a line, but scattered in groups over a large extent, attempted to cross swamps wider than the one we had left behind us, in order to get to the dry land. Without taking any trouble to find a ford, now stumbling over papyrus roots, or heaps of mud, and sinking in the marshy soil, wet from head to foot, after about two hours' struggling we reached the banks, and ran along the road to the hills which led us to the Mpogo village, the residence of Igomero, the son of the king.

It was night, and our efforts to save some of the oxen which had fallen, having been vain, we were obliged to abandon them.

A message from the king, brought by a prince of the royal family, granted the caravan permission to get the necessary supplies of bananas, beans, peas, and sweet potatoes in the fields along our route—but limited to the farms that were near the villages. Stanley, on account of this concession, strictly forbade the members

A WOMAN STOLEN.

of the caravan to take the cattle and property found in the dwellings.

On the 14th of July we arrived at Ruganda, whose chief, Vasingana, is a kinsman of Ntali, where a sad event prevented Stanley from carrying out his plan of an early departure. Some soldiers and porters of the caravan having succeeded in evading the surveillance of the camp, went to a village on the mountains, and tried to steal goats and other property from the huts of the blacks. Not at all frightened by the rapacious invasion, a good many natives attacked the thieves, made six prisoners and seized two guns. Stanley was indignant, with reason; but through the chief of Ruganda he obtained their release and the return of the rifles; but he declared openly that, in the case of similar events taking place, he would abandon the culprits to their fate.

Circumstances had changed. We were no longer among a timid population, frightened by our presence,

NTALI'S PRESENT TO STANLEY.

and running away at our approach; nor with tribes surprised at our presence, diffident but respectful; we were amongst an audacious and cunning population, well aware of their strength, watching our movements, and always trying to take advantage of our passage through their territory.

Intercourse with Uganda, business relationship with merchants, have made of them a provident, sagacious, and thoroughly business-like people. Their assaults on the stragglers gave proof of their enmity to us. On the 22nd they carried off a woman, found at a distance from the caravan.

Promptly pursued and overtaken on the road, the numerous raiders were attacked by Captain Shukri, near the village of Viarua; they defended themselves in the groves of banana-trees, but after a few shots the woman was saved, who, for the sake of her life, had been glad to part with the few things she had with her.

On the 23rd an unusual excitement prevailed in the camp owing to the arrival of King Ntali's son. The Zanzibaris were drawn up in lines; the echo of the mountains resounded with salutes to the king; for the first time we heard the mitrailleuse fired. The king sent two cows; the usual courteous compliments were paid on each side; protection was promised, and, most important of all, we were granted permission to leave the kingdom.

We descended the hills of Viarua, skirted the last mountainous slopes, and reached the river Kagera on the boundary between the States of Nkole and Karagua, on the 23rd. The king welcomed us and sent presents, but his subjects impressed us with a sad remembrance of their country. Half-way between Mavona and Kandakamo an unfortunate Manyema, prostrated by fever and heat, was left behind; he painfully attempted to follow the caravan; and awaiting his wife, who had gone to fetch some water for him, stopped near a group of huts, but the natives rushed on the two poor creatures, and answered their entreaties to have their lives spared with thrusts of their lances, killing them both, and thus giving vent to the hatred hidden in their hearts. A patrol sent in the evening in search of the couple had witnessed the murder without being able to prevent it.

A NEGRESS OF THE CARAVAN CARRIED AWAY BY A LEOPARD.

The river Kagera, called Kitangobe by the Waganda, flows south-westward between two high hills, and is, at Kandakamo, about 330 feet (100 metres) broad; its current has great velocity. At an altitude of about 3800 feet (1160 metres) it finds its way through the mountainous country, and after having received the waters of several tributary rivers, amongst which the principal is the Ruizi, reaches the Victoria Lake by long windings.

The violence of the current renders the crossing of the stream dangerous and long. We had to join two boats strongly together; and part of the caravan ferried over the river on the 27th, the day of our arrival; but the majority were obliged to encamp on the shore.

The valley is full of wild beasts, which manifested their presence to us by sinister roars. At about midnight the whole camp was disturbed by loud shrieks: a leopard had taken away a girl. Everybody started to trace the unlucky woman and try to save her, but in vain. The victim could not be recovered.

On the 28th of July 1889 we entered the Karagua country, which we traversed, by a route ascending hills scattered over the valley, which with long zigzags reaches Ugomoro, and from thence the Ntagata mineral waters, which the inhabitants of the country make great use of for the cure of diseases of the skin. In the territory between the mountainous region in which the river Semliki flows, to the shore of the Victoria Lake, hot springs are plentiful. On the route followed by our caravan we came across a sulphurous spring near Msucali in the Vakongio country, the temperature of the water was 30°·7 Centigrade; in the Usongora territory one drew our attention near Muchora, and its water was 30°·5; and in another at Moshambo, we found the register to be 35°. In the district of Usigno the temperature of the spring called Teko was ascertained to be 33°·16.

The Karagua territory, already known, owing to the account given by Speke in connection with King Rumanika, was conquered by and annexed to Uganda, after having gone through internal commotions, either owing to the caprice of princes or the dissensions of the people. The King of Uganda's first care was to deprive the country of its numerous and beautiful cattle, the main source of the wealth of the population.

Ndàgora, Rumanika's youngest child, is the king of the country, but more from traditional habit than real authority. The Arabs, who once used to have stations there, after the opening of the road to Uganda through Usukuma and the lake, now only make raids in the State at certain times in order to obtain the supply of ivory, compelled to do this by the continual hostility of the natives. Their permanent station, established at Kafuro, was abandoned after the murder of the Arab Bin Salem, treacherously shot with arrows by the natives.

Since my illness, when visiting Lake Ruitan, I had several attacks of fever, but on the 2nd of August 1889, I was taken so very ill that Dr. Parke asked for and obtained from Stanley the necessary porters to carry me.

Every day that passed, I felt weaker, and it was with joy that I welcomed the day of the arrival of the caravan at Mr. Mackay's British Mission station.

At daybreak of August 8, the sky was clouded, and a very cold wind from the south blew violently and rendered our limbs torpid. But the caravan started. We had already ascended the first hill, covered by woods of mimosa, when a terrible rainfall began, driven so strongly by the force of the wind that we could hardly

CASATI ILL, ON THE RETURN.

breathe. The caravan was broken up ; porters dropped their loads, many an imprudent one stopped by blazing fires, and at our arrival at Batenga several individuals were missing, who had died during our journey. On account of the increased number of sick people, and the necessity of making the loads lighter, several boxes of ammunition were thrown into the Urigi, a little lake surrounded by grassy hills, whose waters are of a bright azure. The Urigi has an elongated shape, the greatest distance between the two extremities being about 19 miles (30 kilometres); it is so narrow that from one side, the other can always clearly be seen. Its shore is broken by numerous inlets, thus making the banks of this lake pleasant to the sight.

The Yanghiro district, which is situated on the eastern shore of the Urigi, is a hilly region, scattered over with villages and cultivated fields, as well as with woods of banana-trees.

At ten o'clock A.M. of the 12th of August, we encamped in a wooded plain on the lake shore, not far from the Mtara village; and soon all our people, soldiers, servants, women, and children, started for the purpose of seeking food, of which we were in want.

A few soldiers and Zanzibaris entered the village and forced their society upon a party of natives who were drinking beer. Without the least prudence or sense of reciprocal respect, our men soon began to insult and ill-use the blacks, and, as was their custom, took possession of the vessels of beer, driving their owners away.

The natives did not suffer the insult quietly; but, having called their friends to help, prepared to attack the troublesome guests. Thus a fight ensued, and one of the natives having been killed, the others, raging with fury, doubled their efforts, and succeeded in making some prisoners. The news soon reached the camp, and Stanley sent for particulars of the event and opened an inquiry into the matter.

The natives demanded payment for the loss sustained. Bloodshed does not admit of mercy. Stanley, faithful to his word given at Rugandu, did not condescend to enter into any agreement, but handed over the soldier guilty of murder to the friends of the murdered Negro, to pay with his life for the life of the deceased.

Rejoicing at their success, they dragged the poor fellow away, and, like an automaton, he offered no resistance to his executioners.

The party had not left the camp long when three arrows were already stuck in the back of their victim. The same evening it was told in the camp that, in compliance with the wishes of the angry females, Fatelmula's teeth had been pulled out one by one. The sentence of death passed upon him was to be executed by long and atrocious sufferings.

The *lex talionis* traditional with the natives was on that occasion sanctioned and confirmed by the authority of the *white people*. Great was the discontent felt in the camp at the severe sentence, and the soldiers begged Emin to intervene for the victim; Omar, the Soudanese officer, appealed to him as the direct chief of the Government's people, but the Pasha refused to comply with their requests.

The condition of the caravan was about to change. Since the day we left the Albert Lake it had always been an easy thing to get the necessary supplies. The abundance of products in the countries we had successively crossed, the natural timidity of the natives, as well as the superiority of the armed caravan, removed every obstacle to our catering, and each individual could

DISTRIBUTION OF GOODS.

always and with no difficulty find a plentiful supply to meet his wants.

Already this state of affairs was modified in the Nkole country, where, fortunately, the king granted us permission to get the necessary food for the caravan all along the route we were to follow. But this advantage was now taken from us, and our wants were to be met with by paying for the goods.

On the 14th of August Stanley therefore began to

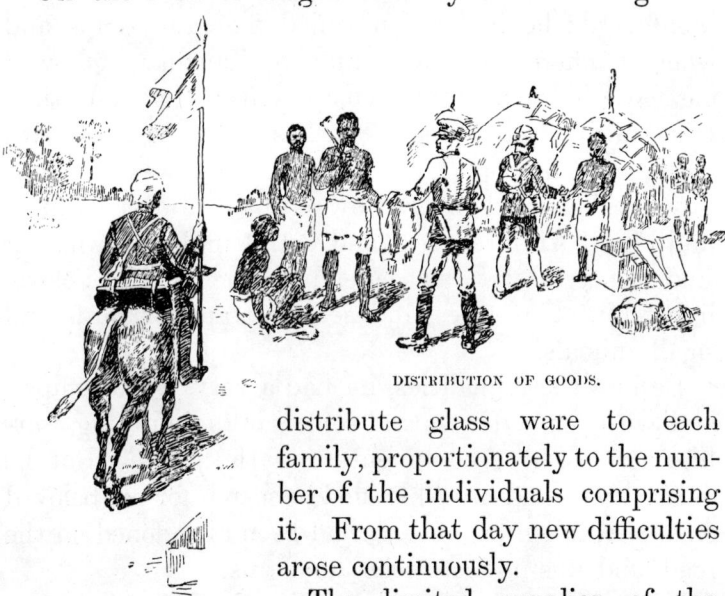

DISTRIBUTION OF GOODS.

distribute glass ware to each family, proportionately to the number of the individuals comprising it. From that day new difficulties arose continuously.

The limited supplies of the caravan, the stock of goods, not always such as to meet the exigencies of the natives, and the ever increasing claims of the vendors, seduced by easy profits on account of the imperious wants of our column, were obstacles of such gravity that we should never have been able to triumph over them if the property of the inhabitants of the country had been duly respected, and if our arrival at the British Mission had been delayed.

The habit prevailing among the servants and porters of the caravan of eating raw manioc roots, in spite of the reiterated warnings of those who knew the dangers of such a practice, had its victims.

On the 15th two young fellows, hungry and impatient, ate some roots which they had bought, without cooking them. During the night both of them died in consequence, after having suffered horrible spasms.

I had an Akka with me whom I had taken from Monfuland; he had accompanied me in my trips, and when I offered to take him to Zanzibar, followed me more from inveterate custom than from affection. His stature was 4 feet 5 inches (1·32 metres), with regular and proportionate limbs; his skin was of a light brown colour, and covered by soft hair all over his arms and legs. An intelligent and artful individual, honest and respectful, he was a splendid archer, and was clever in catching butterflies and setting traps for birds and small animals.

Besides these qualities, he had a very jovial temper, and with comic dances and somersaults, imitating warlike actions, he used to entertain the party. But he fell in love! and my Akka fled to search for his beloved one, who, fallen exhausted, had been abandoned on the road, and was no more seen among us.

We were getting near the Victoria Lake. On the 18th, from the mountains, which we skirted from Kisinge to Guyamogojo for more than four hours, we could see a branch of this lake; we reached its shore next day, near Kissao, in the Ukume district, and marched along its banks as far as Moranda.

August 21.—Woods of mimosa, with huts and villages, surrounded by groves of banana-trees, and cultivated fields, cover the hills.

At Moranda the road leaves the lake, and runs

through woody plains and meadows, with few villages, as far as Usumbiro, the French Mission, which had been recently abandoned for want of water. The villages we came across on our route were enclosed in wooden fences. On the 28th of August the caravan arrived at the establishment of the British Mission.

My heart rejoiced in entering that house! It was the home of a friend, whose rare qualities I knew so well, though he was personally unknown to me. Common dangers and comforts led both, he in Uganda, and I in Unyoro, to very hard experiences. This unknown friend was Mr. Mackay.

When we shook hands, I gazed in his face, and he appeared to me the very man I had fancied him to be. His manners were kind and frank. Intelligent-looking and highly intellectual, though he spoke seldom, when he did it was to the point. After our arrival on the coast, death put an early end to a life devoted wholly and with no ostentation to redemption and civilisation. He died on the field of his contest, and his name will live for a long time on the lips and in the hearts of the Uganda natives, who, with filial affection, venerated him, and will tell his virtues to future generations.

CHAPTER XVI.

ARRIVAL AT BAGAMOYO.

David Livingstone and slavery —Humanity is one and the same everywhere— Explorers and missionaries—Robbers of men in Egypt and Zanzibar—The war in Africa—Europe intervenes—Persecution of the missionaries— Suppression of the slave treaty—The words of Cameron—The means must be adequate to the end—Want of news—Stanley decides on departing —Arrangements for the journey—The districts of Urima and Boniera— Attack by Negroes in the district of Kelia—Four days of hostilities— General flight of the natives—Atrocity committed by a Soudanese porter— *Adansonia digitata*—The chief Mitinginya—The Wanyamuesi—Evil school of the Arabs—The *tembe*—The Masai—Theft of three asses—A Masai saved from deserved punishment—Fauna and flora—The chief Icongo— The Fathers Giraud and Schynse—The forest of sorrows—The river of palms —The cisterns of Makomero—We leave the forest—A remembrance of the caravan for the Wanyamuesi—We set foot in Ugogo—Mualata—The Wagogo —The *tembe* of Ugogo—Sands and desolation—The chief Nianguira—A foolish pretext—Robbery of guns—The caravan at Unyamuesi—Letter from Wissmann to Emin—The village of Mussanga—The forest of Jonyo or of the salt water—A well-merited punishment—At Mpwapwa—Usagara— A lovely region — At Mrogoro — The French missionaries — Captain Gravenreuth—At Kingani—The explorer of the Cassai—At Bagamoyo— Accident to Emin—The return.

"I CAN do nothing more except to wish that the fullest blessings of Heaven may fall on those who will cause the scourge of slavery to disappear from the earth." Such was the last thought of the great man dying, of the man who had consecrated thirty years of toil and suffering to the redemption of the African people—of David Livingstone.

Humanity is the same everywhere: man is of one kind, whatever may be the ethnographical differences that have given rise to a variety of races. Every act that tends to set aside this right of equality is in opposition to the harmonious laws that regulate the universe, and should be opposed by every one.

Slavery, the daughter of oppression and covetousness, degrading human nature, casts strife and barbarity over an immense number of people, whom it reduces to the condition of vile and foolish creatures. To emancipate man from this outrage done to his dignity constitutes a duty for civilisation, intent on the legitimate vindication of the principles of morality and right, and will be consecrated in history as a monument to the honour and glory of our century. It is the cry raised by all humanity, that the poet has repeated with the beauty of lyrical expression :*

> "All are in one great image made,
> In one Redemption all men share;
> In every age, in every clime,
> Where'er we breathe this vital air,
> We all are brethren—by a law
> Condemning him who breaks the chain,
> Who dares to trample on the weak,
> And cause the immortal spirit pain."

In the inhospitable lands of Africa, which, from their climate and the harshness of nature, have been shut from the knowledge of the civilised world from immemorial times, the native chiefs, powerful by audacity or by descent, found pleasure in hunting human creatures for the satisfaction either of their caprice or luxury. And when explorers or missionaries, inspired by a noble enthusiasm, endeavoured to tear away the veil of mystery that enveloped the Dark Country, and to raise brilliant hopes in its forsaken inhabitants, they found in their way—an unpropititious augury— the robbers who traded in human flesh, who had come from Egypt and Zanzibar. But these valorous and enterprising men were not discouraged ; they even

* A. Manzoni—"The Count of Carmagnola."

redoubled their efforts, and, inspired by a noble self-denial, they led the negroes on the road to civilisation, and rendered them by instruction, capable of struggling against their bitter persecutors. Unfortunately, they were few, and they perished in the struggle. The banner of a religion raised only to cover wicked intentions, kindled war and spread desolation on every side. The strife would have still farther extended its evil consequences if Europe, breaking with a noble impulse through all hindrances, had not arisen as the avenger of the violated rights of humanity. She sent her soldiers to the gates of the black continent, thus pledging her honour for the redemption of its inhabitants. The noble pioneers of this rescue, few and isolated, either paid with their life for the boldness of the enterprise to which they had devoted themselves, or were left wandering through those inhospitable regions to await the dawn of the day of requital.

Uncertain of their own future, yet strong and fearless, we found the French missionaries on the shores of Lake Victoria at Ukumbi, fugitives from their various stations, and at Usumbiro the English clergymen previously driven from Uganda and afterwards from Msalala, through the hatred excited against them by the Mussulmans.

An arduous enterprise, and deserving of all attention, of calm study, and prudent action, is the task that Europe has assumed in the conflict between civilisation and barbarism—in the work for the suppression of slavery.

"Those who desire the extirpation of the slave-trade," said Cameron, "should set in motion words, money, and energy."

But in our time is benevolence sufficient for that redemption? And is it possible to collect the enormous sums it would require? Is not the reasonable use of

A SLAVE-CARAVAN.

armed force indispensable for the suppression of slavery? The depopulation of the country by the removal of the slaves; the habit in most of them of forgetting the family from whom they were taken at a tender age, and of adapting themselves to the degradation of their lot; the natural mistrust of the Negro, much increased by the horrors of which he is a witness; his dislike of work, and the readiness with which he leaves his birth-place, are all reasons that should keep us on our guard against being led away by utopian ideas in reflecting on the means available to secure the object of our wishes—that is, the redemption of Africa from barbarism.

Enthusiasm is as easy in Europe as disillusions are in Africa. At the first step the dreamed-of light is changed into darkness, and every unexpected obstruction signifies a disaster.

It is, therefore, necessary that the means should be adequate to the end in view, so that the foot may not recede from the place where it has marked its imprint. Neither should we proceed without first being sure of victory, because the banner of redemption should be a guarantee of lasting protection. Our first care ought to be to satisfy in a just measure the new desires and new needs of the natives; to render social intercourse friendly and sincere; to excite the activity of their minds, and urge them to alacrity in work. A loyal commerce of exchange; cordiality, brotherhood without distinction of races; love and reverence for that which is just and honest, instilled into the hearts by the salutary assistance of religion—without, however, any utilitarian character in it that, for the slavery of the body would often substitute that of the mind—will lead gradually and without great shocks to the redemption of a people who are not deficient in natural gifts, and who occupy a region remarkable for its extent and fertility of soil.

To the slave dealers, however, constant persecution, incessant war, the infamy of the gallows should be given.

The information we received at the British Mission about the road that remained for us to travel over, although it was not of recent date, was not reassuring. The fact even of the non-arrival of the couriers augmented doubt and confirmed the opinion that we should encounter probable peril. The conflict on the coast of Zanzibar, between the troops of the German Government and the rebel Arabs, was still going on, and the territory to the south of the lake, even into the heart of Usagara, was at the mercy of the insurgents.

In consequence of these rumours, Mackay was earnest in dissuading Stanley from ordering the immediate departure of the caravan, and advised him to await the arrival of couriers with more positive intelligence. But Stanley, pre-occupied by the difficulties that would certainly have arisen from this delay, and on the other side confiding in the armed force of the caravan, decided, after having sent on a letter-bearer, to depart on the morning of the 17th of September.

The repose and comfort that we had enjoyed during our stay at the Mission had strengthened our health; and the conviction that the most difficult part of the journey was overcome, and that the way to Zanzibar had been for a long time open to caravans, and therefore presented nothing unknown, made every one feel convinced of the certainty of safely reaching the end of our journey.

On the march to Bagamoyo provisions could no longer be procured by requisitions; they must be obtained by means of payment to the natives, therefore the cloth and beads necessary for exchange were again distributed to each component part of the caravans.

I had a gift from Stanley of some provisions, and I

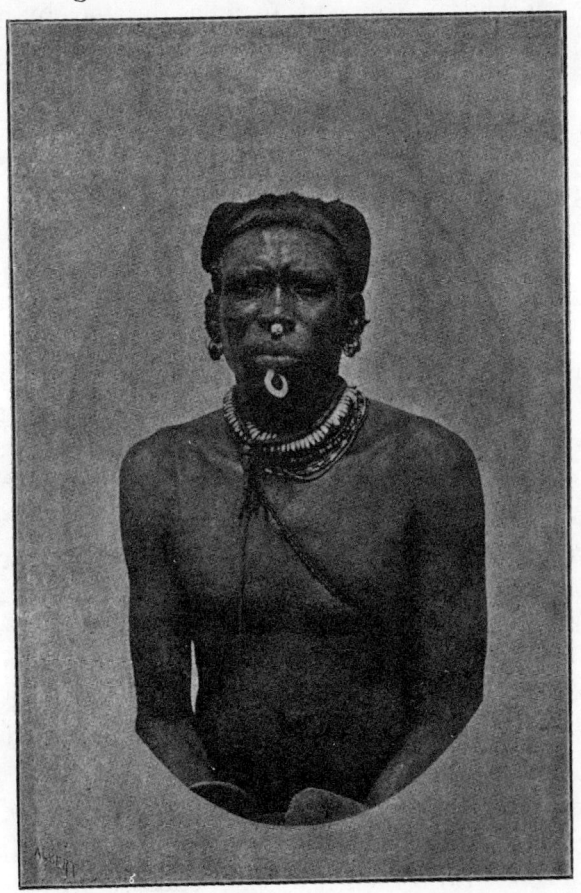

NEGRO OF URIMA.

was able to purchase from the French missionaries some clothes and shoes, besides an ass, which, though old and feeble, and an object of universal commiseration, went on intrepidly, and was of most valuable assistance to me as far as Bagamoyo.

On the 17th of September we took leave of our courteous host, and the caravan, proceeding more carefully than it had even done before, took the road to the district of Urima. This is a low plain covered with short grass, marked by frequent marshes, broken by masses and fragments of rocks, and here and there showing rare trees of *Cucifera thebaica*. After travelling three days, we were in the district of Boniera, a territory shut in by low hills and sprinkled with frequent villages and groups of dwellings, with a large population, who received us, when we stopped to pitch our camp (September 19, 1889), with war cries and offensive actions, to which we replied by silence and indifference.

But the day after (September 20, 1889), having entered the district of Kelia and approached the residence of the chief Malissa, the head of the caravan was suddenly assailed by arrows, shot from behind a pile of enormous stones that, rising up, formed a hill, and amongst which the habitations of the village are constructed. Two Zanzibaris were wounded, and a combat began; the crowd decamped, but other casualties occurred. We were engaged with men posted in ambush, who discharged arrows and musket shots at us. We prudently retired and encamped under the shelter of a group of rocks.

Nor did the audacity of the natives stop here. Leaving very early on the morning of the 21st, we were soon overtaken by the enemy, who closely followed us, joined by others of the territory that we were traversing. We marched on, fighting on the 22nd and 23rd. The flat land, on the way we were pursuing, open all round us, did not present any serious peril of our being smartly attacked. The caravan marched compact and united, as the plain, free

WARRIORS OF THE URIMA DISTRICT.

from all obstacles, permitted it; the flanks and rear were protected by guards posted at a convenient distance. But the paucity of the means of sustenance, the scarcity of water, and the finding ourselves near the entrance of a wood (by which one passes from the district of Usseke to that of Vanianga), obliged us to take an energetic resolution. It was three hours after noon, September 23, 1889. The mass of the natives, firm in its hostile intentions, was increased from the

ATTACK ON THE CARAVAN.

surrounding villages, and redoubled its hostility; the rushes that our men made in different directions no longer sufficed to keep them back. The mitrailleuse was brought up to the front of the camp, its roar resounded, and there was a general flight. We were freed from any further molestation. The dwellings of the neighbouring villages were sacked, and then burnt down; some heads of cattle were surprised and captured, whilst the proprietors were driving them away in their flight.

In the night, from the tent of a Zanzibari porter the groans of a suffering woman brought angry voices from every part where repose had been disturbed. Suddenly a gun shot was heard, and then silence reigned in the darkness. The miserable creature killed was the woman who had groaned; an unhappy being, captured that day, and bound by strong and tight cords to prevent her from taking flight. Her scoundrel of an owner, not being able to silence her by threats, in a fit of rage had committed murder.

Following a direction to the south-east, and then to the south, in six days we traversed the districts of Vanianga and Kisumbe, in which the colossal *Adansonia digitata* (baobab) makes a fine show; and then by the districts of Samie and of Nguro, through a dense population, extensive fields richly cultivated, and lovely woods of umbelliferous plants, we entered into Unyamuesi, stopping in the district (Oct. 1, 1889) of Usongo, where the chief Mitinginya rules.

Mitinginya is the only sovereign of these regions who always shows the same courteous manner towards Europeans, without asking them for tribute. He is satisfied with a gift, often of very little value. He told us that at our return we should bring him two great receptacles in which he could carry water during war and the chase, because the last time he had suffered much from thirst.

Mitinginya is about fifty years of age, but has still a young and fresh countenance. He marches always at the head of his warriors, is the first in the combat, and is a brave chief, beloved and feared by his people. A European power might draw profit from him, and obtain a stable footing in Unyamuesi without great expense.

THE CHIEF MITINGINYA.

If it were possible to find a successor at Mirambo, who would be feared on account of his power, placing by his side a European to instruct and counsel him, much would be gained in favour of peace in the country between Tanganika, Tabora, and Nyanza. The roads would be again secure, and our missionaries could attend to the conversion of the country without being disturbed. Of all the Wanyamuesi princes, Mitinginya seems to me the only one with whom such an experiment might be made with probability of success. The presence of a small force commanded by Europeans would give him such prestige that his name would be sufficient to maintain order, and, on the other side, the Europeans would not be suspected of "wishing to devour the country." The station would have little attraction for a foreigner, but it would be very useful.

Usongo is a slightly undulating country, without woods, as a great part of Unyamuesi is, and comparatively healthy.* Unyamuesi is a rich and productive country; cattle, grain, rice, beans, and tobacco are found in abundance in every village. The population is intelligent, active, strong, and robust, with manifest business-like propensities, but somewhat suspicious, noisy, and prone to malice. To the use (common to all the Negroes) of copious libations they add the fatal hasheesh (*Cannabis indica*), the use of which they learned from the Arabs of Zanzibar. Ground to the finest powder, they use it as snuff; in the leaf they smoke it in great pipes, and they chew it half roasted, as a pastime. To prolong the voluptuous pleasure of the narcotic, they regulate the slow combustion of the leaves with little red-hot stones, amongst which they put the tobacco in the pipe. The noisy sneezes, exces-

* Father Augustus Schynse. *With Stanley and Emin Pasha across Eastern Africa.*

sive, convulsive coughs, wild cries, frequent quarrels, and the constant repetition of the stupid old jests of a hundred of these raving drunkards accompanied the caravan till they reached Bagamoyo. They have no forms of religious faith, but they have very definite and respected traditions about social order and the conduct of each individual.

The villages are formed of scattered and isolated habitations, that occupy almost the whole territory brought into cultivation, and that are called *tembe*. The *tembe* of the Wanyamuesi is a rectangular construction, with a narrow door for entrance in the front. The walls of mud, mixed with chopped grass, and intertwined osiers, reach a height of about ten feet, and are furnished with loopholes for defence. The rooms are distributed all round the interior, the centre of the dwelling has a well of water in it, and is reserved for the shelter of the animals during the night. The number of the family who inhabit it varies with the size of the building. When one arrives in sight of these villages, one is struck by the capricious distribution of the houses, from the roofs of which clouds of pigeons fly; the number of cows and goats, mixed with groups of asses, scattered confusedly around; and the colossal *Adansonia*, which give importance to the vastness of the plain, show in a pleasant and comforting manner the prosperity of the region and the well-being of its inhabitants.

The country is swarming with Masai, called in by Mitinginya to assist him in his war against Simba, the chief of a bordering tribe that at intervals became troublesome by its inroads into Usongo.

"These Masai are agile and robust; they clothe themselves in the skins of animals, and wear real weights of iron in the lobes of their ears, fastened by great pins.

AFRICAN WOMEN OF VARIOUS TRIBES.

They have always a serious manner, and one seldom sees on their lips the appearance of a smile. Their armament consists of a great oval shield made of bull's hide and coloured black, white, and red ; a great lance, the point of which is nearly thirty inches long and more than four inches wide, while at its other end it is furnished with an iron sword thirty inches long. The handle or pole of the lance measures six feet six inches in length. At their crossbelt they wear a sword two feet long, in a wooden sheath. On the upper part of the arm the Masai wear also a little stiletto.

"These warriors despise fire-arms and know (without them) how to make themselves feared by enemies armed with guns ; every owner of cattle is an enemy for them. The young men of this tribe if they are not called on to aid others (in which case the flocks taken remain the latter's property) effect on their own account extensive inroads into the zone of hostilities, taking whatever they can find. They live almost exclusively on their flocks. They plant only a few bananas, and for this reason do not need slaves. Their language differs entirely from the Bantu, and has only deep guttural sounds. It is a rare occurrence to find an interpreter by whom one can communicate with them. Many times Europeans have visited their native country between Kilimanjaro, the mountains of Usagara, and the coast, but they were not always received amicably." *

Of their superiority in audacious rapine we had proofs during the nine days that we encamped at Usongo. One night three asses were stolen from the caravan, and were only returned by the Masai robbers two

* Father Augustus Schynse. *With Stanley and Emin Pasha across Eastern Africa.*

days afterwards, on the authoritative intervention of Mitinginya.

The Masai used to go round our encampment under the pretext of selling us articles of food; and although our men, aware of their tendency to theft, stood on their guard, they had every day to lament some cheating on their part.

One day one of these men with sesame to sell, went to a hut when the wife of an Egyptian employé was alone. For a long time he discussed the quality and quantity of his merchandise, and whilst the woman, annoyed by his importunity, unfolded a piece of cloth to show him, he caught it suddenly, tore it from her, and ran off. The cries of the robbed woman raised an alarm; the thief was soon arrested, and, luckily for him, the intervention of an officer saved him from the clubs of the Soudanese servants.

The place of the encampment was close to the habitation of Stokes, an English merchant, who undertakes to supply and guide caravans from Zanzibar to the regions of Lake Victoria. Stokes has married a daughter of Mitinginya, and such a relationship gives him great influence in the country, and facilitates for him the task of enrolling or engaging Wanyamuesi porters. At this time he was absent, having gone with the Rev. Messrs. Gordon and Walker to Uganda, in order to re-establish the station and the authority of the missionaries.

On the 9th of October 1889, the march began across Unyamuesi. The plain was cut by the sandy beds of dried-up torrents, in which, however, one found water by digging a little way down. It was broken by frequent undulations of hilly ground, and scattered over with numerous villages and fields that were being prepared for the approaching sowing. The *Adansonia*, king of colossal plants, showed its branches, unadorned by leaves; and rows of the *borassus* palm comforted us on the march (troubled by drought) with the hope of finding restorative water. Woods of acacia, the refuge of lions, of leopards, of hyenas, and of lively monkeys, were alternated with grassy plains, on which fed menacing buffaloes; timid antelopes fled at our approach, whilst astonished giraffes surveyed us from the wooded hills. Niava, Muana, Dombolo, Kivalaro, with minor groups of *tembe* (villages), were full of sounds and rumours from their crowded populations, who were always noisy and in motion.

We arrived October 17, 1889, at Gombe Yaicongo, the residence of the chief Icongo, rich in cattle and ruler of an extensive territory.

In this locality there joined us and accompanied the caravan two French missionaries, Fathers Giraud and Schynse, on their journey to Zanzibar. The first was going to Europe to try and recover his failing health; the other accompanied him, according to the rules of the fraternity. They are affable in their manners, intelligent, and active, devoted to Africa and the duties of their noble ministry, as well as to their scientific studies.

At the hour of six in the morning the usual whistle announced our departure, October 20, 1889. There were few *tembe,* few cultivated fields. We entered the wood. It was the Mgunda-Mkali—*the forest of sorrows* —the rising ground that separates Unyamuesi from Ugogo. We saluted the last *Adansonia;* and entered thick woods of thorny shrubs, amongst which the *Mimosa latronum* was the finest.

The way was marked by a narrow path, widening at rare intervals into small grassy glades, by some little dried-up torrents, climbing and descending undulations of ground that was of little elevation. Walking was unpleasant, from the unevenness of the ground, and from the thorny branches that, curving in, formed a continuous gallery, a great hindrance to the carriers of large loads. And worse still was the deficiency of water, from which those imprudent people suffered who had been deaf to the repeated injunctions to make adequate provision of it before starting.

However, fate was propitious to us, and we found a little water in the sands of Makalongo, and in those of Mtikwa, and more abundantly on the twenty-second day (October) at the river Msaka, which the Zanzibaris, not strangers to this road, call Mto Misanzi, the river of the palms, which abundantly fringe its banks. The latitude of this place, according to astronomical observations made by Father Schynse is 5° 29′ S.

October 23, we descended into a vast plain; the acacia trees became thinner, and thus the difficulties of the march were diminished. Three palm trees rose at a distance, a sign of the probable presence of water. We entered a thick wood, and after a struggle of two hours with the insidious brambles we reached the reservoirs of Makomero. They are three pools in a large open plain, scooped out in the rocks by the hand of man, and about eighty feet deep. They contain abundance of water, due to the presence of a subterranean current.

The strength of the caravan preserved us from a peril that frequently occurs to merchants who have to pass through *the forest of sorrows*—that of being assailed by robbers, who, in the recesses of the wood, have rooms in miserable huts, and are ready to fall on incautious loiterers, or on travellers without sufficient means of defence. The numerous fires near each other that we were obliged to keep up in the places of encampment guaranteed us from the assaults of the wild beasts inhabiting the forest; and where the danger of setting fire to anything hindered us from using this means of defence we found spacious enclosures already prepared by hunters, or by caravans that had preceded us, surrounded with hedges of thorny foliage.

On the 24th we traversed a woody road, in the midst of which a plain opened that preserved some traces of culture, and a little further on was a series of dismantled *tembe* in the vicinity of dry pools or mire. We were on the water-shed of Lake Tanganika, sloping towards the Indian Ocean.

The road slowly descended. On the 25th we were at Kapalata on the extreme borders of Mgunda Mkali. The apparent tranquillity of the inhabitants, and the courtesy of the chief gave us confidence; while the Wanyamuesi of the caravan, putting faith in the respect that the force of the expedition must inspire, the next morning early set out and preceded the column by some hours. It was the worse for them, for they were assailed by robbers hidden in the woods, saw themselves robbed of the goats that they drove before them, and owed their own safety to prompt flight.

We left the wood and entered a grassy region scattered over with rocky hills; the road ascended by a winding path strewn with stones, steep and broken, till we reached the first terrace.

Here a wide extent of open plain presented itself to our gaze, whitened by its sandy nature, bare of vegetation, and treeless. It was the arid Ugogo, the country of furious winds, of rarely seen bushes, that produces only poor scanty grain and pumpkins. We continued the descent; then a vast flat area surrounded by low hills, broken by large ponds of water, sprinkled with extensive tracts of cultivation, and sown with numerous *Adansonia,* presented a fine picture. We precipitated ourselves rather than descended, on account of the steepness of the road, and we were in sight of Mualata, an extensive village, which numbered quite sixty large *tembe.* The chief of the village is tributary to the *Mukenge* of Nianguira, who is the most potent prince of Ugogo. "The Wagogo are troublesome and saucy, and it is difficult to get rid of them; besides, they are very dirty. They dye their stuffs (when they wear any, and are not content with a goat skin thrown over their shoulders) a brownish red, the same colour with which they also dye their skin and hair; the lobes of their ears are deformed by their hanging to them circles of wood, pieces of iron, rings, their pipe and tobacco pouch. They are armed with an oval shield of raw ox-hide, with a lance of a different style to those of the Masai, and they also carry bows and arrows.

"They are fairly robust and prolific, rich, and in consequence also impudent; they have the bad habit of exacting large tributes from passing caravans, on which account many of the owners unite to pay a single tribute which, divided amongst many, is not so sensibly felt. The caravans are in their power, because the porters refuse to depart until the tribute question is settled; and besides that, the Wagogo occupy the wells and prevent their getting water. The country is melancholy, and without woods."[*]

The *tembe* of Ugogo are generally constructed in the identical form and with the same kind of material as those in Unyamuesi, the only visible difference is in the position of the entrance door which, instead of being at the front of the house, is at the bottom

[*] Father Augustus Schynse. *With Stanley and Emin Pasha across Eastern Africa.*

THE PLAIN OF UGOGO.

of an open court that occupies the centre of the building.

We had surmounted the circle of heights that form the basin of Mualata, and, passing by woody tracts over successive undulations, we entered (October 28, 1889) the vast plain of Ugogo, broken here and there by

VILLAGE OF UGOGO.

rare bushes, by groups of *borassus* palms near the water courses, and by long tracts of woods of low and thorny trees. The torrents that—as far as we could infer from their winding and deep beds—must in the season of the rains, flow abundantly, were now perfectly dry, and even by digging amongst the sands it was difficult to find sufficient water; in some places one meets with none. The wells that have water in them at this season are carefully guarded by the natives, who refuse to point them out, and when once they have been found demand payment in cloth or tobacco for the water that is drawn from them.

At Nianguira (October 29), the prince with unusual insolence caused Stanley to be told that tribute should be paid for crossing his territory; but knowing that the caravan did not carry ivory, he would be contented if they would heap up a certain quantity of wood for him, as much as he required to construct a *tembe*. This strange request would have deserved a suitable reply; but in the condition of our caravan, prudence counselled that the tribute should be converted into the payment of a limited quantity of cloth.

The next night (October 30), the Wagogo gave us specimens of their tendency to theft. Penetrating into the camp by the entrance in the Kitinku wood, they robbed us of a gun, from the hut in which the Soudanese Captain Shukri slept, and of two others, the property of the Zanzibari porters. Stanley would have liked to give a lesson to this population of robbers, but "I have these women and boys with me," he said, "and they render it impossible for me to do so."

We were at the river Bubo, in a small wood (October 31) that afforded us shelter from the burning rays of the sun; a line of palms cheered us and indicated the path that we ought to follow in our search for water. The presence of a colony of Masai not far from the opposite side of the river kept the people vigilant and united. It was near noon, when cries of gladness arose in the encampment, and there was swift running toward the way by which we had come; messengers had arrived, sent through Usukuma with letters.

They had travelled by the road of the caravan; knowing the direction taken by us, they had hastened their return. They came from Mpwapwa, and brought a letter from Wissmann for Emin. He had started for Zanzibar, leaving Lieutenant Schmidt with troops to await us. The joy of this announcement, removing all further doubts as to the news we had received that morning from a caravan of Wanyamuesi which we met on the road, raised every one's spirits; the journey

DELIVERY OF A LETTER TO EMIN.

presented no further difficulties: Mpwapwa was near, the fatigues that still remained to be borne no longer gave us any uneasiness.

On the 1st of November 1889, very early, we resumed our march in undergrowths and thorny thickets. In little more than five hours we reached the small village of Magombia, in which locality one finds little water, even by digging the ground to a great depth. Nevertheless, in view of the necessity of renewing our provisions, of which the country could furnish as much as we needed, Stanley granted a day's rest.

The road continued from the first amongst briars and thorny woods; then through a grassy plain, with groups of huts scattered over it, it led us to Matako, November 4, 1889. Here and there in the plain there rose isolated little hills, rocky and without vegetation. We marched towards the east; the ground soon became hilly, with many now dried-up torrents, and we halted at Npala. The country here is serrated in the front and at the sides by a chain of mountains.

Through woods of mimosa, and passing over hills of little height, we entered a vast plain, and after a walk of two hours pitched our camp (November 6) at Mussanga, a large village of about fifty *tembe*; some *Adansonia*, groups of mimosa, vast fields, and wells in good number were near the habitations. The plain extends without undulations of any sort, until it reaches the mountains, which border it closely on the north, and still more so on the west, where a cliff, disengaging itself from the chain, projects in proximity to the last *tembe* of the village.

The 8th of November, we encamped at the river Mausea, shut in between two hills; on the 9th we traversed the forest of Jonyo, called by the caravan Marenga Mkali, that is, salt water; we arrived the same day at the foot of the mountains of Usagara. The road runs on the slopes of successive hills, and gradually we gained the summit, descending on the opposite side to Kambi.

On the point of leaving Ugogo, and putting an end to the sufferings of the caravan from the aridity of the soil and the wickedness of its inhabitants, it did not seem amiss to take the opportunity that presented itself of leaving a remembrance of our presence. The

LIEUTENANT ROCHUS SCHMIDT.

herds of the caravan, reduced to a few heads of cattle, whilst being driven to pasture were assailed by about fifty Masai, who thought it an easy prey. But the few Soudanese who had charge of the animals resented their audacity with arms, and the strife was brief, for the Masai, seeing two of their companions fall dead, took to precipitate flight.

The road was fatiguing, nevertheless not a word of complaint was heard (November 10); all were joyous and marched close together, not a break in the ranks, not one of the caravan delayed to rest on the side of the road. We ascended a steep hill, passed the mountain; were soon on the plain; we reposed under the shade of sycamores and acacias on the shore of the torrent, in whose bed ran a fresh and limpid water that fell from the neighbouring mountain; in front of us, on a little hill, was the military station, above which floated the German flag. This station is formed by a stone wall, constructed diligently and solidly by the Soudanese soldiers and Kisuaili, under the direction of German officers. The lieutenant, Rochus Schmidt, as ordered by Major Wissmann, placed himself at the disposal of Emin Pasha. On the 12th of November, early in the morning, the column commenced its march, preceded by Lieutenant Schmidt and his Soudanese soldiers, the German banner in the vanguard.

A rich and fertile country, with abundance of water, rejoicing in verdant pastures and shady trees, made delightful by the balsamic air of the mountains, with inhabitants of gentle character and kindly manners— this is Usagara.

The chain of mountains that extended before us in a semicircle descends to the plain by a series of minor heights, forming first the valleys of the Dambi,

Kidete, and Mokondokua, the principal river of this region. The way, sharp and difficult, opens over the spurs of the chain, amongst bushes and woods shutting in the valley, which grows larger where the Simba pours itself into the Mokondokua. Great acacias, white trunks of *Buttneriaceæ* and the *Palma dóm*, give a gracious and imposing aspect to the region.

At first the spaces under cultivation are small, but

MEETING WITH MAJOR WISSMANN.

they go on augmenting with the extension of the valley, and fine plantations of bananas, fields of grain, and verdant meadows abound on the declivities, that descend gently to the plain.

The dwellings of the natives of Muini Usagara are formed of huts with conical roofs; the villages are generally placed together in the recesses of the valleys and on the hills amidst the woods. On the 20th of November we left the high mountains behind us and entered a beautiful and vast plain, charmingly planted and shaded by umbelliferous trees, and palms, and inhabited by numerous antelopes and gazelles, and next day, by a wood of palms and over a country that begins to present dunes of sand, we arrived at the river Mkate, rapid in its course, and scattered with large stones.

Mrogoro, the altitude of which is 1421 feet (433 metres) opens the plain of the Irrengere, where chief Kinga dwells, an intelligent young man. The French

BAGAMOYO, WHERE EMIN'S ACCIDENT OCCURRED.

missionaries have made a lovely dwelling for themselves on a spur that projects like a terrace from the mountain, and have there a garden charming from the riches and variety of the plants cultivated in it.

By Simbamueni and Mikese—through green woods and following the crests of a series of beautiful hills— we arrived at the river Irrengere, which, after having received the waters of the Mrogoro, falls into the Kingani. The land is transformed by slightly marked undulations, partly covered by grass and thick

THE BANQUET AT BAGAMOYO.

bushes, and at Kisemo reaches an altitude of 335 feet (102 metres).

On Nov. 28 we arrived at Msua, where we were delighted by the arrival of Captain Gravenreuth, "the lion of the coast"—thus called from acts of valour performed by him in combat, during the insurrection of the Mafiti—as well as by the arrival of two correspondents of American journals with provisions for Stanley.

On December 1, 1889, we raised our camp at Msua, and at eight o'clock in the morning of Dec. 4 we arrived at the river Kingani, where we were received by the German Imperial Commissioner, Major Wissmann, the bold explorer of Cassai.

The joy of return, and the festive reception given us by those who had assembled to greet us in Bagamoyo, were marred by the misfortune that befell Emin, happily less serious than we suspected at the time.

* * * * * *

Restored to my country after this long Odyssey of trials and perils, it is with a heart full of gratitude that I offer this public thanksgiving to those who contributed to my safety. And now, presenting these memorial pages, without pretence of learning, and free from personal ambition, I must declare that it has been my constant study to succeed in following the ancient precept :

Amicus Plato, sed magis amica veritas.

APPENDIX.

METEOROLOGICAL OBSERVATIONS IN UNYORO.

METEOROLOGICAL OBSERVATIONS.

JUAYA STATION, ALTITUDE, 3600 FEET (1100 METRES).

Day	Hour.	Hygrometer. Wet.	Hygrometer. Dry.	Aneroid Barometer. No. 1.	Aneroid Barometer. No. 2.	Wind. Direction.	Wind. Force.	Remarks.
1887 Jan. 1	7 a.m.	19.40°	17.60°	645	655	N.E.	0	fair
	2 p.m.	31.00	26.60	644	652	E.	1	,,
	9 p.m.	21.40	21.20	645	654	N.	0	clear
2	7 a.m.	18.00	16.60	944	658	N.	0	,,
	2 p.m.	29.00	24.60	644	657	E.	2	,,
	9 p.m.	18.80	19.00	645	655	N.	0	,,
3	7 a.m.	18.60	16.80	645	656	N.E.	0	fair
	2 p.m.	30.20	26.40	643	653	E.	1	rather cloudy
	9 p.m.	18.80	19.20	643	654	N.	0	clear
4	7 a.m.	18.40	17.00	645	655	N.E.	1	,,
	2 p.m.	26.60	25.60	643	653	E.	1	rather cloudy
	9 p.m.	19.60	19.80	644	653	N.	0	clear
5	7 a.m.	19.80	18.60	644	654	N.E.	0	fair
	2 p.m.	30.00	25.00	643	653	N.E.	1	rather cloudy
	9 p.m.	20.60	20.60	645	655	N.	0	clear
6	7 a.m.	19.60	18.80	644	655	N.E.	0	rather cloudy (1)
	2 p.m.	30.00	25.80	644	653	E.	1	,,
	9 p.m.	18.80	19.20	644	654	N.	0	clear
7	7 a.m.	19.40	18.60	647	657	E.	1	cloudy (2)
	2 p.m.	29.20	25.89	645	655	E.	0	rather cloudy
	9 p.m.	18.60	19.00	645	655	N.	0	clear
8	7 a.m.	18.60	18.60	647	657	E.	0	cloudy (3)
	2 p.m.	18.00	17.80	645	656	S.E.	1	,, (4)
	9 p.m.	16.60	16.80	645	656	N.	0	clear
9	7 a.m.	17.20	16.40	646	646	N.E.	0	,,
	2 p.m.	29.80	26.00	645	655	E.	1	rather cloudy
	9 p.m.	21.00	21.20	645	655	N.	1	clear
10	7 a.m.	20.00	19.80	646	657	N.W.	0	rather cloudy
	2 p.m.	29.60	26.60	645	654	N.E.	1	,, (5)
	9 p.m.	19.80	19.60	645	655	E.	0	cloudy
11	7 a.m.	20.20	19.20	646	656	N.	1	fair
	2 p.m.	26.80	24.20	645	655	N.W.	1	rather cloudy (6)
	9 p.m.	16 80	17.00	645	656	N.	0	clear
12	7 a.m.	16.00	15.20	648	657	N.	0	,,
	2 p.m.	23.00	22.40	648	659	S.E.	1	rather cloudy (7)
	9 p.m.	17.40	17.60	645	656	N.	0	clear
13	7 a.m.	17.00	16.20	647	659	N.	0	,,
	2 p.m.	31.00	25.80	645	655	N.E.	1	fair
	9 p.m.	18.80	18.80	645	655	N.	1	clear
14	7 a.m.	18.40	16.40	646	657	N.	0	,,
	2 p.m.	26.20	23.60	645	655	E.	1	rather cloudy
	9 p.m.	17.80	17.20	645	655	N.	0	clear
15	7 a.m.	17.40	16.40	645	656	N.	0	,,
	2 p.m.	30.00	26.00	645	655	N.E.	1	rather cloudy (8)
	9 p.m.	18.80	18.80	644	652	N.E.	0	,,
16	7 a.m.	19.00	18.20	645	655	N.	0	clear
	2 p.m.	29.00	25.60	644	655	N.W.	1	rather cloudy (9)
	9 p.m.	19.80	19.20	645	655	N.	0	clear
17	7 a.m.	18.40	17.60	645	657	N.E.	0	fair
	2 p.m.	19.20	18.40	644	654	E.	1	rather cloudy (10)
	9 p.m.	17.60	17.60	645	657	N.	0	fair

METEOROLOGICAL OBSERVATIONS.

Day.	Hour.	Hygrometer. Wet.	Dry.	Aneroid Barometer. No. 1.	No. 2.	Wind. Direction.	Force.	Remarks.
1887 Jan. 18	7 a.m.	18.00°	17.40°	648	658	N.E.	1	cloudy
	2 p.m.	23.20	20.40	645	655	N.W.	1	fair (11)
	9 p.m.	19.20	19.00	645	656	N.	0	,,
19	7 a.m.	19.00	18.20	647	658	N.W.	0	rather cloudy
	2 p.m.	21.20	19.80	645	656	N.	1	,,
	9 p.m.	17.40	17.40	645	657	N.E.	0	,,
20	7 a.m.	18.40	17.40	649	658	N.E.	0	,,
	2 p.m.	24.20	28.00	647	657	N.W.	1	fair
	9 p.m.	17.40	17.20	646	657	N.	0	clear
21	7 a.m.	16.60	15.80	647	657	N.	0	,,
	2 p.m.	27.00	24.60	646	657	N.E.	1	rather cloudy (12)
	9 p.m.	15.80	16.60	645	656	N.	0	clear
22	7 a.m.	15.80	14.80	647	657	N.	0	,,
	2 p.m.	26.20	23.40	645	656	N.W.	1	rather cloudy
	9 p.m.	18.60	18.40	646	658	N.	1	fair
23	7 a.m.	16.80	15.60	647	657	N.	0	clear
	2 p.m.	25.60	21.80	647	658	N.W.	1	fair
	9 p.m.	15.80	16.20	645	656	N.	0	clear
24	7 a.m.	15.80	14.80	647	657	N.	0	,,
	2 p.m.	27.00	23.20	647	657	N.W.	1	fair
	9 p.m.	15.40	15.80	645	656	N.	0	clear
25	7 a.m.	18.40	16.40	647	657	N.	0	,,
	2 p.m.	27.20	22.80	647	658	W.	1	fair
	9 p.m.	16.60	16.60	646	658	N.	0	clear
26	7 a.m.	14.60	13.20	647	658	W.	0	fair
	2 p.m.	25.80	22.00	647	657	N.W.	1	rather cloudy
	9 p.m.	16.00	16.00	646	657	N.	0	clear
27	7 a.m.	14.80	13.40	648	659	N.W.	0	,,
	2 p.m.	26.80	23.40	647	657	N.W.	0	,,
	9 p.m.	16.60	16.80	646	658	N.W.	0	,,
28	7 a.m.	16.00	14.40	647	658	N.E.	0	fair
	2 p.m.	25.80	22.20	645	656	N.W.	1	,,
	9 p.m.	15.20	15.40	646	659	N.	0	clear
29	7 a.m.	15.20	13.60	647	659	N.W.	0	,,
	2 p.m.	28.00	22.40	647	657	N.W.	1	,,
	9 p.m.	18.20	18.20	646	658	N.E.	1	fair
30	7 a.m.	15.80	15.40	649	659		0	clear
	2 p.m.	26.20	21.80	648	657	N.W.	1	,,
	9 p.m.	15.40	15.80	647	657	N.	0	,,
31	7 a.m.	16.80	14.80	647	659	N.	0	,,
	2 p.m.	29.00	21.40	646	656	W.	1	,,
	9 p.m.	16.40	14.80	645	655	N.	0	,,
Feb. 1	7 a.m.	16.40	13.20	646	657	N.	0	,,
	2 p.m.	29.40	24.00	645	656	N.	1	,,
	9 p.m.	15.60	15.40	645	656	N.	0	,,
2	7 a.m.	15.20	12.80	647	657	N.	0	,,
	2 p.m.	29.80	22.60	645	656	W.	2	,,
	9 p.m.	16.00	15.60	645	657	N.	0	,,
3	7 a.m.	16.80	14.80	647	657	N.	0	,,
	2 p.m.	29.20	22.20	646	657	W.	1	,,
	9 p.m.	15.40	15.40	646	656	N.	0	,,
4	7 a.m.	13.60	12.40	647	658	N.W.	1	,,
	2 p.m.	30.00	24.80	645	656	W.	1	,,
	9 p.m.	16.60	16.20	645	655	N.	0	,,

METEOROLOGICAL OBSERVATIONS. 319

Day.	Hour.	Hygrometer. Wet.	Hygrometer. Dry.	Aneroid Barometer. No. 1.	Aneroid Barometer. No. 2.	Wind. Direction.	Wind. Force.	Remarks.
1887 Feb. 5	7 a.m.	14.80°	12.60°	647	658	N.	0	clear
	2 p.m.	31.40	23.80	647	657	N.W.	1	,,
	9 p.m.	16.60	16.20	645	656	N.	0	,,
6	7 a.m.	13.60	11.80	648	659	N.	0	,,
	2 p.m.	31.40	24.40	647	657	N.W.	2	,,
	9 p.m.	15.60	15.60	645	655	N.	0	,,
7	7 a.m.	13.40	11.20	648	658	N.	0	,,
	2 p.m.	31.60	24.40	646	657	N.W.	1	,,
	9 p.m.	15.80	15.80	645	655	N.	0	,,
8	7 a.m.	14.80	13.40	647	657	N.	0	,,
	2 p.m.	32.40	24.80	647	656	W.	2	,,
	9 p.m.	12.20	11.40	645	656	N.	0	,,
9	7 a.m.	16.40	14.40	648	658	N.	0	,,
	2 p.m.	31.60	24.20	647	658	N.W.	2	fair
	9 p.m.	17.80	17.40	646	656	N.	0	clear
10	7 a.m.	15.60	14.40	648	659	N.	0	,,
	2 p.m.	33.00	23.40	647	659	W.	2	,,
	9 p.m.	19.20	18.40	647	658	N.E.	1	,,
11	7 a.m.	19.20	17.00	649	660	W.	1	,,
	2 p.m.	31.60	24.60	647	657	W.	2	fair
	9 p.m.	19.60	19.20	646	658	N.E.	1	clear
12	7 a.m.	15.80	14.60	647	657	N.	0	,,
	2 p.m.	31.20	25.40	646	656	N.W.	1	,,
	9 p.m.	18.60	17.80	646	656	N.	0	,,
13	7 a.m.	18.40	17.60	649	660	N.E.	0	,,
	2 p.m.	22.40	21.40	648	660	E.	1	cloudy (13)
	9 p.m.	17.20	17.20	646	658	N.	1	fair
14	7 a.m.	18.20	16.60	648	659	N.	0	clear
	2 p.m.	31.20	25.80	647	657	E.	1	rather cloudy
	9 p.m.	17.20	17.40	646	657	N.E.	0	clear
15	7 a.m.	18.40	17.40	647	658	N.	0	,,
	2 p.m.	28.60	25.40	646	656	E.	1	rather cloudy
	9 p.m.	19.20	18.80	646	657	N.E.	0	clear
16	7 a.m.	22.00	19.80	647	658	E.	2	,,
	2 p.m.	33.60	26.30	648	657	E.	2	,,
	9 p.m.	23.20	20.80	645	657	E.	1	,,
17	7 a.m.	19.80	17.00	646	657	N.	1	rather cloudy
	2 p.m.	32.60	24.20	647	656	E.	2	clear
	9 p.m.	23.40	20.40	645	658	E.	1	,,
18	7 a.m.	19.40	16.80	647	657	E.	1	,,
	2 p.m.	23.20	25.80	645	655	E.	2	rather cloudy
	9 p.m.	19.60	17.60	644	655	N.	0	clear
19	7 a.m.	22.80	18.80	648	658	N.	0	,,
	2 p.m.	32.40	24.80	645	655	E.	1	rather cloudy
	9 p.m.	18.40	18.20	645	655	N.	0	clear
20	7 a.m.	17.40	15.40	645	656	N.W.	0	,,
	2 p.m.	33.60	26.40	645	655	N.E.	2	rather cloudy
	9 p.m.	18.40	15.80	645	655	N.	0	clear
21	7 a.m.	17.60	15.80	647	656	N.	0	,,
	2 p.m.	33.60	25.40	645	655	N.W.	2	rather cloudy
	9 p.m.	19.60	18.40	645	655	N.	0	clear
22	7 a.m.	15.60	14.40	647	657	N.	0	fair
	2 p.m.	33.60	25.80	646	655	W.	1	clear
	9 p.m.	18.00	16.80	645	655	N.	0	,,

METEOROLOGICAL OBSERVATIONS.

Day.	Hour.	Hygrometer. Wet.	Hygrometer. Dry.	Aneroid Barometer. No. 1.	Aneroid Barometer. No. 2.	Wind. Direction.	Wind. Force.	Remarks.
1887 Feb. 23	7 a.m.	15.60°	13.60°	647	656	N.E.	1	rather cloudy
	2 p.m.	30.80	21.20	646	656	N.W.	1	,,
	9 p.m.	16.40	15.80	645	656	E.	0	clear
24	7 a.m.	15.40	13.00	646	657	N.E.	0	,,
	2 p.m.	33.40	26.20	645	655	E.	1	rather cloudy
	9 p.m.	19.80	18.60	645	655	N.E.	0	clear
25	7 a.m.	18.60	16.80	647	658	N.E.	1	fair
	2 p.m.	30.60	25.20	645	655	N.W.	1	rather cloudy
	9 p.m.	21.00	20.40	645	656	E.	0	clear
26	7 a.m.	20.40	18.80	648	659	N.W.	1	rather cloudy
	2 p.m.	27.40	21.60	646	657	N.W.	2	,,
	9 p.m.	18.60	17.80	647	660	E.	1	,,
27	7 a.m.	18.80	17.80	649	660	E.	1	,,
	2 p.m.	22.60	20.80	648	659	N.W.	2	cloudy
	9 p.m.	17.80	17.60	648	660	N.E.	1	clear
28	7 a.m.	16.20	14.60	649	659	N.	0	,,
	2 p.m.	30.60	23.80	647	657	N.W.	2	rather cloudy
	9 p.m.	19.20	18.60	646	657	N.	0	clear
Mar. 1	7 a.m.	18.60	16.60	647	657	N.	0	,,
	2 p.m.	31.40	24.40	645	655	N.W.	2	,,
	9 p.m.	23.00	20.00	645	656	E.	1	fair
2	7 a.m.	20.20	18.20	647	658	N.W.	1	clear
	2 p.m.	30.60	19.60	645	655	W.	2	fair
	9 p.m.	23.00	20.80	645	656	E.	1	cloudy (14)
3	7 a.m.	18.80	18.20	649	657	E.	0	,,
	2 p.m.	27.80	23.40	645	656	E.	1	rather cloudy
	9 p.m.	21.20	20.40	645	656	E.	0	cloudy
4	7 a.m.	20.80	19.80	649	659	E.	1	,, (15)
	2 p.m.	27.40	19.20	648	657	E.	1	rather cloudy
	9 p.m.	21.20	20.40	647	658	N.E.	0	,,
5	7 a.m.	19.00	18.20	647	657	S.E.	1	cloudy (16)
	2 p.m.	22.60	22.00	647	657	S.E.	2	,,
	9 p.m.	18.80	18.40	645	658	E.	0	rather cloudy
6	7 a.m.	16.80	15.80	649	659	N.	0	clear
	2 p.m.	27.60	24.80	647	657	S.E.	1	rather cloudy
	9 p.m.	18.60	18.40	645	657	N.	0	clear
7	7 a.m.	16.40	15.60	649	659	N.	0	,,
	2 p.m.	28.20	25.60	647	656	E.	0	rather cloudy (17)
	9 p.m.	19.80	19.80	646	656	E.	1	clear
8	7 a.m.	20.40	18.80	647	657	E.	1	rather cloudy
	2 p.m.	27.80	24.80	644	655	N.	2	,,
	9 p.m.	19.80	19.20	645	655	N.E.	0	clear
9	7 a.m.	18.80	17.80	647	657	N.	0	fair (18)
	2 p.m.	21.60	19.60	645	655	N.W.	1	cloudy
	9 p.m.	20.40	19.80	645	656	E.	0	clear
10	7 a.m.	20.20	19.20	647	657	N.W.	0	,,
	2 p.m.	28.40	25.00	645	655	N.E.	1	rather cloudy (19)
	9 p.m.	20.00	19.20	646	657	N.W.	0	cloudy
11	7 a.m.	18.20	17.40	648	659	N.	0	fair
	2 p.m.	27.00	24.20	647	657	E.	1	rather cloudy (20)
	9 p.m.	18.00	17.80	646	658	N.E.	0	clear
12	7 a.m.	19.40	18.40	648	658	N.	0	rather cloudy
	2 p.m.	24.40	21.60	648	659	N.	1	,,
	9 p.m.	18.80	18.60	649	660	E.	1	,,

METEOROLOGICAL OBSERVATIONS.

Day.	Hour.	Hygrometer. Wet.	Hygrometer. Dry.	Aneroid Barometer. No. 1.	Aneroid Barometer. No. 2.	Wind. Direction.	Wind. Force.	Remarks.
1887 Mar. 13	7 a.m.	18.00°	17.40°	649	660	E.	0	rather cloudy
	2 p.m.	28.60	24.00	647	657	N.	1	,,
	9 p.m.	20.20	19.80	648	659	E.	0	,,
14	7 a.m.	18.80	17.60	649	659	N.	0	fair
	2 p.m.	22.00	21.40	645	655	N.W.	1	cloudy (21)
	9 p.m.	18.80	18.20	647	659	E.	0	,,
15	7 a.m.	18.80	18.00	649	660	N.	0	rather cloudy
	2 p.m.	22.20	20.00	645	654	W.	1	,, (22)
	9 p.m.	19.20	18.80	646	657	N.E.	1	,,
16	7 a.m.	16.40	15.80	648	658	N.	0	clear (23)
	2 p.m.	26.80	23.40	646	656	W.	1	fair
	9 p.m.	18.80	18.80	648	658	N.	0	clear
17	7 a.m.	19.20	18.20	649	659	N.	0	,, (24)
	2 p.m.	25.80	23.40	645	655	N.W.	1	rather cloudy
	9 p.m.	20.40	19.60	647	659	N.E.	1	,, (25)
18	7 a.m.	18.80	17.20	649	659	N.	0	,,
	2 p.m.	23.20	19.80	647	657	E.	2	,,
	9 p.m.	18.60	18.40	647	658	N.	0	clear
19	7 a.m.	18.00	17.20	648	660	N.W.	0	,,
	2 p.m.	28.40	24.20	646	657	E.	1	,,
	9 p.m.	21.80	21.20	645	656	N.W.	0	rather cloudy
20	7 a.m.	18.60	16.80	646	657	N.E.	1	clear
	2 p.m.	22.40	20.40	645	655	N.	1	rather cloudy (26)
	9 p.m.	20.80	19.60	645	656	N.	0	clear
21	7 a.m.	20.20	18.60	647	657	N.E.	0	,,
	2 p.m.	29.20	24.80	645	655	N.E.	0	rather cloudy (27)
	9 p.m.	19.60	18.80	645	655	N.E.	1	,,
22	7 a.m.	20.00	19.20	647	657	E.	1	,,
	2 p.m.	26.60	24.40	646	656	E.	2	cloudy
	9 p.m.	17.60	17.60	645	657	N.	0	rather cloudy (28)
23	7 a.m.	18.20	17.20	647	656	N.	0	,, (29)
	2 p.m.	21.20	20.00	645	657	E.	1	cloudy
	9 p.m.	19.60	19.40	647	658	E.	0	fair
24	7 a.m.	18.20	17.80	648	659	N.E.	0	cloudy (30)
	2 p.m.	27.60	24.00	647	657	E.	1	fair (31)
	9 p.m.	17.80	17.20	646	658	E.	1	,,
25	7 a.m.	—	—	—	—	—	—	—
	2 p.m.	—	—	—	—	—	—	— (32)
	9 p.m.	—	—	—	—	—	—	—
26	7 a.m.	17.60	16.80	649	660	N.E.	0	clear
	2 p.m.	28.60	25.00	645	657	E.	1	rather cloudy
	9 p.m	18.80	17.80	645	656	N.	0	clear
27	7 a.m.	18.80	17.40	646	657	N.	0	,,
	2 p.m.	27.80	24.80	645	655	N.	1	rather cloudy (33)
	9 p.m.	18.60	18.00	645	655	N.	0	clear
28	7 a.m.	18.60	18.20	645	657	N.E.	0	fair
	2 p.m.	28.60	25.00	647	657	E.	1	rather cloudy
	9 p.m.	18.80	18.40	645	656	N.E.	0	clear
29	7 a.m.	18.20	17.60	649	659	E.	1	rather cloudy (34)
	2 p.m.	27.40	24.80	647	657	E.	1	,, 35)
	9 p.m.	18.80	18.60	646	657	E.	0	,,
30	7 a.m.	18.00	17.60	649	659	N.	0	,, (36)
	2 p.m.	26.60	23.60	649	659	N.W.	1	,,
	9 p.m.	18.00	18.00	645	657	N.E.	0	clear

METEOROLOGICAL OBSERVATIONS.

Day.	Hour.	Hygrometer. Wet.	Hygrometer. Dry.	Aneroid Barometer. No. 1.	Aneroid Barometer. No. 2.	Wind. Direction.	Wind. Force.	Remarks.
Mar. 31	7 a.m.	18.60°	18.00°	649	660	E.	0	rather cloudy
	2 p.m.	25.60	22.40	647	657	N.W.	1	fair
	9 p.m.	19.20	19.00	646	657	N.	0	clear
April 1	7 a.m.	18.60	17.60	649	659	E.	0	rather cloudy
	2 p.m.	21.40	20.40	647	657	S.E.	0	cloudy (37)
	9 p.m.	18.80	18.80	647	658	N.	0	rather cloudy
2	7 a.m.	20.00	19.20	647	657	S.E.	0	,,
	2 p.m.	22.60	21.20	647	656	N.E.	1	cloudy
	9 p.m.	19.60	19.20	646	657	E.	0	rather cloudy (38)
3	7 a.m.	19.20	18.20	648	658	N.W.	0	fair
	2 p.m.	27.00	19.00	645	655	E.	1	rather cloudy (39)
	9 p.m.	20.40	20.00	645	657	N.E.	0	fair
4	7 a.m.	19.60	19.20	647	658	N.E.	0	overcast
	2 p.m.	18.60	18.60	646	656	S.E.	1	clear (40)
	9 p.m.	17.80	17.40	645	657	N.	0	fair
5	7 a.m.	16.80	15.40	647	658	N.E.	0	rather cloudy
	2 p.m.	26.40	23.80	646	656	S.E.	0	clear
	9 p.m.	19.80	19.80	646	656	N.	0	fair
6	7 a.m.	18.20	17.20	649	658	N.E.	1	rather cloudy
	2 p.m.	29.00	25.60	647	657	N.E.	1	fair (41)
	9 p.m.	19.20	18.80	645	657	N.	0	rather cloudy
7	7 a.m.	20.20	18.40	649	660	E.	1	,,
	2 p.m.	28.20	24.60	650	657	S.E.	1	,,
	9 p.m.	19.40	19.40	646	657	N.E.	0	clear
8	7 a.m.	19.60	18.60	649	660	S.E.	1	fair (42)
	2 p.m.	27.80	24.20	647	658	E.	0	clear
	9 p.m.	19.80	20.20	647	657	N.E.	0	,,
9	7 a.m.	17.60	17.00	647	659	S.E.	1	cloudy (43)
	2 p.m.	22.60	21.00	646	657	N.E.	1	rather cloudy
	9 p.m.	18.20	18.60	645	657	E.	0	fair
10	7 a.m.	17.40	16.40	647	657	S.E.	0	,,
	2 p.m.	27.40	23.60	647	657	S.E.	1	,, (44)
	9 p.m.	17.60	17.40	645	655	N.E.	0	clear
11	7 a.m.	19.20	17.80	647	657	N.E.	0	fair
	2 p.m.	28.60	25.00	646	656	N.E.	1	clear
	9 p.m.	19.40	19.20	646	658	N.	0	,,
12	7 a.m.	21.00	19.40	649	659	S.E.	1	,,
	2 p.m.	23.60	22.20	647	655	S.E.	1	,, (45)
	9 p.m.	18.80	18.40	646	657	S.E.	0	rather cloudy
13	7 a.m.	19.20	18.40	649	658	N.E.	0	,,
	2 p.m.	24.80	23.40	648	656	S.E.	2	,, (46)
	9 p.m.	18.60	18.00	650	659	E.	0	overcast
14	7 a.m.	19.60	18.80	650	659	E.	0	rather cloudy
	2 p.m.	24.60	22.60	648	657	S.E.	1	,, (47)
	9 p.m.	18.20	18.20	650	659	N.	0	clear
15	7 a.m.	18.40	17.00	649	659	N.E.	0	,,
	2 p.m.	26.20	24.20	649	658	N.E.	0	rather cloudy
	9 p.m.	20.20	20.00	648	658	N.W.	0	fair
16	7 a.m.	18.60	17.40	648	657	N.E.	0	clear
	2 p.m.	28.20	25.40	647	656	S.E.	1	rather cloudy
	9 p.m.	18.00	18.20	646	655	N.	0	clear
17	7 a.m.	19.20	17.60	648	658	N.	0	,,
	2 p.m.	30.40	26.20	647	655	N.E.	1	rather cloudy
	9 p.m.	20.20	19.80	647	656	S.E.	0	clear

METEOROLOGICAL OBSERVATIONS.

Day.	Hour.	Hygrometer. Wet.	Hygrometer. Dry.	Aneroid Barometer. No. 1.	Aneroid Barometer. No. 2.	Wind. Direction.	Wind. Force.	Remarks.
1887 April 18	7 a.m.	19.80°	19.20°	549	658	S.E.	1	cloudy (48)
	2 p.m.	26.80	23.20	647	657	S.E.	1	rather cloudy
	9 p.m.	19.80	19.60	647	657	N.E.	0	clear
19	7 a.m.	18.40	17.80	649	658	E.	0	fair
	2 p.m.	23.20	22.00	647	659	E.	1	rather cloudy (49)
	9 p.m.	18.20	18.40	649	659	N.	0	clear
20	7 a.m.	19.40	17.40	651	660	N.E.	0	fair
	2 p.m.	28.20	24.80	650	659	N.E.	1	rather cloudy
	9 p.m.	19.80	20.00	650	660	N.	0	clear
21	7 a.m.	19.40	18.40	652	661	N.E.	0	rather cloudy
	2 p.m.	26.60	24.00	650	659	S.E.	1	,,
	9 p.m.	19.80	19.60	649	660	S.E.	0	,,
22	7 a.m.	20.20	18.20	650	660	N.E.	0	clear
	2 p.m.	28.40	25.20	649	658	N.E.	0	rather cloudy
	9 p.m.	19.40	18.80	648	659	N.	0	fair
23	7 a.m.	17.60	16.60	648	657	N.	0	clear
	2 p.m.	29.60	25.40	647	657	N.E.	1	fair
	9 p.m.	19.80	19.40	647	657	N.E.	0	clear
24	7 a.m.	19.80	19.00	648	657	N.E.	0	,,
	2 p.m.	28.80	25.00	647	656	S.E.	1	rather cloudy
	9 p.m.	19.60	19.40	648	659	N.E.	1	,, (50)
25	7 a.m.	19.80	19.60	650	660	S.E.	1	cloudy (51)
	2 p.m.	24.40	22.40	650	659	S.E.	1	rather cloudy
	9 p.m.	17.80	18.00	650	661	N.	0	clear
26	7 a.m.	18.60	17.00	650	660	N.E.	0	,,
	2 p.m.	28.00	24.20	650	657	S.E.	1	rather cloudy
	9 p.m.	19.80	19.40	650	659	N.E.	0	,, (52)
27	7 a.m.	19.60	18.40	649	658	E.	0	,, (53)
	2 p.m.	19.20	19.80	647	657	N.	1	overcast
	9 p.m.	17.80	17.20	647	657	N.E.	0	clear
28	7 a.m.	19.80	19.40	650	659	N.E.	0	rather cloudy (54)
	2 p.m.	25.00	22.80	650	658	S.E.	1	,,
	9 p.m.	18.20	18.40	649	658	N.	0	clear
29	7 a.m.	17.20	17.20	648	657	N.E.	0	fair
	2 p.m.	28.60	25.20	648	657	S.E.	0	,,
	9 p.m.	19.40	19.20	648	657	N.	0	clear
30	7 a.m.	20.20	18.60	650	658	N.E.	0	,,
	2 p.m.	30.00	24.80	649	657	N.E.	2	rather cloudy (55)
	9 p.m.	18.80	18.60	649	658	N.E.	0	,,
May 1	7 a.m.	17.80	16.80	649	659	N.	0	fair
	2 p.m.	28.40	25.40	649	658	S.E.	1	rather cloudy (56)
	9 p.m.	18.80	18.60	648	656	N.E.	0	clear
2	7 a.m.	20.20	19.80	650	659	E.	1	rather cloudy (57)
	2 p.m.	26.60	23.80	648	657	S.E.	1	,, (58)
	9 p.m.	18.60	18.20	650	658	E.	0	fair
3	7 a.m.	19.20	18.40	651	660	N.E.	1	rather cloudy (59)
	2 p.m.	24.80	22.60	649	659	N.E.	0	,,
	9 p.m.	19.80	19.60	650	659	E.	0	,,
4	7 a.m.	18.40	17.60	650	658	N.E.	0	fair (60)
	2 p.m.	20.80	20.20	647	655	N.E.	0	rather cloudy
	9 p.m.	18.20	18.20	651	660	E.	0	,, (61)
5	7 a.m.	19.80	18.80	650	659	N.E.	1	,,
	2 p.m.	25.20	22.60	650	657	N.E.	1	,,
	9 p.m.	19.80	19.80	652	660	S.E.	1	,, (62)

METEOROLOGICAL OBSERVATIONS.

Day.	Hour.	Hygrometer. Wet.	Hygrometer. Dry.	Aneroid Barometer. No. 1.	Aneroid Barometer. No. 2.	Wind. Direction.	Wind. Force.	Remarks.
1887 May 6	7 a.m.	18.00°	17.40°	652	660	N.E.	1	cloudy
	2 p.m.	22.60	20.60	650	659	S.E.	1	rather cloudy
	9 p.m.	18.20	17.80	651	660	N.E.	1	clear
7	7 a.m.	20.20	19.60	652	660	E.	0	,,
	2 p.m.	27.60	24.00	650	659	S.E.	1	rather cloudy (63)
	9 p.m.	19.40	19.20	650	660	S.E.	1	cloudy
8	7 a.m.	20.60	19.40	651	660	S.E.	1	rather cloudy
	2 p.m.	26.80	24.20	650	659	N.E.	1	,,
	9 p.m.	18.60	18.60	651	660	E.	0	clear (64)
9	7 a.m.	17.40	16.00	650	659	N.E.	0	,,
	2 p.m.	27.60	24.60	649	658	S.E.	1	rather cloudy
	9 p.m.	20.40	20.00	650	660	E.	1	,,
10	7 a.m.	20.80	19.40	650	659	S.E.	1	clear
	2 p.m.	28.20	24.20	649	658	S.E.	1	,,
	9 p.m.	18.80	18.60	650	659	E.	0	rather cloudy (65)
11	7 a.m.	—	—	—	—	—	—	—
	2 p.m.	—	—	—	—	—	—	—
	9 p.m.	—	—	—	—	—	—	—
12	7 a.m.	18.80	18.20	651	660	S.E.	0	rather cloudy
	2 p.m.	26.20	23.80	650	659	S.E.	1	,,
	9 p.m.	19.20	18.80	649	659	N.E.	1	fair
13	7 a.m.	19.20	19.20	652	660	S.E.	1	clear
	2 p.m.	27.40	23.60	650	658	S.E.	1	rather cloudy
	9 p.m.	18.80	18.00	650	659	N.E.	1	clear
14	7 a.m.	18.80	17.60	650	660	S.E.	1	,,
	2 p.m.	28.00	24.80	648	658	S.E.	1	,,
	9 p.m.	18.60	18.40	650	658	N.E.	0	,,
15	7 a.m.	16.60	15.60	650	658	N.E.	1	,,
	2 p.m.	28.00	24.80	650	658	S.E.	1	rather cloudy
	9 p.m.	18.60	18.40	650	658	N.E.	0	clear
16	7 a.m.	20.20	18.80	650	659	N.E.	1	fair
	2 p.m.	20.20	19.80	650	657	S.E.	1	cloudy (66)
	9 p.m.	19.80	18.60	649	658	S.E.	1	rather cloudy
17	7 a.m.	19.20	18.40	651	660	E.	1	,, (67)
	2 p.m.	26.20	23.20	652	660	S.E.	1	,,
	9 p.m.	18.20	18.20	649	657	E.	0	clear
18	7 a.m.	18.60	17.80	650	659	E.	0	rather cloudy
	2 p.m.	27.20	24.20	649	658	S.E.	1	,,
	9 p.m.	19.20	18.20	650	660	E.	1	overcast
19	7 a.m.	17.20	15.40	649	659	N.E.	0	clear
	2 p.m.	27.80	24.60	650	659	N.E.	1	rather cloudy
	9 p.m.	17.60	17.40	651	660	N.E.	1	clear
20	7 a.m.	18.20	17.20	652	660	E.	0	rather cloudy
	2 p.m.	28.00	24.60	652	660	S.E.	1	,,
	9 p.m.	18.60	18.60	651	660	S.E.	1	,, (68)
21	7 a.m.	19.40	18.80	652	660	E.	0	cloudy
	2 p.m.	25.60	23.40	651	660	E.	1	rather cloudy
	9 p.m.	18.60	17.80	650	660	S.E.	0	fair
22	7 a.m.	19.40	18.40	652	660	S.E.	1	rather cloudy
	2 p.m.	23.40	22.60	651	660	S.E.	1	cloudy
	9 p.m.	17.60	17.00	652	660	S.E.	1	fair (69)
23	7 a.m.	16.40	15.40	650	660	E.	0	,,
	2 p.m.	27.40	23.60	650	660	S.E.	1	rather cloudy
	9 p.m.	18.20	18.00	652	660	S.E.	0	fair (70)

METEOROLOGICAL OBSERVATIONS.

Day.	Hour.	Hygrometer. Wet.	Hygrometer. Dry.	Aneroid Barometer. No. 1.	Aneroid Barometer. No. 2.	Wind. Direction.	Wind. Force.	Remarks.
1887 May 24	7 a.m.	19.60°	17.40°	652	261	E.	1	cloudy
	2 p.m.	26.80	23.80	652	660	S.E.	1	rather cloudy
	9 p.m.	19.80	19.20	651	661	E.	0	clear
25	7 a.m.	17.60	17.20	650	660	E.	1	fair
	2 p.m.	27.40	24.20	650	660	E.	1	,,
	9 p.m.	19.20	19.40	651	660	E.	0	clear
26	7 a.m.	17.40	16.20	651	660	E.	0	,,
	2 p.m.	28.40	24.80	650	660	E.	1	rather cloudy
	9 p.m.	17.60	17.20	650	658	S.E.	0	clear
27	7 a.m.	17.40	15.60	650	660	E.	0	,,
	2 p.m.	25.60	23.60	648	658	S.E.	1	rather cloudy
	9 p.m.	19.20	19.00	649	658	E.	0	clear
28	7 a.m.	16.60	15.80	649	657	E.	0	fair
	2 p.m.	27.80	23.60	648	657	E.	1	,,
	9 p.m.	17.60	17.20	650	659	N.	1	rather cloudy
29	7 a.m.	19.80	19.60	651	659	E.	1	fair
	2 p.m.	26.00	23.60	650	658	N.E.	1	rather cloudy (71)
	9 p.m.	17.20	17.40	650	659	E.	0	fair
30	7 a.m.	18.40	16.80	650	660	N.E.	0	clear
	2 p.m.	27.60	24.60	650	659	N.E.	1	rather cloudy
	9 p.m.	18.40	18.20	649	659	E.	0	clear
31	7 a.m.	16.40	15.40	651	660	N.E.	0	,,
	2 p.m.	26.40	23.80	649	657	E.	1	rather cloudy
	9 p.m.	18.40	18.60	650	659	N.E.	1	fair (72)
June 1	7 a.m.	—	—	—	—	—	—	—
	2 p.m.	—	—	—	—	—	—	—
	9 p.m.	—	—	—	—	—	—	—
2	7 a.m.	18.40	17.60	650	660	E.	0	cloudy
	2 p.m.	24.40	22.40	650	660	E.	1	,,
	9 p.m.	17.40	17.20	650	660	E.	0	clear (73)
3	7 a.m.	15.40	14.40	650	660	E.	0	,,
	2 p.m.	26.40	23.20	651	660	E.	0	rather cloudy
	9 p.m.	18.40	18.00	650	659	E.	0	clear
4	7 a.m.	19.80	18.80	651	660	S.E.	0	rather cloudy
	2 p.m.	25.40	23.00	649	658	E.	1	,, (74)
	9 p.m.	17.20	17.20	649	660	S.E.	0	clear
5	7 a.m.	19.20	18.40	650	661	N.E.	1	rather cloudy
	2 p.m.	26.20	22.40	650	661	N.E.	2	,,
	9 p.m.	19.40	19.00	651	659	N.E.	1	,,
6	7 a.m.	18.80	17.40	650	660	E.	1	,,
	2 p.m.	27.80	24.20	650	658	E.	1	,,
	9 p.m.	18.80	18.20	650	660	E.	0	clear
7	7 a.m.	15.60	15.40	650	660	N.E.	0	,,
	2 p.m.	26.60	21.80	650	660	S.E.	1	rather cloudy
	9 p.m.	18.20	17.80	650	660	E.	0	clear
8	7 a.m.	14.60	13.20	649	659	N.E.	0	,,
	2 p.m.	27.80	20.60	650	660	S.E.	1	fair
	9 p.m.	18.60	17.60	650	659	E.	0	clear
9	7 a.m.	14.80	13.20	650	660	N.E.	0	,,
	2 p.m.	27.40	23.40	651	660	S.E.	1	fair
	9 p.m.	18.20	18.20	650	660	S.E.	1	clear
10	7 a.m.	18.80	17.40	650	660	S.E.	1	,,
	2 p.m.	29.00	24.80	650	659	S.E.	1	rather cloudy
	9 p.m.	19.20	18.80	650	660	S.E.	1	,,

METEOROLOGICAL OBSERVATIONS.

Day.	Hour.	Hygrometer. Wet.	Hygrometer. Dry.	Aneroid Barometer. No. 1.	Aneroid Barometer. No. 2.	Wind. Direction.	Wind. Force.	Remarks.
1887 June 11	7 a.m.	17.60°	15.60°	651	660	S.E.	0	clear
	2 p.m.	26.00	22.60	649	658	S.E.	1	rather cloudy (75)
	9 p.m.	18.60	17.80	649	660	N.E.	1	cloudy
12	7 a.m.	17.80	17.40	650	659	E.	0	rather cloudy
	2 p.m.	23.20	21.40	650	660	S.E.	1	cloudy
	9 p.m.	17.60	17.40	650	660	N.E.	0	rather cloudy
13	7 a.m.	15.40	14.80	650	661	E.	0	clear
	2 p.m.	24.00	22.20	651	660	S.E.	1	rather cloudy (76)
	9 p.m.	17.20	17.20	651	660	E.	0	clear
14	7 a.m.	14.80	13.80	651	660	N.E.	0	fair
	2 p.m.	25.20	23.00	652	662	N.	1	rather cloudy
	9 p.m.	18.40	18.00	651	660	E.	1	clear
15	7 a.m.	16.80	15.80	651	660	N.E.	0	rather cloudy
	2 p.m.	21.40	19.60	650	660	N.E.	1	cloudy
	9 p.m.	13.80	14.20	651	660	E.	1	clear
16	7 a.m.	18.40	17.40	651	660	N.E.	0	rather cloudy
	2 p.m.	24.60	23.00	651	660	E.	1	,,
	9 p.m.	17.40	17.40	650	660	N.E.	1	clear
17	7 a.m.	19.40	18.40	651	661	N.E.	0	rather cloudy
	2 p.m.	25.60	22.80	650	660	E.	1	,, (77)
	9 p.m.	17.60	17.60	650	659	E.	0	,,
18	7 a.m.	18.60	17.60	650	659	E.	0	fair
	2 p.m.	25.20	22.40	650	659	N.E.	1	rather cloudy
	9 p.m.	17.40	17.40	651	660	E.	0	clear
19	7 a.m.	17.20	17.20	651	660	S.E.	1	fair
	2 p.m.	25.40	22.60	651	660	S.E.	0	rather cloudy
	9 p.m.	17.60	17.80	650	660	N.W.	0	clear
20	7 a.m.	16.60	15.40	650	660	N.E.	0	rather cloudy
	2 p.m.	25.20	22.80	650	660	N.W.	1	fair
	9 p.m.	18.60	18.00	651	660	N.E.	0	clear
21	7 a.m.	18.40	17.40	650	661	E.	0	fair
	2 p.m.	26.00	23.80	650	659	S.E.	1	rather cloudy (78)
	9 p.m.	17.60	17.80	649	658	N.E.	0	clear
22	7 a.m.	18.80	17.40	649	657	N.E.	0	fair
	2 p.m.	26.60	23.60	647	657	E.	9	rather cloudy
	9 p.m.	16.60	16.40	648	657	N.E.	0	clear
23	7 a.m.	19.00	18.00	649	659	N.E.	0	,,
	2 p.m.	24.00	21.40	647	655	S.E.	1	rather cloudy (79)
	9 p.m.	18.40	18.20	649	658	E.	0	,,
24	7 a.m.	18.00	16.40	647	657	S.E.	1	clear
	2 p.m.	21.40	20.40	647	658	S.E.	1	rather cloudy (80)
	9 p.m.	16.20	16.40	648	657	E.	1	,, (81)
25	7 a.m.	17.80	17.60	650	660	N.E.	0	,,
	2 p.m.	21.00	19.80	651	660	S.E.	1	cloudy
	9 p.m.	14.80	15.20	650	659	E.	0	clear (82)
26	7 a.m.	17.40	16.60	650	660	E	1	rather cloudy
	2 p.m.	24.40	21.80	650	660	S.E.	1	,, (83)
	9 p.m.	18.20	17.80	651	661	S.E.	1	clear
27	7 a.m.	17.60	16.80	650	660	S.E.	0	fair
	2 p.m.	25.80	23.00	650	659	E.	1	,, (84)
	9 p.m.	17.40	17.00	648	657	S.E.	0	,,
28	7 a.m.	18.40	17.20	650	660	E.	0	rather cloudy
	2 p.m.	24.60	23.00	649	659	S.E.	1	,,
	9 p.m.	18.40	17.40	650	659	S.E.	0	fair

METEOROLOGICAL OBSERVATIONS. 327

Day.	Hour.	Hygrometer. Wet.	Dry.	Aneroid Barometer. No. 1.	No. 2.	Wind. Direction.	Force.	Remarks.
1887 June 29	7 a.m.	18.80°	18.00°	651	660	N.E.	1	rather cloudy (85)
	2 p.m.	20.60	19.80	649	658	S.E.	2	cloudy
	9 p.m.	18.20	17.40	650	659	E.	0	clear (86)
30	7 a.m.	17.40	16.80	650	659	E.	0	cloudy
	2 p.m.	25.40	22.20	650	660	S.	1	rather cloudy (87)
	9 p.m.	16.60	16.40	650	660	E.	0	clear
July 1	7 a.m.	17.40	16.60	650	660	E.	0	cloudy (88)
	2 p.m.	25.40	22.40	651	660	N.E.	1	fair
	9 p.m.	17.60	19.40	650	659	E.	0	cloudy (89)
2	7 a.m.	17.80	17.40	650	659	S.E.	1	,,
	2 p.m.	26.40	23.40	649	659	S.	1	rather cloudy
	9 p.m.	17.40	17.20	649	658	E.	0	clear
3	7 a.m.	15.40	14.80	650	659	E.	0	,,
	2 p.m.	26.20	22.80	650	660	S.E.	1	rather cloudy
	9 p.m.	18.60	18.40	650	660	E.	0	clear
4	7 a.m.	16.80	16.20	650	660	E.	0	rather cloudy
	2 p.m.	26.40	23.40	652	661	E.	2	,,
	9 p.m.	17.20	16.80	652	660	S.E.	0	,,
5	7 a.m.	17.00	16.40	652	662	S.E.	0	,,
	2 p.m.	26.40	21.80	652	661	S.	1	,, (90)
	9 p.m.	17.80	17.80	650	661	E.	0	,,
6	7 a.m.	18.40	17.40	650	660	E.	0	,,
	2 p.m.	25.60	23.40	651	660	S.E.	1	,, (91)
	9 p.m.	18.40	18.60	651	660	S.E.	0	clear
7	7 a.m.	17.40	17.20	650	660	S.E.	0	rather cloudy
	2 p.m.	26.80	24.20	648	659	S.E.	1	clear
	9 p.m.	19.40	19.20	650	660	S.E.	1	,,
8	7 a.m.	19.40	18.20	649	660	S.E.	0	fair
	2 p.m.	26.80	24.20	650	659	E.	0	rather cloudy
	9 p.m.	19.40	19.20	649	660	E.	0	,,
9	7 a.m.	19.00	17.60	651	661	E.	0	clear
	2 p.m.	25.00	22.40	650	659	S.	1	overcast (92)
	9 p.m.	17.20	16.40	650	660	S.E.	1	,,
10	7 a.m.	17.60	17.20	651	660	S.E.	0	,,
	2 p.m.	23.60	21.40	651	660	S.E.	1	rather cloudy
	9 p.m.	17.20	16.80	651	660	E.	1	clear
11	7 a.m.	16.60	16.20	650	660	E.	0	fair
	2 p.m.	25.40	22.80	653	661	S.	1	rather cloudy
	9 p.m.	19.40	19.60	651	659	E.	0	fair
12	7 a.m.	18.80	18.40	651	660	E.	0	rather cloudy
	2 p.m.	25.40	22.80	651	660	S.E.	1	,,
	9 p.m.	19.20	18.40	652	660	S.E.	0	cloudy (93)
13	7 a.m.	18.60	17.80	653	662	N.W.	0	overcast
	2 p.m.	25.40	23.80	652	661	S.E.	1	rather cloudy (94)
	9 p.m.	17.20	16.80	652	660	N.E.	0	clear
14	7 a.m.	17.80	17.40	661	659	N.W.	0	rather cloudy
	2 p.m.	24.20	22.20	651	660	S.W.	1	,, (95)
	9 p.m.	18.80	18.60	652	660	S.	0	,,
15	7 a.m.	18.40	18.00	651	660	S.E.	0	cloudy (96)
	2 p.m,	22.80	21.40	651	660	S.	1	,,
	9 p.m.	19.20	18.80	650	660	N.E.	0	rather cloud
16	7 a.m.	18.80	16.20	650	660	E.	0	,,
	2 p.m.	23.80	22.40	650	660	S.E.	0	,,
	9 p.m.	16.80	16.60	650	660	N.E.	0	clear

METEOROLOGICAL OBSERVATIONS.

Day.	Hour.	Hygrometer. Wet.	Hygrometer. Dry.	Aneroid Barometer. No. 1.	Aneroid Barometer. No. 2.	Wind. Direction.	Wind. Force.	Remarks.
1887 July 17	7 a.m.	18.40°	18.00°	651	661	N.E.	1	fair
	2 p.m.	25.00	21.20	650	660	S.E.	1	rather cloudy
	9 p.m.	18.60	18.20	651	660	E.	0	clear (97)
18	7 a.m.	19.20	18.00	650	660	S.E.	0	fair
	2 p.m.	26.00	23.20	650	660	E.	1	rather cloudy
	9 p.m.	18.20	18.20	650	660	N.E.	0	clear
19	7 a.m.	18.00	17.20	650	660	E.	0	rather cloudy
	2 p.m.	26.20	23.80	651	660	S.E.	1	,,
	9 p.m.	19.20	19.20	651	660	N.E.	0	clear
20	7 a.m.	18.80	18.60	651	660	N.E.	0	rather cloudy
	2 p.m.	24.20	21.80	649	659	E.	2	,,
	9 p.m.	19.20	18.20	650	660	S.E.	0	cloudy
21	7 a.m.	18.20	17.40	648	659	N.E.	0	rather cloudy (98)
	2 p.m.	24.20	22.40	649	659	N.E.	0	,,
	9 p.m.	17.60	17.60	650	660	E.	0	fair (99)
22	7 a.m.	18.20	17.00	650	660	E.	1	rather cloudy (100)
	2 p.m.	23.40	21.60	650	660	S.E.	0	,,
	9 p.m.	17.60	17.60	648	659	N.E.	0	,,
23	7 a.m.	19.20	18.40	651	660	E.	0	,,
	2 p.m.	23.00	21.60	654	662	N.	2	,,
	9 p.m.	16.20	16.00	650	660	E.	0	clear
24	7 a.m.	15.20	14.60	650	660	E.	0	,,
	2 p.m.	25.80	22.40	650	659	S.	1	rather cloudy (101)
	9 p.m.	18.20	18.00	651	660	S.E.	0	fair
25	7 a.m.	16.20	15.40	649	658	N.E.	0	clear
	2 p.m.	24.80	22.40	649	659	N.	1	rather cloudy
	9 p.m.	18.40	18.20	650	660	N.E.	2	,,
26	7 a.m.	16.60	15.00	650	659	N.E.	0	,,
	2 p.m.	23.80	22.60	650	659	N.E.	1	,,
	9 p.m.	19.40	19.20	650	659	N.E.	0	cloudy
27	7 a.m.	18.20	17.80	650	660	S.E.	0	overcast (102)
	2 p.m.	20.80	19.80	649	659	E.	1	rather cloudy
	9 p.m.	18.40	18.60	651	660	E.	0	fair
28	7 a.m.	18.00	17.00	649	658	E.	0	clear
	2 p.m.	25.20	22.60	650	659	E.	1	rather cloudy
	9 p.m.	19.20	19.00	651	660	S.E.	1	cloudy
29	7 a.m.	18.20	17.40	650	660	N.E.	0	rather cloudy (103)
	2 p.m.	25.80	23.40	652	660	S.E.	0	,, (104)
	9 p.m.	17.20	17.00	651	660	S.E.	2	cloudy
30	7 a.m.	16.80	16.40	649	659	S.E.	0	fair (105)
	2 p.m.	20.80	19.80	650	660	S.W.	1	cloudy
	9 p.m.	15.60	15.80	650	660	E.	0	bright
31	7 a.m.	16.40	16.20	649	659	N.E.	0	fair
	2 p.m.	25.20	23.20	650	659	N.E.	1	rather cloudy
	9 p.m.	18.40	18.60	651	660	S.E.	0	clear
Aug. 1	7 a.m.	18.20	17.40	651	660	E.	1	fair
	2 p.m.	21.40	19.80	652	660	N.E.	1	rather cloudy (106)
	9 p.m.	17.00	16.40	650	660	E.	0	clear
2	7 a.m.	14.80	13.60	649	660	E.	0	,,
	2 p.m.	24.40	22.80	650	660	E.	0	rather cloudy (107)
	9 p.m.	17.60	17.40	650	660	E.	0	clear
3	7 a.m.	17.20	16.20	649	659	N.	1	cloudy (108)
	2 p.m.	21.40	19.80	649	658	N.W.	1	rather cloudy
	9 p.m.	16.20	16.00	650	660	E.	0	clear

METEOROLOGICAL OBSERVATIONS.

Day.	Hour.	Hygrometer. Wet.	Hygrometer. Dry.	Aneroid Barometer. No. 1.	Aneroid Barometer. No. 2.	Wind. Direction.	Wind. Force.	Remarks.
1887 Aug. 4	7 a.m.	17.60°	16.80°	651	661	E.	0	rather cloudy
	2 p.m.	25.40	23.00	650	660	S.E.	1	,, (109)
	9 p.m.	17.20	16.80	649	660	E.	1	fair
5	7 a.m.	19.80	18.60	649	659	N.W.	0	,,
	2 p.m.	25.20	23.00	650	659	N.	2	rather cloudy (110)
	9 p.m.	17.20	17.20	649	660	N.E.	0	fair
6	7 a.m.	17.80	16.80	649	659	N.E.	0	clear
	2 p.m.	26.20	24.00	649	658	N.E.	1	rather cloudy
	9 p.m.	18.20	17.80	650	659	E.	1	cloudy
7	7 a.m.	16.80	16.20	649	658	N.E.	0	rather cloudy
	2 p.m.	24.80	21.40	647	657	N.E.	1	,,
	9 p.m.	19.20	17.80	648	657	E.	2	clear
8	7 a.m.	17.80	16.80	648	657	N.E.	1	,,
	2 p.m.	26.80	23.00	649	659	N.E.	1	rather cloudy (111)
	9 p.m.	17.80	17.80	649	658	E.	0	clear
9	7 a.m.	16.80	16.40	649	659	N.E.	0	fair
	2 p.m.	25.00	22.60	650	659	S.E.	1	rather cloudy (112)
	9 p.m.	18.20	17.80	650	660	S.E.	0	clear
10	7 a.m.	17.60	16.20	650	660	N.E.	0	,,
	2 p.m.	25.60	23.80	650	659	N.E.	1	rather cloudy
	9 p.m.	18.00	18.20	649	658	E.	0	clear
11	7 a.m.	15.80	14.80	648	657	N.E.	0	,,
	2 p.m.	28.40	24.20	650	659	S.E.	1	rather cloudy (113)
	9 p.m.	16.60	16.40	650	660	E.	0	clear
12	7 a.m.	15.40	14.80	648	658	E.	0	fair
	2 p.m.	27.80	23.40	649	657	S.E.	2	rather cloudy (114)
	9 p.m.	17.20	17.20	648	657	N.E.	0	clear
13	7 a.m.	15.20	15.00	650	659	N.E.	0	,,
	2 p.m.	27.80	22.60	647	657	E.	0	fair
	9 p.m.	19.20	18.20	648	657	N.E.	0	clear
14	7 a.m.	16.20	15.40	647	657	N.E.	0	rather cloudy
	2 p.m.	23.80	21.80	647	657	N.E.	1	,,
	9 p.m.	16.40	16.40	647	647	E.	0	clear
15	7 a.m.	14.80	13.40	647	657	N.E.	0	,,
	2 p.m.	29.00	23.60	647	657	N.	1	rather cloudy
	9 p.m.	18.20	18.00	648	658	N.E.	0	clear
16	7 a.m.	18.00	16.40	649	659	N.E.	0	,,
	2 p.m.	27.60	19.00	648	658	N.E.	1	rather cloudy
	9 p.m.	18.40	18.20	650	660	E.	0	clear
17	7 a.m.	16.20	16.20	649	658	N.E.	0	,,
	2 p.m.	23.60	23.00	647	657	S.	2	overcast (115)
	9 p.m.	17.60	17.40	650	660	E.	1	clear
18	7 a.m.	16.40	14.60	649	660	N.E.	0	fair
	2 p.m,	24.80	20.60	649	659	S.E.	1	rather cloudy
	9 p.m.	17.40	17.00	649	658	E.	0	,,
19	7 a.m.	15.60	14.20	647	657	E.	0	clear
	2 p.m.	27.20	23.80	648	658	S.E.	1	fair
	9 p m	17.40	17.20	650	660	S.E.	0	clear
20	7 a.m.	17.80	16.80	650	659	S.W.	1	,,
	2 p.m.	28.80	24.00	649	659	S.W.	1	fair (116)
	9 p.m.	16.60	16.40	650	660	N.E.	0	overcast
21	7 a.m.	17.20	16.40	649	658	E.	0	fair
	2 p.m.	26.20	23.00	648	657	N.	1	clear
	9 p.m.	18.20	18.20	649	659	N.W.	0	fair

METEOROLOGICAL OBSERVATIONS.

Day.	Hour.	Hygrometer. Wet.	Hygrometer. Dry.	Aneroid Barometer. No. 1.	Aneroid Barometer. No. 2.	Wind. Direction.	Wind. Force.	Remarks.
1887 Aug. 22	7 a.m.	17.00°	16.00°	649	659	N.E.	0	rather cloudy
	2 p.m.	24.00	22.20	647	656	N.E.	1	,,
	9 p.m.	17.60	17.20	650	660	E.	0	,,
23	7 a.m.	17.80	17.40	650	660	N.E.	0	,,
	2 p.m.	26.60	23.80	650	660	N.	1	fair
	9 p.m.	17.60	17.40	649	659	E.	0	clear
24	7 a.m.	19.40	18.40	650	659	N.E.	0	rather cloudy (117)
	2 p.m.	23.40	21.80	649	658	N.	1	clear
	9 p.m.	17.60	16.60	650	660	E.	2	,,
25	7 a.m.	18.20	16.80	650	658	N.E.	0	rather cloudy
	2 p.m.	27.20	23.80	648	660	N.	2	fair
	9 p.m.	18.80	19.00	650	660	N.E.	0	clear
26	7 a.m.	17.80	17.20	650	661	N.	0	rather cloudy
	2 p.m.	18.40	17.60	647	656	S.	2	cloudy (118)
	9 p.m.	16.60	16.40	649	659	E.	0	fair
27	7 a.m.	17.40	16.60	649	659	N.E.	0	,,
	2 p.m.	27.20	24.40	648	658	N.E.	0	rather cloudy (119)
	9 p.m.	17.40	17.60	650	660	S.E.	0	cloudy
28	7 a.m.	15.20	14.80	647	657	N.E.	0	clear
	2 p.m.	25.60	23.60	647	656	N.E.	1	fair (120)
	9 p.m.	17.40	17.20	649	658	E.	0	clear
29	7 a.m.	17.40	16.20	649	659	N.E.	0	rather cloudy (121)
	2 p.m.	19.40	18.40	649	659	N.E.	1	,,
	9 p.m.	13.40	13.20	648	658	N.E.	0	clear
30	7 a.m.	13.80	13.00	647	657	N.E.	0	fair
	2 p.m.	25.40	23.40	650	660	N.E.	0	,,
	9 p.m.	17.40	17.40	649	659	S.E.	0	,,
31	7 a.m.	16.20	15.20	649	659	N.E.	1	clear
	2 p.m.	26.00	22.60	649	658	S.E.	1	rather cloudy
	9 p.m.	17.00	16.80	650	660	S.E.	0	fair

NOTES ON THE METEOROLOGICAL OBSERVATIONS.

1. Rain from 3.30 A.M. till 4 A.M.
2. Rain from 7 A.M. till 7.15 A.M.
3. Rain from 5 A.M. till 6 A.M.
4. Rain from 11 A.M. till 3 P.M.
5. Rain from 3 P.M. till 4 P.M. and from 8 P.M. till 1 A.M.
6. Thunder and lightning with a little rain from 3 P.M. till 4 P.M.
7. Thunder and lightning with rain from 1 P.M. till 1.30 P.M. and from 2 P.M. till 3 P.M.
8. Thunder and lightning from 3 P.M. till 3.25 P.M. without rain.
9. Thunder and lightning with rain from 3 P.M. till 3.25 P.M.
10. Thunder and lightning, south-east wind, with rain from 12 noon till 1.45 P.M.
11. Rain from 12 noon till 1.30 P.M. and from 10 P.M. till 3 A.M.
12. Rain from 3 P.M. till 4 P.M.
13. Thunder and lightning with rain from 1.30 P.M. till 3.30 P.M.
14. A little rain from 9.30 P.M. and for about two hours in the night.
15. Rain from 1 A.M. till 2 A.M. and from 11 A.M. till 11.30 A.M.
16. A little rain in the night and from 9 A.M. till 10 A.M.
17. Rain from 2.30 P.M. till 3 P.M.
18. Thunder and lightning, strong northerly wind, with rain from 11 A.M. till 12 noon.
19. Thunder in the west.
20. Thunder in the west.
21. Thunder and lightning, with easterly wind; rain from 11 A.M. till 1 P.M. and from 6 P.M. till 8.30 P.M.
22. Rain from 12 noon till 1 P.M.
23. Thunder and lightning, strong north-east wind, rain from 11 P.M. till 12.30 A.M. and from 3 P.M. till 4 P.M.
24. Rain from 3 A.M. till 4 A.M.
25. Thunder in the north.
26. Thunder in the north-east.
27. Thunder in the north-east, thunder and lightning, hail, rain from 2.30 P.M. till 3.30 P.M. and from 12.30 A.M. till 2 A.M.
28. Rain from 2.30 P.M. till 3.30 P.M.
29. Rain from 12.30 A.M. till 2 A.M. and from 11 A.M. till 12 noon.
30. Rain from 6.30 A.M. till 8 A.M.
31. Thunder and lightning with easterly wind and rain from 2.30 P.M. till 8 P.M.
32. Thunder and lightning with strong easterly wind and rain from 7 P.M. till 9 P.M.
33. Thunder in the north.
34. Rain from 7 A.M. till 8 A.M.

35. Thunder and lightning with rain from 2.30 P.M. till 4.30 P.M.
36. Heavy rain in the night at intervals.
37. Rain from 1 P.M. till 3 P.M.
38. Rain from 3 P.M. till 4 P.M.
39. Lightning in the north.
40. Rain from 1 P.M. till 5 P.M.
41. Thunder and lightning, south-east wind and rain from 3.30 P.M. till 4.30 P.M.
42. Rain from 1 A.M. till 3 A.M.
43. Thunder and lightning, rain from 3 A.M. till 11 A.M.
44. Thunder in the north.
45. Rain from 3 P.M. till 5 P.M.; thunder and lightning, rain from 7 P.M. till 11 P.M.
46. Rain from 2.30 P.M. till 3 P.M., from 4 P.M. till 5 P.M., and from 8.30 P.M. till 11 P.M.
47. Rain from 2.30 P.M. till 4 P.M.
48. Thunder and lightning, rain from 1 A.M. till 5 A.M.
49. Rain from 1.30 P.M. till 2 P.M.
50. Rain from 4 P.M. till 5 P.M.
51. Rain from 3 A.M. till 4 A.M.
52. Rain from 4 P.M. till 5 P.M.
53. Thunder and lightning, rain from 1 P.M. till 2.30 P.M.
54. A little rain during the night.
55. Thunder and lightning, northerly wind, rain from 5 P.M. till 6 P.M.
56. Thunder and lightning, northerly wind, rain from 3.30 P.M. till 4.30 P.M.
57. Rain from 3.30 A.M. till 7 A.M.
58. Thunder and lightning, south-east wind, with rain from 5 P.M. till 7 P.M.
59. Rain from 2 A.M. till 5 A.M. and from 9 A.M. till 10 A.M.
60. Rain with northerly wind from 10.30 A.M. till 12 noon.
61. Rain from 10.30 P.M. till 12 midnight.
62. Rain from 8.30 P.M. till 3.30 A.M.
63. Thunder and lightning, easterly wind, with rain from 4.30 P.M. till 8 P.M.
64. Rain from 4 P.M. till 8 P.M.
65. Rain from 6 P.M. till 7 P.M.
66. Rain from 12.30 P.M. till 1.30 P.M., with some thunder and lightning.
67. Rain from 1 A.M. till 2 A.M.
68. Rain from 12 noon till 2 P.M.
69. Rain from 3 P.M. till 4 P.M.
70. Rain from 12 midnight till 3 A.M.
71. Thunder and lightning, easterly wind, with rain from 3 P.M. till 5 P.M.
72. Rain from 4 P.M. till 5 P.M.
73. Rain from 3 P.M. till 4 P.M.
74. Rain from 10.30 A.M. till 12 noon and 3.30 P.M. till 4.30 P.M.
75. Thunder and lightning, southerly wind, with rain from 3 P.M. till 4.30 P.M.
76. Thunder and lightning, south-east wind, with a little hail and rain from 3.30 P.M. till 5.30 P.M.

NOTES ON OBSERVATIONS.

77. Thunder and lightning, south-east wind, with heavy rain from 3 P.M. till 4 P.M.
78. Rain from 2.30 P.M. till 6 P.M
79. Rain from 3 P.M. till 4 P.M.
80. Rain from 1.30 P.M. till 2.30 P.M. and from 4 P.M. till 5 P.M.
81. Rain from 1 A.M. till 3 A.M.
82. Rain from 1 P.M. till 3 P.M.
83. Rain from 11 A.M. till 12 noon.
84. Rain from 1 P.M. till 2.30 P.M. and from 1 P.M. till 5 P.M.
85. Rain from 1 A.M. till 5 A.M.
86. Rain from 6 P.M. till 6.30 P.M.
87. Rain from 2 P.M. till 3 P.M.
88. Rain from 5 A.M. till 6 A.M.
89. Rain from 9 P.M. till 10 P.M.
90. Thunder and lightning, north-east wind, rain from 3.30 P.M. till 5 P.M.
91. Thunder and lightning, south-west wind, rain from 7 P.M. till 8 P.M.
92. Thunder and lightning, rain from 1.30 P.M. till 4 P.M. and from 7 P.M. till 3 A.M.
93. Rain from 9.30 P.M. till 10 P.M.
94. Thunder and lightning, rain from 2.30 P.M. till 3.45 P.M.
95. Thunder and lightning, southerly wind, rain from 3.30 P.M. till 4.30 P.M.
96. Rain from 1 A.M. till 5 A.M.
97. A little rain at 5 P.M.
98. A little rain at 10.30 P.M.
99. Rain from 4 P.M. till 4.30 P.M.
100. Thunder and lightning, south-west wind, rain from 4 P.M. till 8 P.M., hail from 4 P.M. till 4.30 P.M., rain from 9 P.M. till 11 P.M.
101. Thunder and lightning, southerly wind, rain from 5 P.M. till 6 P.M.
102. Rain from 6 A.M. till 8 A.M.
103. Rain from 11 P.M. till 12 midnight.
104. Rain from 3 P.M. till 4 P.M., from 5 P.M. till 5.30 P.M., and from 10 P.M. till 11 P.M.
105. Rain from 8 A.M. till 10 A.M.
106. Thunder and lightning, south-west wind, with rain from 2.30 P.M. till 4 P.M.
107. Thunder and lightning, north-west wind, with rain from 3 P.M. till 3.30 P.M.
108. Light rain from 5 A.M. till 8 A.M.
109. Thunder and lightning, southerly wind, with rain from 4.30 P.M. till 7 P.M.
110. Thunder and lightning, southerly wind, with rain from 2.30 P.M. till 3.30 P.M.
111. Southerly wind with rain from 2 P.M. till 5 P.M.
112. Thunder and lightning, southerly wind, from 3 P.M. till 3.45 P.M.
113. Thunder and lightning, southerly wind, and rain from 3.30 P.M. till 4.15 P.M.
114. Rain from 3 P.M. till 3.30 P.M. and from 5.30 P.M. till 6 P.M.
115. Thunder and lightning, southerly wind, and rain from 2 P.M. till 3 P.M.

116. Thunder and lightning, strong north-east wind, with rain from 7 P.M. till 11 P.M.
117. Thunder and lightning, northerly wind, with rain from 11 A.M. till 12 noon.
118. Thunder and lightning, southerly wind, with rain from 12.30 P.M. till 4 P.M.
119. Thunder and lightning, south-west wind, with rain from 7 P.M. till 11 P.M.
120. Rain from 12 midday till 1 P.M. and from 5 P.M. till 5.30 P.M.
121. Rain from 8 A.M. till 11 A.M.

INDEX.

INDEX TO VOLUME II.

ABBA, ISLAND OF, 1
Abd Rehman, 21, 24, 67, 90
Abdallah Menze, 174
Abd-el-Aziz river, 201
Abd-el-Bein Aga Shialai, Lieut., 301
Abd-el-Kader Pasha, 3, 4
Abdul-Waab Effendi, 166
    death of, 199
Abu-Hableh, 4
Abu Klea, 12
Abu Saoud, 2
Abu Zeir, ford of, 3
Acoi, chief, 139
Adansonia digitata, 296, 300, 301, 304
Ahmed Akkad, 66, 67
Ahmed Asuti, 206
Ahmed Dinkani, 177, 179
Ahmed Mahmoud, 166
Ala-el-Din Pasha, 4
    death of, 5
Albert, lake, 38, 47, 48, 138, 209, 231
    Emin places his steamers on, 70
    Sir S. Baker discovers, 127
Ali Aga, 148, 150, 199
Ali Giabur, 182, 187
VOL. II.

Alloba, 5
Amara, chief, 117
Amat, Lieut., 197
Ambatsh, 123, 134, 136
Amina, little, 260
Amkongo, village of, 269
Antina, chief, 28
Arabi Pasha, 236
Arabs, the, 23, 31, 190, 274, 292
Aruwimi river, 156, 157, 231, 256
Asraël, 1
Assua river, 132
Assuti, Captain, death of, 206
Attikende, chief, 209
Ayu station, 204

BABEDONGO, CHIEF, 27, 70, 85, 146, 163, 210, 226
Bachit Aga Bargut, 200
Bachit Aga Mohammed, 199
Bagamoyo, 125, 288, 292, 293
Baganghese, 44
    invasion of, 74
Baggara, the, 171
Bagonza, chief, 27
Bahr-el-Ghazal, 130

INDEX

Baker Pasha, 5, 7, 25
Baker, Sir S., 127, 130
Ballula, chief, 92, 142
Banalya, 213, 214
Banana Point, 213
Bananas, beer made of, 54
Banassura, the, 61, 65, 66, 69, 80, 89, 93, 95, 99
    arms of, 80
Bangala, 213
Bantu, the, 44, 299
Barabra, chief, 112
Bari, the, 127, 147, 194
    as *banassura*, 62
    as hunters of crocodiles, 195
Baringo, lake, 157
Barttelot, Major, 213
Basili, clerk, 267
Bassua, the, 265
Batata edulis—see Potato
Beatrice, gulf, 129
Bedden, 128, 131, 175, 194
Beer, 54, 55
Befo, chief, 150
Berber, 9, 11, 12, 130
Bidongo, woods of, 77
Biri, Mohammed, 73, 75, 89, 91, 95, 99
    at Juaya, 97
    at Wadelai, 28
    bound to a tree, 102
    departs for Uganda, 26
    prevented from entering Unyoro, 21
    servant of, arrested, 69
    starts for Kibiro, 25
Blood-brotherhood, 81, 98
Bodo, fort, 152, 157, 213
Boki, chief, 139, 209
    death of, 210
Bomokandi river, 157
Boneira, territory of, 294

Bonny, William, 213, 226
    arrival at Were of, 225
Bor, 127
Bora, village of, 197
Bubo river, 306
Buemba, 81
Buffaloes, 119, 138, 301
Buguera, 225, 230, 231, 234
Buhogo, village of, 262
Bujungue, 262
Bukorongo, 270
Burial customs, 210
    of the Wanyoro, 59
Bwasse, battle near, 266

CABACA, KING OF UGANDA'S TITLE, 22
Cairo, 3, 4, 223, 244, 251
Cameron, B. L., 127, 290
Canoes, building of, 87
Casati, Major, 249
    arrives at Buguera, 230
    arrives at the British Mission, 287
    bound to a tree, 102
    dwelling of, ransacked, 108
    escape of, 111, 122, 124
    goes to Emin at Msua, 146
    goes to see Guakamatera, 101
    illness of, 282
    Kagoro shelters, 112
    outrage on, 102–110
    proposals of, to Emin, 220
    starts for Were, 229
Chimpanzees, 40, 232, 233
Chippendale, 128
Chua, King (Kabba Rega), 16, 38
    abandons Juaya, 35
    cows of, 19

INDEX. 339

Chua, King, Court of, 52
   Muanga wages war against, 16
   obese women of, 71
   sentences of, 52
Condo, order of, 50
Congo Free State, 155, 156, 161, 213
Crocodiles—
   on the Victoria Nile, 136
   the Bari as hunters of, 195
Cyprea moneta, 56

DAMBI RIVER, 310
Deki river, 231
Dinka, the, 119
   as snake charmers, 196
Dispensers of rain, 57
Dombolo, village of, 301
Donagla, the, 172, 208
Dongola, 111
Duemme, 4
Dufilé, 88, 105, 128, 129, 142, 149, 176, 184, 196, 197, 204, 207

EARLE, GENERAL, 12
Egyptians, the, 2, 180, 236
Elephants, 39, 138
Eleusina coracana, 38
El-Obeid, 3
El-Teb, battle of, 8
Emin Pasha—
   a prisoner at Dufilé, 177
   and the mutineers, 176
   arrival at Tunguru of, 167
   charges against, 166
   collection of birds of, 211
   embarks for Msua, 145
   en route to Wadelai, 192

Emin Pasha—
   flees to Muggi, 150
   goes to Dufilé, 149
   goes to Wadelai, 149
   has words with Stanley, 248, 249
   house of, searched, 188
   letter of, to Selim Matera, 216
   one of the servants of, killed, 266
   plots against, 28
   searches for the Expedition, 146
Equatoria, Province of, 81, 92, 118, 128, 161
   lakes of, 133, 155
Erica arborea, 266
Euphorbia candelabra, 268
Euphorbia venefica, 37, 134

FABLES, 45
Fabo station, 177, 197
Fadibek, defeat of the Shooli at, 30
Fadl, 118, 123
   promotion of, 142
Farajak, forests of, 41, 111
Fatelmula Aga, 172, 173, 177, 181, 186, 208, 226, 228, 239
Fatiko, 30, 44, 172, 197
Felkin, Dr., 154, 156
Ferida, Emin's daughter, 188
Fish, in the Victoria Nile, 137
Fola, waterfall of, 129, 132
Foweira station, 53, 128

GALLA, THE, 47
Gessi Pasha completes the ex-

INDEX.

ploration of the Albert Lake, 127, 128
Ghiaden Aga, 148
Giegler Pasha, 3
Giglioli, Professor, on chimpanzees, 41
Giraud, Father, 301
Gombe Yaicongo, 301
Gondokoro, 150, 174
    Sir S. Baker's arrival at, 127
Gordon, Col., 132
Gordon, General, 7, 13
    death of, 14
    despatches a flotilla, 11
    occupies Bor, 127
    proclaims the independence of the Soudan at Berber, 6
    writes from Lado, 128
Grant, Capt., 126
Graham, General, 9
Gravenreuth, Capt., 313
Guakamatera, chief, 83, 85, 89, 98, 101, 102, 104, 107, 109, 110, 112, 114, 144
Guamirma, Chua retires to, 77
Gubat, 12
Gumangi, death of, 27

HADENDOWA, THE, 5
Hamid Aga, Major, 147, 183
    death of, 201
Hamis, the merchant, 86
Hannington, Bishop, 16, 275
Hassan, Vita, 152, 169, 187, 190, 229, 249
    prisoner at Dufilé, 177
Hawashi Effendi, Major, 147, 148, 167, 173, 183, 184, 207, 245, 247

Hicks, General, 4
    death of, 5
Hippopotami, 119, 138
Hurshid, Circassian soldier, 119, 121, 140
    death of, 142
Hassan Bey, 6
Hellem, Capt. Ibrahim, 244, 245
Helmia bulbifera, 38
Hyenas, destruction of, 40, 301

IRANGARA, ISLAND OF, 269
Ireta, chief, 48, 70, 226
Irrengere river, 312
Ismail Pasha, the Khedive, 127, 246
Ituri river, 215, 231
    waterparting of, 262
Ivory, 17, 22, 54, 56, 75, 85, 89, 155, 162, 273, 282

JEBEL KADAR, 2
Jephson, A. J., 160, 168, 177, 238, 258
    as a sportsman, 212
    departure of, from Msua, 216
Jikombi, 276
Joddo, 260
Jongolo, the, 254
Jonyo, forest of, 308
Juaya, 17, 41, 44, 84, 148
    birth of Amina at, 260
    Chua abandons, 35
    sacrifices to the *Mapingo* at, 33
    tableland of, 38
    tanners in, 55
    trades in the markets of, 54, 55

INDEX. 341

Juguro, mountains of, 135, 138
    chief of, 163
Junker, Dr., 24, 29, 156, 157

KABBA REGA, KING, *see* Chua
Kabamiro, Chua's brother, 18, 38, 60
    death of, 18
Kabonga, chief, 260
Kadar, mount, 3
Kafu, or river of death, 38, 69, 81, 89, 108
Kagera river, 272, 280, 281
Kagoro, chief of Kibiro, 112, 146
Kambi, village of, 308
Kamissua, 82
    murder of, 53
Kamrasi, King, 17, 32, 61, 81
    burial of, 59
Katenta, 252
Katikiro, Muanga's minister, 273
Katongoli, chief, 82, 83
Kapalata, 303
Kapidi, chief, 116
Karagua, 272, 281
Karema, King, 275, 282
Kategora, King Chua's minister, 21, 60, 93
    death of, 26
Katonzi, chief, 211, 225
Katto, chief, 89, 209
Katua station, 48
    arrival of the Expedition at, 268
Kauto, chief, 77
Kavalla, death of, 266
Kavalli, camp at, 196, 215, 264, 266
Kavarongli river, 84
Kavira, Muanga's brother, 275
Kelia, district of, 294

Khartoum, 127, 128, 130, 201, 263
    fall of, 12
    death of Gordon at, 14
Khor Ayu, 176
Kiambali, 268
Kiani, 83, 90
Kiani Cassangoro, 81
Kibararo, 78
Kibiro, 25, 41, 70, 81, 111, 134
    Emin leaves, 89
    massacre at, 164
    salt at, 137
Kidete river, 311
Kieya, 48, 134, 211, 226
Kio, lake, 48, 268
Kiriangobi, forest of, 38, 41, 134, 138
    tableland of, 38
Kirota, 128
Kirri station, 128, 131, 147, 173, 190, 194
Kisa, chief, 22
    death of, 27
Kitana, tableland of, 38, 111
    mountain of, 134
Kitega, 245, 276
Kitindi, forest of, 269
Kolikio, chief, 141, 209
Koran, extracts from the, 233, 244
Kordofan, 4
Korti, 11
Kudurma, 24
Kumbiere, 254

LABORÉ STATION, 128, 175, 177, 198
Lado, 131, 133
    Government transferred to, 128

INDEX.

Lango, the, 62, 80, 92, 144
    tournaments of, 31
Lendu, 93
Leopards, 40, 281, 301
Lions, 39, 68, 301
Livingstone, David, 126, 127, 288
Lur, the, 120, 138, 139, 164, 224, 241
    of Melindwa, 48

MABITU, THE, 17, 50
Mackay, Mr., 66, 243, 274, 287
Mackinnon, Sir William, 155
Madundi, 43, 44
Magnoro, the, 49, 61, 95
Magombia, village of, 307
Magungo, 43, 117
    peninsula of, 38
Magaya, 43, 44
Magungo Baba, 138
Mahatuk, 4
Mahdi, the, 1, 2, 12
    occupies Kordofan, 3
    coins of, 204
Mahmoud Ahmed, 194
Maize, 38, 40, 271
Makama, title of the King of Unyoro, 22, 58, 71, 91, 120
Makamba, 92, 93
Makavaro, chief, 70
Makiera, Governor's interpreter, 144
Makomero, reservoirs of, 302
Makongo, 49
Makua river, 153, 159
Malemba river, *see* Semliki
Malissa, chief, 294
Manioc, 38, 272, 286
Manyema, the, 235, 258, 260, 266, 267, 280

Manzoca, 254
Marco, Greek merchant, 196, 249, 267
Masai, the, 298, 306, 309, 310
    arms of, 299
    agriculture of, 299
    country, 155
    language of, 299
Mason, Colonel, 129
Matako, 308
Matamure (granaries), 15, 79
Matungoli, 49; 121, 144
Matunzi, chief, 85
Mausea river, 308
Mavona, village of, 280
Mazamboni, chief, 239, 255
Mbagungue river, 254
Mboga, 48, 86, 93, 262, 264
Mbuti, village of, 252
Mbuzi, Munga's envoy, 30
Meikambi, 89
Melbes, 5
Melindwa, heights of, 135
    chief of the Lur of, 139, 241
Melino, chief, 117
Merawe, cataract of, 11
Meshra-el-Dahi, battle of, 4
Messedaglia, Colonel, 4
    his account of El-Teb, 8
Metemmeh, 12
Meteorological observations, 315–330
    notes on, 331, 332
Menakulia, 89
Mergian Aga Danassuri, 121
Mgunda-Mkali, forest of, 301, 303
Miani, 126
Milk ceremony, 53
Miro, village of, 252

INDEX.

Mitinginya, chief, 296, 297, 298, 300
Mina, cape, 136
Mkate river, 312
Mohammed Ahmed, *see* Mahdi
Mohren-el-Bohur, 130
Mogo, chief, 152, 212
Mokondokua river, 311
Mombasa, 161
Moncrief, Captain, 5
Monkeys, 40, 41
Moon, mountains of the, 36, 272
Moranda, 286
  hills of, 77
  tableland of, 38
Mpango, ceremony of the, 32, 50
Mpigwa, chief, 139, 158, 212, 234
Mpinga, chief, 252
Mpogo, swamp, 277
Mrogoro river, 312
Mruli, 38, 48, 128
Msaka river, 302
Msiri, 38
Msoga, 56
Msua, 22, 81, 135, 138, 313
Msucali, village of, 265
  sulphurous spring in, 281
Mtara, village of, 283
Mtesa, King, 129
Mualata, basin of, 305
Muanga, King of Uganda, 16, 64, 273, 274
  escape of, 275
Muchora, 267
Muenghe, 38, 44
  Kamissua murdered at, 53
Muggi, 132, 174
  Emin flies to, 150
Muicu, village of, 254

Muimba, 35
  the natives leave, 70
  the king abandons, 75
  abandonment and burning of, 77
Muninga, 254
Mussanga, 308
Mustapha Ahmed, 183

Naunga country, 265
Ndagora, King, 282
Ndinda, chief, 254
Nelson, Capt., 237, 246, 258
Ngussi river, 38, 41, 134
Ngazi, *see* Semliki
Nguro, Ntali's envoy, 21, 274
Nianguira, 306
Niangabo, 239, 253, 254, 260
Niebetembe river, 229-231
Nile, the, 127, 132
  basins of, 130
  cataracts of, 132
  country bordering, 130-135
  navigation on, 135
  rapids of, 132
Nkole, 21
  warriors of, 155, 271
No, lake, 130
Nparo, tableland of, 38
  Chua retires to, 75
Nsabaco, 254
Nsabe, 136
Ntagata, mineral waters of, 281
Ntali, King, 272
Ntiabo, 116
Nubar Pasha, 158
Nuer, the, 130
Nur Angara, 12
Nusranduru, 38
Nyamsanzi, 136, 152
Nyassa, lake, 125

INDEX.

Nyassa, Livingstone reaches, 126
Nymphea lotus, 38

OAKIBI, WAGANDA GENERAL, 77
Oakil, 187
    death of, 263
Obangi-Makua, 153
Okello, chief, 209
Okuza, chief, 142, 209
Omar, 251
Omar Saleh, commander of the Mahdi's troops, 201
Omdurman, 4, 204
Osman Digna, 5
Osman Latif, 187, 222, 223, 247
    dismissal of, 168

PALMS, 306
    borassus, 301
    Palma dôm, 37, 311
    Palma phœnix, 268
    wild date, 134
Panyatoli, 128
Papyrus, 20, 36, 134, 194, 277
    islands of, 132
Parrots (*Psittacus erythacus*), 40
Parke, Dr., attends Stanley, 255
Pipes, 114, 304
Potatoes, sweet, 272, 278
    Batata edulis, 38, 111, 138, 252
Protshamma, 30

RAOUF PASHA, 3
Rashid Bey, 2
Rejaf, massacre at, 187

Rehan, Stanley's servant, 254, 256
    hanging of, 257
Rehan Aga, Major, death of, 147
Reichart, Professor, on chimpanzees, 41
Rionga, chief, 82
Ripon Falls, 126
Roali river, 270
Roconcona, chief, 112
Rokora, chief, 72
    village of, 118
Rosher, 126
Ruanda, territory of, 272
Rubanga, 89
Ruganda, village of, 278, 284
Ruitan, lake, 48, 129, 133, 262, 268
Ruizi river, 277, 281
Rumanika, King, 282
Ruroi river, 270
Ruwengabi-Coanga forest, 77
Ruwenzori mountain, 49, 235

SABRI, CLERK, 183
Sacrifices, 51, 59, 83, 209
    new moon, 50
    of the *mpango*, 32, 50
Sagwa, village of, 252
Said Barghash, 24
Saleh, Stanley's servant, 247
Sandeh, the, 41
    mode of capturing monkeys by, 232, 333
Saura, village, arrival of the Expedition at, 266
Schmidt, Lieut., 307, 310
Schweinfurth, Dr., on chimpanzees, 41
Schynse, Father, 301, 302
Sedgiomocoro, mountain, 38, 78

INDEX.

Segadi, 4
Selim Matera, 186, 191, 219
   letter from, 201, 204
   promotion of, 221
Semliki river, 48, 86
   waterparting of, 262, 264, 265, 267
Sennaar, 3
Sesame, 54, 56, 138, 158, 300
Shukri, Capt., 212, 233, 270, 280, 306
Shefalu, the, 28, 43, 44
Shooli, the, 30, 43, 110
Simba, chief, 298
   river, 311
Singoma, the guard, 107, 161
Sinkat, 7
   fall of, 9
Slave trade, the, evils of, 289
   enterprise against, 290
   how to abolish, 291
Sobat river, Gordon builds a station on, 127
Solyman Aga, 171, 178
Solyman Dand, 18
Speke, J. H., 125
   discovers Victoria Lake, 126
Spermania Africana, 232
Stanley, H. M., 127
   arrives in the Were roadstead, 157
   arrives at Kavalli, 157
   discovers the watershed between Victoria and Ruitan lakes, 129
   illness of, 255
   letter from, 152
   letter of, to Jephson, 313–315
   loses his temper, 249
   manifesto from, 227
   news of, 212

Stanley, H. M., news of arrival of, 48
   opens the march, 258
   oclamation of, 175
   the "stone-breaker," 237
Stairs, Lieutenant, 253, 258
   explores the Virika Peaks, 266
Stewart, Colonel, 4, 7
   death of, 11
   shells Berber, 11
Stewart, General, 12
Stokes, the merchant, 300
Stone, General 189
Suakim, 9
Soudanese, the 180, 251, 306
Suez, return of the British to, 9
Sunga, chief, 22, 209
Surur, Corporal, 29 105, 107, 111
Suuna, King of Uganda, 51
   bead cultivation, 51, 52

TABORA, 125
Tabatt, 246
Taib, clerk, 183
Tamai, 9
Tanganika, lake, 125–127
   discovery of, 125
   watershed of, 303
Tel-el-Kebir, battle of, 4
Telabun porridge, 54
Tembe (villages), 298, 301, 303, 304, 308
Tendiabro, village of, 254
Termites, 41, 42
Tin river, 201
Tobacco, 39, 273
Tokar, 5, 7
   surrender of, 9
Tokongia, 115

Toru, 48
Trifolium intermedium, 232
Tunguru, 22
    woods of, 135
Troglodytes niger, 41; see Monkeys
Troglodytes Schweinfurthii, 41; see Monkeys

UGANDA, 21, 36
    Speke reaches, 126, 272
Ugogo, 303
    inhabitants of, 304, 306
Ugomoro, 281
Ukongio, territory of, 267
Umma, chief, 143
Unyampaka, 269, 271
Unyamuesi country, 296, 297
Unyamwambi river, 269
Unyoro, 36
    population of, 54
    superstitions in, 53, 54
Urigi lake, 283
Urima, district of, 294
Usagara, mountains of, 308
    territory of, 310
Usimba, territory of, 271
Usongo, 297
Usongora station, 48, 264
Usukuma, the, 77, 275, 282
Usumbiro, French Mission of, 287

VAKONGIO, THE, 49, 235, 265
    kill one of Emin's servants, 266
Vanianga, 296
Varicampanga, the, 235
Vasingana, chief, 278
Vavra, the, 234, 254
Viarua, village of, 280

Victoria, lake, 286
    discovery of, 126
Virika, see Ruwenzori, 262, 264, 265
Vochumbe, village of, 262
Vugorama, village of, 265
Vurvira mountain, 142

WADELAI, projected attack upon, 70
    arrival at, 180
Waganda, the, 16
    army of, 79
    attack the Wanyoro, 78
    deputation of, 31
    language of, 44
Wagogo, the, 304, 306
    arms of, 304
    habitations of, 304
Wahuma, the, 43, 44, 138, 234, 246, 254, 270
    customs of, 47, 48
    shepherds of, 48
Walegga, the, as hunters of chimpanzees, 233
    mountains of, 267
Wamba, country of, 265
Wanyamuesi, the, 297
    burial customs of, 59
    dwellings of, 298
Wanyoro, the, 15, 43, 44
    customs of, 57
    dwellings of, 57
    language of, 44
    put to flight by Emin, 72
Watson, Captain, 130
Waviasi, the, 234
Were, 136, 224
    arrival of Bonny at, 225
Wilson, Colonel, 12

INDEX.

Wilson, C. T., missionary, on languages, 44
  on the use of bark, 55
Wissmann, Major, 310, 313
  letter from, 307
Wolseley, General, starts with an expedition, 11

YAMBUYA, 152, 254
Yanghiro, district of 283

Yussuf Fahmi, 198
Yussuf Pasha, 3

ZANZIBAR, 88, 93, 125, 128, 155, 157, 160, 163, 289, 292, 297
  merchants of, 56
Zanzibaris, the, 21, 157, 158, 213 256, 257, 294

FUNDERBURG LIBRARY

MANCHESTER COLLEGE

916.7
C264t
v.2